THE VALUE OF
VIOLENCE

THE VALUE OF VIOLENCE

BENJAMIN GINSBERG

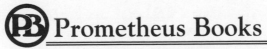

Prometheus Books

59 John Glenn Drive
Amherst, New York 14228–2119

Published 2013 by Prometheus Books

Trademarks: In an effort to acknowledge trademarked names of products mentioned in this work, we have placed ® or ™ after the product name in the first instance of its use in each chapter. Subsequent mentions of the name within a given chapter appear without the symbol.

Cover photo © 2013 Media Bakery
Cover design by Jacqueline Nasso Cooke

Inquiries should be addressed to
Prometheus Books
59 John Glenn Drive
Amherst, New York 14228–2119
VOICE: 716–691–0133
FAX: 716–691–0137
WWW.PROMETHEUSBOOKS.COM

17 16 15 14 13   5 4 3 2 1

Library of Congress Cataloging-in-Publication Data

Ginsberg, Benjamin.
    The value of violence / by Benjamin Ginsberg.
        pages cm
    Includes bibliographical references and index.
    ISBN 978-1-61614-831-7 (hardcover)
    ISBN 978-1-61614-832-4 (ebook)
    1. Political violence. 2. State-sponsored terrorism. I. Title.

JC328.6.G52 2013
303.6—dc23

2013022345

Printed in the United States of America

As Always, For Sandy

CONTENTS

ACKNOWLEDGMENTS

In writing this book I benefited from many faculty club discussions with colleagues from diverse fields, including Matthew Crenson, Howard Egeth, John Irwin, and Robert Kargon. I am also indebted to Alexander B. Ginsberg for contributing a good deal to my understanding of the legal and philosophical issues addressed in this book. Finally, I wish to thank the editorial staff at Prometheus Books, including Steven L. Mitchell, Julia DeGraf, and Catherine Roberts-Abel, and my agent, Claire Gerus, for helping me through the various stages of converting an idea into a book.

INTRODUCTION
VIOLENCE OFTEN
IS THE ANSWER

My friend and sometime co-author Matthew Crenson is fond of criticizing my work for its lack of what he calls "analytic tension." By this he means that I generally present the main argument of a book in the first paragraph or two rather than challenge the reader to unravel its mysteries as I proceed. During the course of writing two books and several papers together, we argued more about this issue than any other. In the present volume, as I am not burdened by having to accommodate Crenson, I will summarily dispel all analytic tensions and anxieties by offering this preview of the chapters and arguments to follow.

1. Violence is the driving force of politics. The importance of violence derives from the dominance it usually manifests over other forms of political action, from its destructive and politically transformative power and from the capacity of violence to serve as an instrument of political mobilization. These three factors explain why Chairman Mao was correct in his assertion that political power emanated from the gun barrel.

2. In using violence, states generally have a number of advantages vis-à-vis other actors. One advantage is bureaucracy. Anyone can be violent, but serious violence generally requires the support of a bureaucratic organization to overcome the natural, human, and moral limits of violence. Bureaucracy is one of the mechanisms through which states sometimes achieve the monopoly of force to which Max Weber famously referred.

3. Most states do not rely upon naked violence as an instrument of governance but seek to refine violence and make it a more effective tool. Domestically, states employ various forms of legitimation as well as the rule of law to refine their use of violence. In the international realm,

refined violence is sometimes called soft power. Legitimation, law, and soft power are not substitutes for force but instead are, in military parlance, "force multipliers" that increase the effectiveness of a given quantity of force, allowing the same result to be achieved with less effort.

4. Another instrument that reduces the state's need to rely upon overt violence is public welfare. Welfare is more a substitute for force than a force multiplier. It is the carrot rather than the stick, reward rather than punishment. The U.S., slow to build a welfare state, has chosen to rely more upon punishment than reward internally, which is why America has an enormous prison system. This internal reliance upon force has had consequences for America's external relations, as well. In fact, the weakness of its welfare state helps to explain why the U.S. is among the most overtly violent states on the face of the earth. This might be seen as the dark side of American exceptionalism.

5. Governments, even liberal democracies, use violence against their citizens every day. But when, if ever, is it appropriate for citizens to use violence against the state?

6. Violence is terrible, but it is the great engine of political change. The next generation, perceiving itself to have been the beneficiary, is often grateful for the violent acts of the previous generation. Mechanisms designed to discourage popular violence, including political reform and peaceful modes of political participation, are generally tactics designed to delimit change.

Now that I have allayed all possible analytic tensions, I invite the reader to enjoy a calm and peaceful journey through what might otherwise be an unsettling topic.

><

I should mention, for those not familiar with my work, that I am often accused of being unduly cynical. My response is simple. It is not possible to be too cynical when assessing political events. Americans, in my view, seem to be especially lacking in the requisite level of political cynicism. Many take seriously the constant admonitions by politicians and the media to involve themselves in political life, to pay attention to the issues, to vote for the best candidates, and, above all, to avoid succumbing to political apathy and cynicism. The unpleasant truth, though, is that for most individuals, most of the time, politics is a rather unrewarding enterprise. Clausewitz was, at least in this respect, correct to equate war and politics. Both are nasty, sometimes brutish activities from which ordinary participants secure few benefits. And yet, like war, politics is sometimes forced upon us and we must defend ourselves.

Self-defense requires some understanding of the realities of political struggle. To begin with, much of what we see and hear in the political world consists of lies and deceptions. The issues addressed by competing cliques of politicians are typically developed for tactical purposes and cannot be taken at face value. Politicians are generally, albeit not always, a currish lot, driven by a desire to acquire power or status or wealth, not by some commitment to the public interest. Indeed, since politicians, political parties, and other political actors habitually lie, citizens who heed the frequent injunction to abjure cynicism are likely to be duped into contributing their tax dollars and even their lives for dubious purposes, such as building democracy in Iraq. Those who actually work in the political arena—politicians, journalists, consultants, lobbyists and other political practitioners—are a notoriously cynical bunch. While encouraging ordinary citizens to trust the government and the political class, members of the political class are not so foolish as to trust one another.

As I have noted elsewhere, for more than 200 years, the tale of George Washington and the cherry tree has symbolized the virtue of America's first president and, by his example, the importance of integrity as an attribute of political leadership. Unfortunately, the cherry tree story is a myth, concocted in 1806 by an enterprising preacher, Mason L. Weems, who hoped to bolster the flagging sales of his rather shallow biography of Washington.[1]

While it may seem ironic that an anecdote designed to highlight the importance of truth telling is, itself, a fabrication, this irony is precisely the significance of the story. Parson Weems's fable helps to illustrate the duplicity and hypocrisy so often at the heart of the political process. Politics is a realm in which bold assertions about the importance of the truth are often lies and charges about the duplicity of others are typically hypocritical efforts to divert attention from the speaker's own misdeeds.

Take the never-ending debate between Democrats and Republicans on the question of ethics. Could anything be more obviously hypocritical and dishonest than the tiresome daily spectacle of duplicitous party functionaries accusing one another of ethics violations? In 2006, Republican lobbying and fund-raising improprieties helped Democrats trounce the GOP at the polls as similar scandals had helped Republicans turn out the Democrats in 1994. Not surprisingly, once they regained power, Democrats again had trouble finding their own ethical footing. Within a week of the election and in clear violation of congressional rules, Rep. William Jefferson (D-LA) sent out a franked letter on official stationery to solicit contributions to retire his campaign debt.[2] Of course, by Rep. Jefferson's standards, this was a minor ethical lapse. While sending out solicitation letters at taxpayer expense, the congressman was also busy explaining to federal investigators how he came to have $90,000 in cash hidden in a freezer in his Capitol Hill home. Rather than be known by their current donkey and elephant symbols, the two parties should be identified as the pots and the kettles. This terminology would give voters a better understanding of the meaning of the steady barrage of partisan charges and countercharges to which they are subjected.

Perhaps political figures should be forgiven for their hypocrisy. Like other human beings, politicians are usually driven by personal desires and private ambitions. Yet, individuals in public life are compelled to provide publicly acceptable justifications for their actions. Accordingly, they explain what often is self-interested conduct in terms of high-minded goals, civic needs, and national interests. Honesty would so frequently be politically damaging that virtually all politicians and public officials become practiced liars.

Critics, though, who insist on pointing out the regular discrepancies between politicians' claims and their true purposes are inevitably accused of fostering public cynicism. The news media, in particular, are regularly charged with promoting cynicism through their negative coverage of politicians and government officials. This charge is made so often that even many journalists have come to believe it. Nearly 40 percent of the journalists responding to a recent survey agreed that journalists were too cynical.[3] Some analysts assert that public doubts about the government and politicians diminish popular participation and undermine political institutions. Harvard political scientist Joseph Nye has said that cynicism about the political process tends to reduce the "quality" of American democracy.[4] Several scholars have recently proposed that the government and private institutions should work to develop educational programs and other initiatives to promote popular political trust.[5] A number of states, indeed, have already launched civic education campaigns designed to combat political cynicism among young people.[6] And, even as they regularly present rather unflattering accounts of the governmental and political processes, members of the national news media frequently urge Americans to eschew cynicism. "Cynicism can destroy our nation as readily as enemy bombs," wrote one columnist who apparently loves hyperbole as much as he abhors cynicism.[7]

These condemnations of cynicism, though, seem rather misguided. Perhaps members of the nation's political class have reason to be concerned about cynicism. After all, cynical citizens hardly make enthusiastic subjects or reliable followers. Yet, popular cynicism is hardly an aberration or malady to be cured through the dissemination of more effective propaganda materials. Instead, cynicism should be understood as a reasonable, if mainly intuitive, popular response to the realities of politics. Millions of Americans see over and over again that politicians and government officials routinely deceive, mislead, and misinform them, offering pretexts while masking their true plans and purposes.[8]

"I have previously stated and I repeat now that the United States plans no military intervention in Cuba," said President John F. Kennedy in 1961 as he planned military action in Cuba. "As president, it is my duty to the American people to report that renewed hostile actions against United States ships on the high seas in the Gulf of Tonkin have today required me to order the military forces of the United States to take action in reply," said President Lyndon Johnson in 1964 as he fabricated an incident to justify expansion of American involvement in Vietnam. "We did not, I repeat, did not trade weapons or anything else [to Iran] for hostages, nor will we," said President Ronald Reagan in November 1986, four months before admitting that U.S. arms had been traded to Iran in exchange for Americans being held hostage there. "Simply stated, there is no doubt that Saddam Hussein now has weapons of mass destruction," said Vice President Dick Cheney in 2002. When it turned out that these weapons did not exist, Assistant Defense Secretary Paul Wolfowitz explained, "For bureaucratic reasons, we settled on one issue, weapons of mass destruction (as justification for invading Iraq) because it was the one reason everyone could agree on."[9] In 2012, President Obama correctly accused his opponent Mitt Romney of suffering from "Romnesia" for seemingly forgetting which principles he had previously advocated and then abandoned for the sake of expedience. Obama himself, however, had difficulty deciding whether it was more expedient to tell voters that the U.S. ambassador to Libya had been murdered by organized terrorists or by unorganized thugs. The story seemed to change on a daily basis.

Since politicians and public officials are hypocrites, it is quite appropriate for ordinary citizens to be cynics. Ambrose Bierce defined a cynic as a "blackguard whose faulty vision sees things as they are, not as they ought to be."[10] If anything, too many Americans lack a requisite sense of cynicism. About half of those responding to University of Michigan surveys say the government *can be trusted* most of the time, and nearly two-thirds *disagree* with the proposition that public officials don't really care what people think. These recent percentages actually represent an increase in public trust after some decline between the 1960s and 1990s.[11] But shouldn't every American be just a bit distrustful of a class of individuals whose most prominent members, contrary to all logic and evidence, claim never to have inhaled, aver that they hardly even knew that pesky Ms. Lewinsky, or suggest they reluctantly agreed to forego the opportunity to serve in Vietnam in order to undertake the more onerous task of defending the air space over Texas? For that matter, can anyone truly believe the legions of lesser politicians who portentously declare that they are driven by an overwhelming urge to "fight" for the right of every last geezer to receive a pension check? Far from being a pathological condition, cynicism is a useful defense against such duplicity.

Yet, cynicism alone is hardly an adequate guide to the reality of politics. Political cynics often see through the lies of politicians only to fall prey to even more bizarre fantasies. Millions of Americans, for example, who don't trust the government also believe that federal officials are hiding evidence of extraterrestrial visitors at a secret base in New Mexico.[12] These individuals are ready to spurn official claims but, in their place, accept science fiction tales as reality. An understanding of politics requires not only a willingness to reject falsehoods but also the ability to assess objective evidence and arrive at the truth. The Chinese call this marriage of cynicism and objectivity "cynical realism," connoting an effort to substitute a true and accurate picture of political life for the lies told by the authorities.[13]

Cynics are sometimes accused of being without principles. Cynical realism, however, is based upon three core principles of political analysis. The first is that politics mainly revolves around self-interest. In particular, actors generally compete in the political arena to increase their resources and stature. Individuals strive to enhance their own wealth, their own power, and their own status rather than for more altruistic or public-spirited purposes. Second, even if political actors actually have less selfish aims, they must almost always, nevertheless, work to acquire wealth, power, or status to achieve these other goals. As Machiavelli observed, prophets generally must arm themselves if they hope to succeed.[14] Unfortunately, though, the effort to maximize these interests often becomes an end in and of itself even if it was not a political actor's primary initial goal. The quest for power can be as corrupting as its exercise. Third, the issues and ideas publicly espoused by political actors are more often the weapons of political struggle than its actual goals. What politicians say may be important but cannot be taken at face value.

The idea that political action is governed by selfish motives is hardly novel. Indeed, for centuries, political and social theorists have conceived self-interested conduct to be a fundamental reflection of human nature. "For it may be said of men in general," said Machiavelli, "That they are ungrateful, voluble, dissemblers, anxious to avoid danger, and covetous of gain."[15] This rather bleak view of human nature has a substantial scientific basis. Evolutionary psychologists argue that power, status, and possession of material resources have been associated with reproductive success throughout the evolution of the human species. Hence, the desire to acquire these assets is a potent driving force. Psychologist Steven Pinker writes that while humans have not evolved the rigid pecking orders characteristic of some animal species, in all human societies "high-ranking men are deferred to, have a greater voice in group decisions . . . and always have more wives, more lovers, and more affairs with other men's wives."[16] Of course, individuals vary enormously in the extent to which they are driven by greed or the lust for power and status. Yet, those drawn to political life are, by virtue of self selection, more likely than others to desire the substance, trappings, and privileges of rank.[17]

A telling example from antiquity is that of the Athenian general Alcibiades, a man who, according to Plutarch, had an inordinate love of distinction and fame.[18] After losing a political struggle in Athens, Alcibiades took advantage of his family's ties to members of the Spartan elite and sought to make himself a leader in Sparta, Athens' mortal enemy. After his political foes came to power in Sparta, Alcibiades sought to make himself a leader among the Persians. And, after losing favor with the Persians, Alcibiades was able to take command of an Athenian army. In every instance, Alcibiades appealed to the patriotic sentiments of his followers, calling upon them to fight and die for their country, while he was, himself, prepared to change countries whenever it suited his interests.

Perhaps Alcibiades's modern-day equivalent is the General Motors' Company. General Motors, which recently needed a government bailout mainly to compensate for the cupidity and stupidity of its managers, is well known for ad campaigns based upon nationalistic slogans such as "Keep America Rolling" and "Our Country—Our Trucks." GM also is justifiably proud of its contribution to America's defense effort, especially in World War II when its aircraft engines powered many of the nation's bombers and fighters. GM, however, seldom mentions the fact that during that same war, the company also made a major contribution to Germany's military efforts. While GM built equipment for the U.S. army, its German subsidiary, Adam Opel, built trucks, aircraft engines, and torpedoes for the Germans.[19] And, indeed, as corporate officials exhorted American workers to make an all-out effort to defeat the Germans, their colleagues in Germany urged German workers to do the same to defeat the Americans. The company profited from military contracts in both countries. Indeed, in the United States the company took a huge tax deduction for allegedly abandoning its German plants—which it reclaimed after the war—and then collected reparations from the U.S. government for bombing its German plants during the war. Alcibiades would have been proud.

With a nod to the crafty Athenian—or was he a Spartan or, perhaps, a Persian?—let us turn to our discussion of the unpleasant realities of violence in political life.

CHAPTER 1

VIOLENCE

THE DRIVING FORCE OF POLITICAL LIFE

Recent events such as the Boston Marathon bombing remind us that violence is brutal and terrible. Yet, while we may shrink from violence we should not shrink from attempting to analyze and understand violence. A capacity for violence has always been an important facet of human nature. Humans, and perhaps their pre-human ancestors as well, have engaged in murder and mayhem, as individuals and in groups, for hundreds of thousands of years.[1] And, at least since the advent of recorded history, violence and politics have been intimately related. States practice violence against internal and external foes. Political dissidents engage in violence against states. Competing political forces inflict violence upon one another. Writing in 1924, Winston Churchill declared—and not without reason—that "the story of the human race is war."[2]

Academic discussions of the relationship between violence and politics fall into three main schools. Some authors see violence as instrumentally related to politics. Hobbes, for example, viewed violence as a rational means by which individuals sought to achieve such political goals as territory, safety, and glory.[3] In a similar vein, Clausewitz famously referred to war as the continuation of politics by other means.[4] A second group of authors views violence as typically resulting from political failures and miscalculations. The title of an influential paper on the origins of the American Civil War by historian James Randall, "The Blundering Generation," exemplifies this idea.[5] A third group, most recently exemplified by psychologist Steven Pinker, views violence as a form of pathological behavior that is, perhaps, diminishing in frequency with the onward march of civilization.[6] Some proponents of this perspective have even declared that violence is essentially a public health problem.[7]

Whatever their differences of emphasis, each of these perspectives assigns violence a subordinate role in political life—a secondary means of achieving political goals, a result of political miscalculations, an expression of political pathology, and so forth. There is, as Hannah Arendt once noted, an alternative view that assigns violence a superordinate role in politics.[8] This perspective is implied by Mao Zedong's well-known aphorism that political power "grows out of the barrel of a gun." For Mao, violence is the driving force in the political arena while more peaceful forms of political engagement serve to fill in the details or, perhaps, merely to offer post-hoc justifications for the outcomes of violent struggles. Chairman Mao essentially turns Clausewitz on his head by characterizing politics as a sequel or even epiphenomenon of violent struggles— a continuation of violence by other means. Unfortunately, Mao seemed to have an inordinate fondness for mayhem and bloodshed. He did, after all, suggest that the quality of a revolutionary should be judged by the number of people he or she had killed.[9] Yet, our revulsion at the Chairman's practices should not blind us to the accuracy of his observation. Violence and the threat of violence are, in fact, the most potent forces in political life.

It is, to be sure, often averred that problems can never truly be solved by the use of force. Violence, the saying goes, is not the answer. This adage certainly appeals to our moral sensibilities. But whether or not violence is the answer presumably depends upon the question being asked. For better or worse, it is violence that usually provides the most definitive answers to three of the major questions of political life—statehood, territoriality, and power. Violent struggle, in the form of war, revolution, civil war, terrorism, and the like, more than any other immediate factor, determines what states will exist and their relative power, what territories they will occupy, and which groups will and will not exercise power within them.

In the case of statehood, there are occasional circumstances under which a state may be built by and endure mainly through peaceful means. These are, however, the rather rare exceptions. As Charles Tilly has observed, most of today's regimes are the survivors or descendants of a thousand-year-long culling process in which those states capable of creating and sustaining powerful military forces prevailed, while those that could not or would not fight were conquered or absorbed by others.[10] Similarly, when it comes to control of territory, virtually every square inch on the planet is currently occupied by groups that forcibly dispossessed—sometimes exterminated—the land's previous claimants. Thus far, at least, the meek have not inherited very much of the earth. Indeed, the West's global dominance for most of the past millennium is as much a function of its capacity for violence as any other factor.[11]

In some instances, of course, those deprived of their land raise serious objections and moral questions. Ongoing land disputes are particularly manifest in today's Middle East, where the Israelis are accused of pursuing an ongoing policy of stealing Arab land. Indeed, it is often asserted by Palestinians and by other Arabs and their left-liberal supporters in the West that the very existence of the State of Israel represents an illegitimate theft of Arab land. The creation of the State of Israel is seen in these quarters as a supreme tragedy or catastrophe (*al nakba* in Arabic).[12] Certainly, one can make this argument. Indeed, Arabs and Jews and possibly others, as well, have historic, religious, and legal land claims in the Middle East that merit attention. Yet, Jewish assertions of rightful ownership of the land of Israel do not seem any more or less lacking in legitimacy than any other contemporary territorial claims. It hardly needs to be said that the United States occupies millions of square miles of territory stolen from the Native Americans as well as land taken by force from the Mexicans whose Spanish forebears had previously stolen it from Native Americans. The ancestors of the modern-day Europeans stole their land too. But since these land thefts occurred long ago, the rightful ownership of Western European territory is only occasionally contested these days. In the case of America, the original land owners were largely exterminated by the European settlers and, so, are not in a position to press their claims with much vigor.

The main difference between the Israelis and other contemporary land owners might seem to be that Israel has only existed as a state for a few decades. Israel, moreover, unlike the United States and others, failed to launch a sustained campaign of annihilation against the previous land owners who therefore remain quite able to vocally and violently assert their irredentist claims. Should Israel, however, deserve relegation to the status of a pariah for having been insufficiently murderous? Those nations currently occupying lands whose previous inhabitants they exterminated might seem more blameworthy than those who did not pursue a genocidal program. The point here is not to absolve Israel from reproach but is, rather, to point to the many moral ambiguities surrounding questions of land ownership. The fact of the matter, however unfortunate it may seem, is that territory "belongs" to whatever group is able to seize and hold it.

In the case of power, within every state the composition of the ruling class, if not always the identity of the particular rulers, is generally shaped by the use or threat of what Walter Benjamin called law-making violence.[13] The availability of elections and the correlative peaceful modes of leadership selection that have become common in some parts of the world over the past two centuries does not contravene this last point. Barack Obama, America's first black president, was chosen at the polls. The possibility, however, that a black person could become a member of America's social and political elite was established through sometimes violent and often disruptive protest four decades earlier— to say nothing of the bloody war fifteen decades earlier that freed black people from chattel slavery.

Generally speaking, electoral politics is an arena in which success requires substantial economic, institutional, educational, and organizational resources. Consequently, elections in the Western world are usually fought among competing factions of the bourgeoisie—a social stratum whose power was established in a series of violent struggles that began in Europe in the seventeenth century.[14] Electoral outcomes reflect more than they affect this stratum's power in Western society. Some awareness of the limits of electoral politics seems to underlie the economic protests that developed throughout Western Europe and the United States in 2011. One young Spanish protestor quoted in the American media said, "Our parents are grateful because they're voting. We're the first generation to say that voting is worthless."[15] We shall return to elections in chapter 6.

In the United States over the past two centuries those elected to high political office have mainly been individuals drawn from the middle and upper classes.[16] For new groups, social and economic mobility have generally preceded electoral success. And, if by some chance, significant discrepancies do emerge between electoral results and the actual distribution of power in society, the verdict of the polls is likely to be challenged, often by forcible means. In the United States, for example, such a situation manifested itself in the South during the late 1860s and early 1870s when black electoral success was negated by white-organized paramilitary forces.[17]

Once the basic questions of statehood, territoriality, and power are answered, subsidiary matters might be addressed without a resort to force. But whether some form of peaceful political discourse is likely to emerge in the aftermath of a violent struggle depends in no small measure upon the decisiveness of the struggle's outcome. Decisiveness refers to the relationships among the winners and losers that emerge in the wake of a violent political conflict. An outcome is most decisive when a more or less unitary actor, such as an organized political party, nation-state, revolutionary army, or similar entity—say, the Bolsheviks or Chinese Communist Party—achieves a complete and clear-cut victory over its foes. Decisiveness is reduced when the nominal losers retain the ability to renew hostilities at some future date, or when victory is shared by a loosely knit alliance or coalition whose members' relationships to one another have as yet to be determined.

Generally speaking, more decisive outcomes bring a more certain end to violence but often also lead to the construction of hegemonic national or international regimes. Lack of decisiveness, on the other hand, may leave the road open to continuing or recurrent violence but can also pave the way for the emergence of polyarchical politics and a more liberal national or international order. If the losing parties to a violent conflict are not decisively defeated they may seek to avenge their defeat months, years, or even decades later. Those who are not able to defeat their foes decisively must be prepared to develop programs and policies designed to win the support of their defeated but still dangerous enemies if they wish to avert further hostilities. Thus, in 1066 the Normans defeated the Saxons but were not able to completely destroy the latter's military capabilities. Accordingly, Norman rulers were compelled to incorporate elements of the Saxon nobility into the ruling class and military, and to promote intermarriage and assimilation. Unable to defeat their adversaries more decisively, the Normans found it necessary to rule them more graciously. In a similar vein, though the Bulgarian Empire was conquered by the Byzantines in 1018, the Bulgarian nobility retained significant military strength. Accordingly, Byzantine emperor Basil II allowed Bulgarian nobles to retain their local powers and incorporated them into the Byzantine aristocracy. This policy was successful in preventing revolts, and its reversal after Basil's death sparked a series of rebellions by the selfsame noble families and the eventual overthrow of Byzantine rule.[18]

Decisiveness is also lessened when success in a violent struggle is achieved by a coalition or loosely affiliated set of forces rather than a single entity. Victory won by a coalition may be decisive vis-à-vis the losers but is often followed by disputes among the winners that can produce a renewed threat of violence. The coalition that won a decisive victory over Nazi Germany and Imperial Japan in the Second World War, for example, soon split into hostile camps that faced one another in a protracted and occasionally violent "Cold War." If they wish to avoid internecine disputes, winning coalitions must usually construct institutions and develop rules for peaceful conflict resolution. If the winning coalition involves nations, these arrangements may take the form of complex treaty agreements or super-national organizations like the League of Nations or the United Nations. If the successful coalition consists of groups or entities within a nation, the erstwhile coalition partners may endeavor to develop a constitutional power-sharing arrangement. In the aftermath of the American Revolutionary War, for example, members of the victorious coalition of thirteen states agreed to the Articles of Confederation and, later, the Constitution to provide for the discussion of common issues and the peaceful resolution of problems.

Neither the League of Nations nor the United Nations, nor for that matter the Articles of Confederation and Constitution proved fully effective in preventing the emergence of conflicts among their various members and signatories. There can be little doubt that a decisive resolution of violent national or international conflict offers a surer path to peace than an indecisive conclusion. However, while a decisive end to violent struggle is more certain to yield peace, an indecisive conclusion opens the way for politics. Though it may sometimes recede into the background, the use or threat of violence never truly disappears from governance and politics. Every government routinely employs coercion against those who challenge its power, and most will respond quite forcefully to internal as well as external threats to their autonomy or territorial integrity.

Since many political issues have at least potential implications for the balance of political power within or between states, the threat of violence can lie just beneath the surface of even the most peaceful political discussion. In 2010, for example, the prosaic issue of health care reform seemed, albeit rather obliquely, to raise questions about the relative influence of competing social forces in the U.S. This soon brought intimations if not actual threats of violence by and against foes of the Obama administration's plans as well as ruminations by some politicians about the legalities of state secession from the Union.[19] Should a mundane discussion come to have more direct implications for a nation's territorial integrity or the distribution of power in society, the latent possibility of violence can quickly become manifest. Thomas Jefferson was shocked in 1820 when what had appeared to be a routine debate over the admission of new states suddenly threatened to bring about the violent dissolution of the Union when the issue was seen to have major implications for the balance of power between Northern and Southern elites. It was a "fire bell in the night," Jefferson famously declared. Four decades later, when the fire bell rang again, the national government expended 600,000 lives to crush the South's effort to secede.

The political importance of violence derives mainly from four factors. First is the dominance usually manifested by violence over other forms of political action. Second is the agenda-setting power of violence. Third is the destructive and politically transformative power of violence. Fourth is the capacity of violence to serve as a catalyst for political mobilization. Taken together, these attributes of violent political action explain why the gun barrel is, indeed, such an important source of political power.

DOMINANCE

As to the first of these factors, dominance, political forces willing and able to employ violence to achieve their goals will generally best their less bellicose adversaries, overturning the results of elections, negating the actions of parliamentary bodies, riding roughshod over peaceful expressions of political opinion, and so forth. Indeed, the mere threat of violence is often enough to instill fear in and compel acquiescence on the part of those unwilling or unable to forcefully defend themselves. Violent groups can usually be defeated only by adversaries able to block their use of mayhem or to employ superior force against them. Those who cannot or will not make use of violence seldom achieve their goals over the opposition of those who are not similarly constrained. As Machiavelli observed, things have seldom turned out well for unarmed prophets.[20]

In recent decades, for example, armed insurgents have employed violence or the threat of violence to overthrow a number of established regimes. The African continent alone has experienced some eighty-five successful military coups during the past sixty years. Once in power, such groups can usually only be overthrown by subsequent armed coups or insurrections. They tend not to be very responsive to opinion polls, voting, or other polite forms of political expression. Occasionally, perhaps, a regime steeped in violence can be successfully confronted via peaceful means, but these are exceptional cases. East Germany collapsed in the face of peaceful protests in 1989 when its Soviet sponsor, having decided to rid itself of its satellite empire, would not allow the German Democratic Republic's feared security services to be mobilized. Or, to cite another example, Chilean dictator Augusto Pinochet actually stepped down after losing a plebiscite in 1988, some fifteen years after he had seized power in a bloody military coup. Yet, even Pinochet's departure from office came on the heels of an assassination attempt and five years of increasingly violent demonstrations that undermined the Chilean economy and convinced many military officers that it was time to return power to a civilian government.

As the past century's history of coups, insurrections, civil wars, and invasions suggest, East Germany and Chile are unusual cases. Generally speaking, force can only be defeated by force. When peaceful dissidents confront tanks the result is more likely to resemble the Tiananmen Square bloodletting than the fall of the Berlin Wall. This lesson was learned repeatedly throughout the Middle East in 2011. Peaceful protestors in Libya and Syria quickly found that they were no match for the tanks and machine guns their rulers were only too happy to deploy against them. Only when Libyan insurgents resorted to force backed by NATO air strikes were they able to defeat the Gaddafi regime. Only through force could Syrian protestors confront the Assad government. And, in Egypt, President Hosni Mubarak was ousted more or less peacefully only because the army calculated that it could most easily retain control of the nation by acceding to demands for a new president.

Much attention, of course, is given to the putative effectiveness of non-violence as a political method. Nonviolent tactics are often said, for example, to have been instrumental in ending segregation in the U.S., Communist rule in Eastern Europe and British rule in India, and, certainly, political leaders espousing a philosophy of nonviolence—Martin Luther King, Vaclav Havel, Mahatma Gandhi—played important roles in these cases. Indeed, as an interesting study by Erica Chenoweth and Maria Stephan has shown, various forms of nominally nonviolent civil resistance can be quite effective.[21] A troublesome and disruptive group can wrest concessions from a government without having to resort to mayhem and bloodshed. In some instances, a regime may see the costs of such concessions as less than the costs and risks of a harsh response. This calculus was the basis for Saul Alinsky's well-known "rules for radicals."[22] I shall return to this topic in chapter 5.

However, far from being nonviolent, the protest tactics—strikes, boycotts, demonstrations, and the like—employed by such leaders as King and Gandhi were designed to produce economic and social disruption and, in some instances, to provoke violent responses from their opponents. Violent attacks on apparently peaceful protestors would, it was hoped, elicit sympathy for the innocent victims of bloodshed and perhaps encourage powerful external forces to intervene on their behalf. Their success was predicated upon the availability of allies who could be drawn into the fray in support of the victims of violence.

Take, for example, one of the tactics employed by Dr. Martin Luther King in his effort to undermine the Southern *apartheid* system and secure civil rights for African Americans. On a number of occasions, Dr. King led groups of peaceful protestors into hostile Southern communities where he could be confident that the local authorities could be provoked into employing violence against his followers. This, in turn, would help to build support for his cause and demands for the federal government's intervention on its behalf by convincing Northern audiences that the Southern Jim Crow system was brutal, evil, and fundamentally un-American.[23] In his efforts, Dr. King counted upon the support of an alliance of Northern white liberals, segments of the business community, and important elements of the national news media. The media not only saw a powerful story, but also saw an opportunity to castigate the conservative coalition of Southern Democrats and right-wing Republicans that had tormented journalists and broadcasters over their alleged Communist ties during the 1940s and 1950s. This alliance gave Dr. King extraordinarily good access to the nation's television screens, helped him to sway public opinion in favor of his cause and to secure the intervention of federal authorities who then forcibly suppressed Southern white resistance to the enfranchisement of blacks.

One of the most famous protests organized by Dr. King, the April 1965 march at Selma, Alabama, is instructive in this regard. King targeted Selma for a concerted campaign of protest activity partly because racial discrimination in Selma and surrounding Dallas County was so starkly obvious. For example, because of systematic black disfranchisement, only 2 percent of the county's registered voters were black, even though blacks comprised 58 percent of the county's residents.[24] Selma had been chosen, however, not only because of its record of discrimination but also because Dr. King was confident that state and county political leaders were fools. He expected them to respond to peaceful protests with violence and, in the process, imprint themselves upon the collective consciousness of a national television audience as the brutal oppressors of heroic and defenseless crusaders seeking freedom and democracy.[25] Alabama and Dallas County authorities played their assigned roles convincingly. With network cameras watching, Alabama state troopers launched a vicious attack against protestors on the Edmund Pettus Bridge, leaving forty demonstrators seriously injured in what the media dubbed "Bloody Sunday."[26]

From the perspective of protest leaders and the national media, Dallas County sheriff Jim Clark might have been sent by central casting to play his part in the drama. Clark displayed a violent temper on camera, wore a "Never" button in his lapel, and armed his deputies with electric cattle prods. Clark unwittingly contributed so much to Dr. King's efforts that the protestors made him an honorary member of the Southern Christian Leadership Conference (SCLC) as well as the Student Nonviolent Coordinating Committee (SNCC) and the National Association for the Advancement of Colored People (NAACP).[27] Clark certainly deserved his awards. Nationally televised images of the violence unleashed upon peaceful protestors generated enormous sympathy for the civil rights cause and helped create the setting for the enactment of the 1965 Voting Rights Act, which sent an army of federal law enforcement officials into the South with the power to suppress white resistance to the registration of black voters. In essence, nominally nonviolent protest succeeded because the protestors' allies had an even greater capacity for violence than their foes. Where, as in the case of Tiananmen Square, powerful allies are not available to deploy or at least threaten the use of force, nonviolent protest is almost always doomed to failure.

VIOLENCE DRIVES THE POLITICAL AGENDA

Violence or, in some cases, even the threat of violence tends to drive other issues and considerations from the political agenda. Whatever the underlying causes of a political dispute, once violence erupts, it generally takes center stage with other issues and considerations forced to the margins. The course of the dispute is driven and its outcome heavily influenced if not always fully determined by the violence to which it gave rise. In essence, once ignited, violence takes on a life of its own and becomes, to use a phrase coined by President George W. Bush, the decider.

Take the events leading up to the American Civil War. The war had many contributing causes—sectional economic rivalries, the tariff, slavery, and so forth. Yet, none of these, whether singly or in combination, need have produced a military confrontation. In some measure, the proximate cause of the war was violence itself.

The first state to secede from the Union was, of course, South Carolina. During the constitutional crises of the 1830s and early 1850s, the propertied interests that dominated South Carolina politics had urged caution and moderation in the South's response to Northern criticism and to efforts to limit the expansion of slavery. By the late 1850s, though, the views of South Carolina's planters shifted dramatically. The new Republican Party, a political entity that made opposition to slavery a major plank in its political platform, won the 1858 national congressional elections. In 1859, news of John Brown's raid at Harpers Ferry, Virginia, threw the entire South into an uproar. And, in early 1860, the Republicans nominated as their presidential candidate Abraham Lincoln, an individual seen throughout the South, albeit incorrectly, as a mortal foe of slavery. These developments led even the most moderate among South Carolina's planters to believe that secession from the Union might become necessary. In 1859, planters supported the gubernatorial candidacy of F. W. Pickens, an individual who had been a "Nullie," or outspoken advocate of the idea that states could nullify federal laws within their own borders, in 1852 and had previously been dismissed as a hothead by men of property and substance. Before the war, South Carolina's governors were chosen by the state legislature. The legislature chose Pickens, and a general agreement emerged among the planters that if Lincoln was elected, the state would secede and would defend itself if attacked.

In November 1860, of course, Lincoln won the presidency. The next month, South Carolinians held a state-wide convention that voted to secede from the Union. South Carolina now considered itself an independent nation and prepared to go to war if this should become necessary to maintain its independence. Six other states, Texas, Louisiana, Mississippi, Florida, Alabama, and Georgia, followed South Carolina out of the Union and banded together as the Confederate States of America. This new Confederacy chose Mississippi senator Jefferson Davis as its president. Despite these developments, many politicians in both the North and South continued to hope that some compromise might be reached and the crisis defused. Several of the Southern states, including Virginia, the South's most important state, had not seceded, and their unionist politicians continued, in the spring of 1861, to search for some formula to avert the breakup of the United States. Perhaps such a formula might have been found, but violent events in Charleston's harbor soon made compromise impossible.

At the mouth of Charleston's harbor sits a tiny artificial island, Fort Sumter, constructed after the War of 1812 as part of America's system of coastal defenses. Sumter's artillery, along with guns positioned at Fort Moultrie, a point of land on Sullivan's Island across the harbor from Fort Sumter, guarded the approaches to Charleston. The Charleston forts and one Florida fort were the only federal installations in the seceded states that had not been quickly abandoned by federal authorities. On December 26, 1860, the federal commander in Charleston, Major Robert Anderson, evacuated his troops from the indefensible Fort Moultrie to the more secure Fort Sumter and waited for orders from Washington. An attempt by the U.S. Navy to resupply Fort Sumter in January failed when South Carolina artillery, in response to an order issued by Governor Pickens opened fire on the supply ship *Star of the West* and drove it away.

The standoff at Fort Sumter continued through Lincoln's inauguration in March 1861. At this point, Confederate commissioners traveled to Washington to demand the surrender of the fort. They were officially rebuffed but received tacit assurances from Secretary of State Seward that the government would not attempt to reinforce the fort while discussions and deliberations continued. Both in Washington and the temporary Confederate capital, Montgomery, Alabama, many influential politicians argued for a cautious approach. A number of Confederate officials thought secession could be accomplished without war. A number of federal officials hoped a peaceful resolution to the Sumter question would help persuade Virginia to remain in the Union. By April, though, Sumter's supplies were running out and President Lincoln ordered a relief expedition to leave for Charleston. Confederate President Davis, in turn, ordered Southern artillery to open fire on the fort. Sumter's guns replied, and for two days the citizens of Charleston cheered the artillery barrages from the waterfront.[28] Finally, Major Anderson indicated that he was ready to surrender, and a triumphal flotilla of soldiers and civilians headed for the little island.

News of the fighting at Fort Sumter spread quickly via telegraph. President Lincoln asked the loyal states for 75,000 troops to suppress the rebellion. With Lincoln's call for troops, voices of moderation in Virginia, Arkansas, North Carolina, and Tennessee were drowned out, and these states seceded and joined the Confederacy. Thus, while secession and war had not been planned or even desired by most major policy makers, once sparked, violence drove the political agenda, relegating the other issues and causes of the war to a subordinate status. Students of history will note that a similar story could be told about the outbreak of World War I.

DESTRUCTION AND TRANSFORMATION

Third, violence is a major instrument—perhaps the major instrument—of social and political transformation both in the international system and within given states. Violence is usually necessary to bring about the destruction of existing institutions and social forces and, thus, to pave the way for new developments. As the always prescient Chairman Mao put it, without violence "it is impossible to accomplish any leap in social development."[29]

The likely impact of violence upon "social development" is related to its level of intensity. At a low level of intensity, violence is generally associated with maintenance of the political status quo. States and individual bureaucracies within states usually construct police and security forces and more or less continually employ a low level of violence to intimidate or subdue their opponents and to prevent disruptive or even modestly violent activities on the part of disaffected groups—protests, demonstrations, and the like—from having much effect upon their behavior. Even contemporary American students of public management are taught to be prepared to deal with "public outcries, insults and demonstrations," without allowing these to divert them from their "program goals."[30] At the same time, a low level of violence on the part of disaffected groups can actually help to maintain political order by allowing governments an opportunity to demonstrate their power, to impress all and sundry with their forbearance in the face of provocation and, as sociologist Kai T. Erikson once observed, to strengthen communal solidarity by clearly demarcating the boundary between acceptable and unacceptable political activity.[31]

Violence at a high level of intensity, on the other hand, is often associated with political and social change. First, practiced by states against one another intense violence can transform, indeed, is usually a necessary condition for transformation of the world order. The current international system, dominated by the United States is, like its predecessors, in large part a product of wars and other episodes of violence that created some states, eliminated others, and determined the balance of power among the survivors. Today, forces intent on changing the shape of that order are working assiduously to develop military capabilities that will allow them to challenge the United States or whatever regional powers stand in the way of their ambitions. Thus, Iran is seeking to develop nuclear weapons that might give it a dominant role in the Middle East; China is building naval, air, and ground forces that could make the PRC the dominant power in Asia, while a variety of less-well-endowed states and even non-state entities are counting upon terrorism and other forms of asymmetric warfare to advance their interests. For their part, the U.S. and other established powers constantly endeavor to strengthen their own military forces and frequently wage war to thwart these adversaries.

Intense violence practiced by states against one another not only shapes the international system but also influences the internal politics and institutional development of the states within that system. Acts of violence that are of short duration can often become at least a temporary source of social cohesion as members of a community bond together in shock and indignation. The 9-11 terror attacks, for example, initially produced a sense of national solidarity or "rally-round-the-flag effect" in the United States that seemed to transcend the nation's usual social and political divisions.

If, on the other hand, violence persists for a longer period of time, its human and pecuniary costs can lead to stresses that expose and exacerbate whatever divisions may already exist in a particular society. Thus, for example, most Americans initially supported each of the major military conflicts in which the nation has engaged over the past two centuries, but as these struggles wore on, they aggravated the nation's underlying social, economic, racial, and regional divisions and produced major anti-war movements. During the War of 1812, for example, New England, whose commercial interests were adversely affected by the national government's war policies, nearly seceded from the Union. During the Civil War, the Democratic Party called for a negotiated settlement with the South and nearly ousted President Abraham Lincoln in the 1864 elections. World War I led to political division and resistance to conscription. Similarly, America's wars in Korea, Indochina, and the Middle East sparked political opposition and the eventual defeat of the politicians and parties associated with leading the nation into war. Only World War II failed to generate significant domestic conflict. Though many Americans had voiced isolationist sentiment and had been opposed to the nation's involvement in the war, once America was attacked, few could see any alternative but to fight until Japan and Germany had been defeated.

Over very long periods of time violence between states is associated with the construction and consolidation of state power. Historical sociologist Charles Tilly described the state as the functional equivalent of a protection racket, offering its citizens security in exchange for their taxes, service, and obedience—whether they want protection or not.[32] Citizens are more likely to want protection when they face real threats, hence long periods of international or internecine violence provide rulers with excellent opportunities to expand their power. Over time, moreover, protracted violence operates in a quasi-Darwinian manner to promote the emergence of powerful states. During the course of centuries of conflict, particularly in Europe, the states that survived did so because they were able not only to construct powerful military forces, but also the bureaucracies, tax collection agencies, and administrative procedures needed to extract resources from the citizenry, ensure popular obedience, bolster economic strength, and so forth. Over time, as Tilly put it, "war made states."[33]

Like conflict between states, violence within states can bring about major social and institutional transformations. Practiced by dissident groups against regimes or by regimes against their domestic foes, violence can sweep away established institutions and social forces and help to empower new ones. Violent transformations are particularly important in two realms. First, violence is far more likely than peaceful change to bring new groups and forces to power. Second, violence is one of the few instruments that can uproot established political institutions and bureaucratic agencies.

As to the first of these realms, violence is the most important vehicle through which the power of established social forces can be suppressed. Thus, for example, the terror campaigns launched by Stalin during the 1920s and 1930s were aimed at weakening or eradicating social forces such as the intelligentsia, the upper peasantry or "Kulaks" and, later, the Jews regarded as potential sources of opposition to the regime. Through violence, the Soviet regime worked to fundamentally change the structure of the society it inherited and purge it of groups that might be disloyal or stand in the way of the regime's objectives. The result was the consolidation of Soviet power albeit at the cost of widespread suffering.[34]

By the same token, violence can serve as an important vehicle for groups from society's lower rungs seeking to ascend the ladder of political power. In a series of studies completed during the late 1960s, political scientist Harold Lasswell and his associates examined the revolutionary elites—Soviet, Nazi, Italian Fascist, and Chinese Communist—who changed the face of the world during the early decades of the twentieth century.[35] Each of these political forces used violence to seize power and to stamp out opposition. The Nazis, to be sure, also had some success at the polls, but their electoral tactics included violence and intimidation directed against voters and opposition candidates.[36]

Most of the founders and early leaders of all four revolutionary movements, including the Nazi Party, were intellectual ideologues with middle- or upper-middle-class social origins and, in many cases, a good deal of formal education. These were the individuals with the backgrounds and training necessary to organize political movements and to articulate political ideologies. More important, though, all four movements allowed members of previously subordinate social groups to make their way to the pinnacles of national power. The chief Nazi administrators, for example, were generally recruited from the lower strata of German society. Italian Fascism brought to the fore individuals from the lower middle classes. In Russia and China the revolutionary seizure of power by Communist movements ultimately allowed individuals from the lower classes, including the peasantry, to achieve high positions. In general, leaving aside the intellectuals who founded the four movements, power in the regimes that resulted from the success of these movements was inversely related to success and position in the preexisting society.[37] In all four cases, violent political action served as a vehicle for a social revolution through which subordinate groups were able to displace established elites and seize power.

Just as it can sweep away established elites, violence can also uproot and destroy established governmental and political institutions that might otherwise be impervious to change. Bureaucratic institutions, as Max Weber noted, are extremely difficult to alter or abolish once they are firmly established.[38] Generally speaking, bureaucracies are created to give more or less permanent effect to some set of programs and policies so that they continue on after their initial sponsors pass from the scene. Accordingly, those who create bureaucracies generally surround these institutions with rules and procedures designed to safeguard their autonomy and to prevent potentially hostile forces from gaining control of them and subverting their purposes. Hence, even in a democratic context, bureaucracies are staffed primarily through an appointment process that they, themselves, control, develop their own administrative procedures and promulgate their own rules for the implementation of programs and policies within their bureaucratic domains. In the U.S., these ideas have been enshrined by the courts under the rubric of "deference" to agency decisions.[39]

Once they are established, bureaucratic agencies generally endeavor to protect their institutional and procedural autonomy by sinking taproots into the political economy. They work to build lasting ties of mutual interest to social constituencies, interest groups, and politicians who will, in turn, defend them from criticism.[40] In the United States, relationships between bureaucracies, clientele groups, and politicians are sometimes known as "iron triangles" because of their political power and ability to ward off political adversaries. For example, during the 1980 presidential campaign, Ronald Reagan promised to abolish the Department of Education as part of his effort to get the government "off the backs" of the American people. After his election, Reagan even appointed a Secretary of Education who was publicly committed to eliminating the agency. Nevertheless, the Department was able to rally the support of its allies in Congress as well as the teachers unions, government contractors, and other clientele groups that benefited from its programs. Reagan's efforts were quickly deflected.

Over the years, bureaucratic agencies will sometimes depart from their original missions and evolve new goals and procedures designed to advance both the internal and external goals of their leadership cadres. That is, agency executives will seek to identify a mission that justifies their agency's budgetary claims and power vis-à-vis other institutions, strengthens clientele support, and reinforces the established structure of power within the agency by affirming the importance of the particular leadership group that claims to be uniquely qualified to carry out the agency's core mission.

In time, this mission and associated practices can become so deeply ingrained in the minds of agency executives and staffers that adherence to it becomes a matter of habit and reflex. Students of bureaucracy refer to this set of established pattern of practices and beliefs about the organization's role and purpose as the agency's institutional "culture."[41] Political scientist James Q. Wilson observed that "every organization has a culture . . . a persistent, patterned way of thinking about the central tasks of and human relationships within an organization. Culture is to an organization what personality is to an individual . . . it is passed from one generation to the next. It changes slowly, if at all."[42]

As in the case of efforts to abolish bureaucratic entities, agencies will strenuously resist attempts to redefine their missions, since agency leaders are likely to view these efforts as endangering their own power and position and will mobilize their supporters and clients to drive off such threats. As a result, many agencies seem to cling tenaciously to missions and procedures whose purposes seem no longer to have much validity. It may be recalled that efforts by the battleship admirals who controlled the U.S. Navy to resist the introduction of aircraft carriers were ended only when the Japanese sank several of the enormously expensive but militarily irrelevant leviathans.

Perhaps one of the lessons of the Pearl Harbor attack is that violence is sometimes the most effective way to compel established bureaucracies to alter their behavior. Bureaucracies are almost always protected by rules and procedures designed to prevent external interference in their affairs. Violence, however, is outside the rules and practices that safeguard bureaucratic autonomy. Mechanisms of leadership selection, procedural rules, bureaucratic culture, and the like become irrelevant when an institution is confronted by violent threats to its facilities and personnel.

Take, for example, the relationship between African Americans and America's police forces, school systems, social service agencies, and other urban service bureaucracies. Prior to the 1960s, these institutions generally viewed blacks as problems rather than clients. Many big-city police forces, in particular, routinely subjected blacks to harassment and were far more likely to employ brutality against blacks than against the whites with whom they came into contact. Police officials justified what they viewed as aggressive policing by averring that extraordinary force was needed to maintain order in the black community.[43]

This notion that blacks were generally a troublesome or criminal element also rendered police officials insensitive to the demeaning treatment, insults, and indignities that black citizens frequently suffered in encounters with patrol officers. Even well-educated, middle-class blacks often found themselves subjected to racial epithets and other insulting language and were far more likely than whites to be questioned, searched, or detained by the police. At the same time, police services in black communities were generally far worse than in white areas, with the police responding slowly to calls and ignoring a range of illegal activities such as drug abuse and prostitution that they would not have tolerated in white areas.[44] All of these practices, according to criminologist Robert Fogelson, were attributable to the ideology and experience of the police and were a routine element of their bureaucratic culture.[45]

Efforts by African Americans to persuade police agencies to alter their practices had generally been unsuccessful. In New Orleans, for example, after 1945 more than thirty organizations were established by African American leaders to protest police misconduct in the black community. Groups such as the Police Brutality Committee and the Committee for Accountable Police met with politicians and police officials and held numerous protest meetings all to no avail.[46] In New Orleans, as in other cities, police administrators declared that black criticisms were merely efforts to undermine the effectiveness of law enforcement.[47]

Urban police departments were compelled to modify their conduct in the black community by an outbreak of intense rioting and violence—much of it directed at the police—during the 1960s. Major riots took place in New York (1964), Philadelphia (1964), Rochester (1964), Jersey City (1964), Atlanta (1966), Chicago (1966), Detroit (1967), Tampa (1967), and Washington, DC (1968), while lesser disturbances occurred in a host of other cities. Virtually all these riots were sparked by confrontations between African Americans and the police. In New York an off-duty police officer killed a black teenager, in Atlanta a patrolman wounded a black auto theft suspect, in Detroit the police raided an after-hours black tavern, and so forth.[48] In most cases, too, rioters directed the bulk of their anger and fury at the local police, who suffered numerous injuries, as well as some fatalities at the hands of rioters. National guard troops, mobilized to restore order, were generally treated courteously in the black community.[49]

In the wake of the riots, investigations by a number of official bodies such as the U.S. Commission on Civil Rights, the National Advisory Commission on Civil Disorders, and the President's Commission on Law Enforcement and Administration of Justice, came to the obvious conclusion that police practices had been a major precipitant of urban violence and recommended a number of reforms that were gradually imposed upon police bureaucracies by local and federal officials determined to prevent a renewal of the violence that had already cost billions of dollars in property damage. These reforms included the appointment of larger numbers of black police officers and their assignment to patrol black neighborhoods, the promotion of black officers to command positions including the highest ranks of urban departments, the introduction of a variety of police–community relations programs, and the promulgation of rules and regulations designed to compel officers to behave courteously toward black citizens.[50] Two years of violence had forced urban police departments to at least begin a series of reforms they had previously rejected.

Of course, bureaucracies can be sufficiently resilient to withstand even the most violent attacks. In 1966, Mao Zedong unleashed the first of a decade-long series of blows against the Chinese state and Communist Party apparatus that came to be called Mao's "Cultural Revolution." Fearing that foes, whether real or imagined, within the state and party bureaucracies might unite against him, Mao mobilized hundreds of thousands of students calling themselves "Red Guards" to struggle against those deemed enemies of the Revolution. Most of these putative enemies were state functionaries and party cadres from the lowest to the very highest levels of power, including such luminaries as Marshal Lin Biao, Liu Shaoqi, and Deng Xiaoping. Tens of thousands of officials were exiled to the countryside and forced to engage in hard labor; many thousands of others were murdered, beaten, imprisoned, tortured, humiliated, and driven to suicide.[51] After Mao's death in 1976, however, his closest associates were arrested, and many of the high-ranking party cadres and state functionaries purged during the Cultural Revolution were returned to positions of power. These included Deng Xiaoping, who became China's de facto leader. Even a number of the ministries that had been abolished by Mao and the Red Guards were reopened. Ten years of violent attacks, orchestrated by the nation's paramount leader, had shaken but not uprooted the bureaucracy.

MOBILIZATION

Finally, violence can serve as a powerful catalyst for political mobilization, bringing new or previously marginal groups into the political arena. Some groups may be drawn into the political arena in an effort to bring an end to violence. In the United States, for example, opponents of the Mexican War, the Civil War, World War I, the Vietnam War, and other conflicts were able to organize rallies, demonstrations, resistance to conscription, and widespread electoral opposition to the government's war policies. Opposition to America's war in Vietnam played an important role in bringing young people into the political arena, first as demonstrators and then as voters when the Democratic Party sought to take advantage of this politically mobilized youth by pressing for the enactment of the Twenty-Sixth Amendment, lowering the voting age to eighteen.

At the same time, those who actually fight and sacrifice expect to derive some benefit for themselves and, perhaps, for their ethnic, regional, or confessional compatriots. Such benefits often include a larger role in public life. Thus, in both America and Europe periods of warfare and violence were often associated with suffrage expansion as soldiers demanded voting rights in exchange for their martial efforts, and governments saw political participation as an instrument for inspiring citizens to fight for their country. A nineteenth-century Swedish slogan that captured this notion was "One man, one vote, one gun." In recent years, of course, this slogan has been abbreviated and its original meaning forgotten. World War I, in particular, was associated with a great wave of suffrage expansion in Europe and North America as governments sought to mobilize support for the war effort.[52] In Canada, for example, under the Wartimes Election Act, women with relatives serving in the armed services were given the right to vote for the duration of the war. The government apparently believed that a woman with a vote would have reason to urge her husband, son, or brother to make whatever sacrifice was needed for victory.[53]

Still a third way in which violence can contribute to political mobilization is through its emotive power. For some individuals—perhaps particularly young men from social strata in which what Pinker calls a culture of combative masculinity has taken root—the opportunity to engage in violence exerts a powerful attraction.[54] National military services play on this desire with their recruiting slogans such as "We're looking for a few good men," with its assurance of adventure and promise of a chance to demonstrate one's masculinity by becoming a fierce warrior.

In the political realm, violent movements have sometimes found that it is their very propensity for violence that is attractive to some potential adherents. Take, for example, the appeal of the Nazi movement to some German workers as Hitler bid for power during the 1930s. In contrast to German workers' established Social Democratic leaders, the Nazis did not speak of complex, long-term solutions to the problems faced by the working class. Instead, the Nazis engaged in direct and violent action against immediate and visible targets. To a far greater extent than even other parties of the radical right, the Nazis exulted in acts of violence—in beatings, riots, desecrations, pogroms, and murders. As historian Peter Pulzer has observed, the ferocity of the Nazi's tactics had an enormous allure for desperate and angry workers.[55]

In a similar vein, contemporary terrorist groups often vie with one another for prestige and adherents by planning and executing more spectacular and destructive acts than those committed by their ideological or factional rivals. As political scientist Martha Crenshaw points out, within the Palestinian resistance movement, competing factions have often planned ever more violent attacks against Israeli civilians not so much to intimidate the Israeli government as to enhance their own prestige and to attract recruits to their respective camps.[56] Violence seems especially attractive to those who suffer from a sense of powerlessness and see membership in a violent struggle as a form of personal and communal reaffirmation. Thus, the allure of violence can reshape the political landscape by drawing previously marginal elements into political life. It was the violent struggle launched by Hamas, for example, that inspired thousands of previously quiescent young Palestinians to enter the political arena. Similarly, the violence unleashed in Algeria during the 1990s by the Mouvement Islamique Armé (MIA) inspired political involvement by the young urban poor who had previously been apolitical and mocked as *hittistes*, or persons who spent the day leaning against a wall.[57] In Pakistan, according to anthropologist Oskar Verkaaik, some young men are drawn to violent political movements because they see such involvement essentially as an opportunity for "fun" in otherwise boring lives that provide few chances for meaningful self-expression.[58]

SOLUTIONS FOR VIOLENCE?

The importance of violence in political affairs would seem to be clear. Because violence can be so terrible, however, there is a persistent tendency to treat violence as a problem to be solved rather than the main solution that nation-states, competing political forces, and even individuals employ to solve their most important political problems. As noted above, some see political violence both between and within nations as a disease or public health problem that can be cured through the alleviation of such factors as poverty and inequality. This position has been articulated by the National Institute of Mental Health, the American Psychological Association, and such political luminaries as former Attorney General Ramsey Clark and President Lyndon Johnson, who said that "all of us know" that violence is caused by ignorance, discrimination, poverty, and disease.[59]

This idea seems somewhat misguided. Even if we overlook the overt acts of mayhem committed by wealthy and powerful individuals, groups, and nations, we certainly should not ignore what Walter Benjamin called law-preserving violence or what contemporary social theorist Slavoj Žižek calls "systemic violence," namely the ongoing forms of coercion and threats of violence used by the powerful—mainly, albeit not exclusively, through the governments they control—to intimidate the lower orders and protect their privileged positions.[60]

In the United States, for example, we are inclined to be aware of the petty forms of criminal violence often committed by the poor. These are catalogued each year as "crimes known to the police" in the statistics reported by the Federal Bureau of Investigation and heavily publicized by the national media. Yet, we are less aware of what might be deemed "coercion committed by the state." During any given year, more than 1 percent of America's adults, 2.5 million individuals, are incarcerated in America's prisons and jails with nearly five million more on parole, probation, or temporarily free on bail awaiting trial. The majority of these persons are guilty of nonviolent crimes, and perhaps half have committed victimless offenses such as drug possession, gambling, prostitution, and so forth. In recent years, under what is sometimes called the "broken windows" theory of law enforcement, harsh punishments have been meted out for these and petty forms of disorderly conduct such as panhandling, mainly engaged in by poor people, in order to maintain a level of public order that would make "respectable" people comfortable.[61] In this case as in so many others, systemic violence is a deliberate solution imposed on behalf of the better classes, not an unfortunate and inadvertent problem caused by poverty and inequality.

A second group sees violence as a political problem that can be solved through the development of appropriate forms of political organization. This group follows two main schools of thought, the Hobbesian and the Kantian. For Hobbes, the solution to the problem of violence was the creation of a powerful sovereign authority that would put an end to strife and violent conflict.[62] For Kant, concerned primarily with international conflict, the solution was an increase in the number of republican governments, a type of regime that, in his view, was extremely reluctant to engage in acts of armed aggression.[63] Those

modern-day neo-Hobbesians who are chiefly concerned with international violence favor the construction and empowerment of supra-national organizations,
while those concerned mainly with domestic violence look to strong states able
to suppress violence within their borders. Steven Pinker seems to be a prominent recent addition to this school.[64] Modern-day neo-Kantians count upon the
spread of liberal democracy to bring about a "democratic peace." Each of these
solutions is problematic. Let us first consider the Hobbesian case.

Hobbes famously wrote that in the state of nature, the life of man was
"solitary, poor, nasty, brutish and short," and constantly afflicted by insecu-
rity and violence. The solution was submission to a government with absolute
power. Hobbes wrote, "The only way to erect such a common power, as may
be able to defend them from the invasion of foreigners and the injuries of one
another . . . is to confer all their power and strength upon one man, or assembly
of men, that may reduce all their wills, by plurality of voices, unto one will."[65]
In the Hobbesian Commonwealth, war and violence were to be eliminated by
the complete subordination of the wills of members of the populace to the will
of the sovereign. The possibility of strife was then foreclosed by the sovereign's
absolute authority.[66] This sovereign must, indeed, be absolute according to
Hobbes since any limitations upon its power would open the way to disputes,
which might, in turn, lead to violence. Thus, the Hobbesian solution to the
problem of violence was, in effect, acceptance of tyranny. For Hobbes, tyranny
was to be preferred to anarchy and violence. "Sovereign power is not so hurtful
as the want of it," he averred.[67]

The Hobbesian solution to the problem of violence is problematic in at
least two ways. To begin with, it is not clear that tyranny is to be preferred to
violence and disorder. The prevalence of popular revolution in the contemporary world might suggest that large numbers of individuals prefer violence to
tyranny. In recent years, thousands of Libyans, Syrians. Tunisians, Egyptians,
and so forth seemed to choose the former over the latter even in the face of tanks
and machine guns. In a similar vein, the former German Democratic Republic
(DDR) was a very orderly place, but during its four decades as a nation, hundreds of thousands of its citizens risked their lives, leaving it for the disorder and
uncertainty of life in the West.

Second, the Hobbesian solution to the problem of violence would seem
to require a great deal of violence for its implementation. Hobbes indicates
that men might "agree amongst themselves to submit" to the sovereign. If not,
however, they must be compelled to submit "by natural force" or "by war."[68]

And, once a Hobbesian Commonwealth is established, considerable violence is likely to be required to maintain its power. The DDR, as noted in chapter 1, kept the peace by a program of surveillance, intimidation, and punishment that enrolled nearly a quarter of the populace in the regime's various security forces or as informers. Behind an orderly facade was a very violent place.

Perhaps there are cases where a Hobbesian "agreement" might be reached peacefully, but these would seem most likely to be instances in which states or other entities already have few or relatively manageable antagonisms toward one another and see submission to a single authority as a means of advancing their mutual interests. The thirteen American states in 1789 or the economically advanced Western European states today are examples. The imposition of some sort of sovereign authority over mutually antagonistic states and political forces would seem likely to require considerable violence and a continuing regime of coercion. In other words, it would entail an imperial project that seems more a recipe than a cure for violence.

Now, as to the neo-Kantians, there is support for the idea that democracies are less likely than other sorts of states to go to war, especially with one another. The statistical evidence, however, is far from conclusive.[69] Moreover, the world's premier liberal democracy, the United States of America, as we shall see in chapter 3, is among the most bellicose nations on the face of the earth. Since the Civil War, American forces have been deployed abroad on hundreds of occasions for major conflicts as well as minor skirmishes. And, of course, America's military arsenal and defense budget dwarfs those of the other nations of the world. Ironically, America has justified many of its wars, including the 2002 Iraq War, by the claim that its goal was to transform its adversary into a peaceful liberal democracy. This might cause some concern that Kant's democratic peace might require a good deal of bloodshed to compel unwilling states to become liberal democracies.

There is, of course, a final school of thought that views violence as a moral problem that can be addressed through proper moral education and example. No doubt, moral education can be effective and, certainly, if all could be persuaded of the desirability of forswearing violence, peace would prevail. However, even those who would like to reject violence should be wary of others not as enlightened as themselves. The Moriori of the Chatham Islands remained true to their pacifist principles when attacked by the Taranaki Maori. The result, though, was that most of the Moriori were enslaved or killed, even eaten, by the Maori invaders.

Of course, most groups and nations that avow strong commitments to peace are somewhat less principled than the unfortunate Moriori. Indeed, several forms of pacifism are less peaceful than might meet the eye. Though professing a commitment to peace, some practitioners of nonviolent protest count upon the violence of their opponents to bring intervention by even more powerful and potentially more violent forces. Hence, nonviolence might be seen as a tactic of fomenting rather than engaging in violence. Also quite common is what might be called contingent pacifism. Often, political actors denounce the use of force by some groups or nations while casting a tolerant eye at the use of violence by others. Politically progressive elements typically denounce military actions by the United States while accepting the need for third-world regimes to resort to violence. Politically conservative groups generally take the opposite view. Finally worth noting is what might be called liberal pacifism. Tolerant, politically liberal individuals shrink from using violence under almost any circumstance. Most, however, accept the protection of the government and its military and police forces, paying taxes to support the systemic violence that preserves their often comfortable lives. And, in the international realm, by opposing violence they are effectively condemning many peoples to live under tyranny.[70]

CHAPTER 2

BUREAUCRACY AND VIOLENCE

Acts of violence are certainly not uncommon. In the United States, alone, nearly one and a half million individuals become the victims of violence every year—pushed, kicked, pummeled, stabbed, and shot—while tens of thousands of others are the perpetrators of these same acts. These numbers do not include the many thousands of American soldiers who, each year, inflict and suffer violence in the nation's seemingly interminable armed conflicts.

Minor acts of violence, involving few individuals, entail little in the way of planning, preparation, or resources. Many begin with a flash of anger and an uncontrolled impulse and reach a quick conclusion. If, however, a larger number of individuals are involved and, perhaps, multiple acts of violence must be sustained for some period of time, at least a modicum of planning and organization becomes necessary. Every human activity that lasts more than a few hours requires food and supplies, and violent activity on a larger scale may also require arms and ammunition and elaborate plans for their provision. An American infantry division in battle, for example, is likely to consume more than six hundred tons of supplies every day.[1] Elaborate planning and organization is needed to bring these materials to soldiers who may be fighting in remote and inhospitable areas.

Severe and protracted violence requires more than some rudimentary level of organization. Generally speaking, sustaining a high level of violent activity over a prolonged period of time requires the construction of a bureaucracy dedicated to this purpose. At first blush, it may seem odd to link violence and bureaucracy. After all, the literal meaning of bureaucracy is a government of desks, and these desks are often occupied by the most bland and mild-mannered functionaries. More than any other form of social organization, however, bureaucracy makes large-scale and long-term violence possible. Their usually superior bureaucracies often give states an advantage vis-à-vis other actors when it comes to employing violence to achieve their ends.

45

Bureaucracies facilitate violence in three ways. First, bureaucracy can overcome what might be called the natural limits of violence, allowing violence to grow from a small-scale to a large-scale activity. Second, bureaucracy can help to overcome the human limits of violence, allowing the many individuals who are not inclined to engage in violent action to peacefully provide support for their more violent fellows. Finally, bureaucracy helps to overcome the moral limits of violence, overcoming and circumventing what Hannah Arendt called the "animal pity by which all normal men are affected in the presence of physical suffering."[2]

BUREAUCRACY AND THE NATURAL LIMITS OF VIOLENCE

Most violent actions are limited in scope and duration. Two-thirds of the acts of violence committed in the United States, for example, are simple assaults usually concluded in a matter of minutes. Even mayhem on a larger scale, such as a riot, is usually short-lived. For example, America's 1992 Los Angeles riot, which caused fifty-three deaths and more than $1 billion in property damage, was over in six days. Similarly, the 1967 Detroit riot, associated with forty-three deaths and thousands of injuries lasted fewer than five days. The largest urban riot in American history, the 1863 New York City draft riot, resulted in more than one hundred deaths and the destruction of commercial and residential property throughout the city but also sputtered to a halt in about five days.[3]

Spontaneous forms of violence appear to have a kind of natural limit. The number of individuals actually engaged in violence tends to be small, though occasionally a large number may be engaged for a short period of time. The duration of spontaneous acts of violence, moreover, is usually measured in minutes, hours, and days. After a relatively short period of time, rioters, protestors, and the like run short of energy and supplies. Disparate groups of participants are likely to drift off or engage in disputes with one another. In many instances, the police or other authorities mobilized to suppress riotous conduct find it expedient to avoid inflammatory confrontations with rioters and allow the disturbances to come to an end of their own accord. This was precisely the strategy employed by General John A. Dix, whose troops were called in to quell the New York draft riots.[4]

Overcoming these natural limits requires organization. Indeed, groups that carry out acts of violence on a protracted basis almost inevitably construct elaborate bureaucracies to plan, equip, organize, supply, and sustain their efforts. The 1994 Rwandan genocide, for example, in which nearly 1 million individuals were murdered, is sometimes depicted as a spontaneous paroxysm of rage by machete-wielding Hutu, actually entailed intensive preparation and logistical support by the Rwandan government, which organized the militia forces that did most of the killing, built an effective command-and-control apparatus, and imported and distributed arms, including more than 500,000 machetes to be used in the murder of the Tutsi.[5]

Modern armies, of course, are noted for their sometimes enormous bureaucratic organizations. The United States Department of Defense (DoD), which employs more than two million military and civilian personnel, is a huge and complex bureaucratic entity whose organization charts fill many pages in the official "Department of Defense Organizations and Functions Guidebook."[6] Reporting to the Secretary of Defense are twenty-seven assistant secretaries, undersecretaries, and directors, each commanding hundreds of staffers and charged with such responsibilities as health affairs, budgets, acquisitions, testing and evaluation of equipment, and legal affairs. Laboring beneath these functionaries are thirty-one agencies, employing tens of thousands of individuals. These include National Security, Geospatial Intelligence, Defense Intelligence, Missile Defense, and so forth. These and numerous other entities help to plan and sustain America's seemingly unending military efforts and allow America to put tens of thousands of actual combat troops into the field.

This set of structures, of course, does not even include the actual military services. Each of the three services possesses its own civilian and military bureaucracies to administer and support its combat forces. A U.S. Army division, for example, will include, in addition to its combat troops, large numbers of military personnel, civilian employees, and civilian contractors organized into units whose functions include supply, maintenance, ordnance, ammunition support, quartermaster, transportation, finance, life support, signal infrastructure, public information, civil affairs, and administration. In the modern U.S. Army, approximately three non-combat personnel are devoted to the support of each combat soldier. This figure is sometimes known as the "tooth-to-tail ratio," and some military analysts believe the Army's "tail" should be even longer to properly support its combat operations.[7] American combat forces are, themselves, exemplars of organizational complexity. A U.S. Army division, for instance, typically deploying between ten and seventeen thousand troops, is usually composed of four brigades, which are, in turn, divided into battalions, which, in their turn, are composed of combat companies, each consisting of three platoons. Along with its combat companies (teeth) the division will include a host of logistical, administrative, and service units (tail) to provide the food, fuel, ammunition, and other supplies and services needed to support the division's activities.[8]

This entire military structure is, of course, supported by the vast industrial contracting system that developed during the Cold War, which produces the aircraft, missiles, warships, tanks, electronics, transport systems, and other materiel and supplies upon which the military depends. Though nominally civilian entities, such firms as Boeing*, Lockheed Martin*, Raytheon*, Northrop Grumman*, and General Dynamics* are heavily dependent upon military contracts and are functionally integrated into the military bureaucracies. Many of the executives of these firms, indeed, are retired military officers able to work closely with their still-serving counterparts. Military planning and research is undertaken by another set of private and quasi-private firms such as the RAND Corporation and the Institute for Defense Analyses (IDA). RAND and several of the others are technically Federally Funded Research and Development Centers (FFRDCs), independent nonprofit corporations working for the federal government. RAND was originally created by the Douglas Aircraft Company to undertake research for the Air Force and continues to work primarily on Air Force projects.[9]

Lest it be thought that the American military is unusual in its level of organizational complexity, it is worth pointing out that even shadowy terrorist groups find it necessary to rely upon bureaucratic modes of organization to achieve their military goals. Some terrorists, to be sure, operate as solitary individuals—lone wolves—and some groups are short-lived. Larger and more persistent terrorist groups like al-Qaeda, however, rely upon standard bureaucratic mechanisms, including reporting requirements, organization charts, and expense reports to plan their actions, to communicate with members, and to provide funding and logistical support for their operations.[10] Thus, even terrorists have tails to support their teeth.

Some military organizations are, to be sure, said to be overly rigid. Many analysts have argued that the disastrous performance of the French army in the spring of 1940 was a function of its inflexible organization and rigid adherence to plans that were quickly rendered obsolete by events on the battlefield.[11] Similarly, though less disastrously, the American advance through Western Europe in 1944 was sometimes impeded by the fact that every decision passed through multiple and competing bureaucratic layers before it could be implemented. One authority compared the Allied Expeditionary Force to a reverse brontosaurus, that is, a creature with a huge brain and small body.[12] Nevertheless, without a capacity for planning, coordination, supply, and so forth, no military force can engage in large-scale violence on a long-term basis. Brontosaurus or not, the Allies did, after all, defeat the *Wehrmacht*. If it is not sustained by a bureaucratic organization, within a short period of time—days at most—military violence reaches its natural limits and eases, or sputters, to a halt.

In the ancient world and in early modern times, armies seldom possessed enough supplies and materiel to remain in the field for more than a brief period, and battles seldom lasted longer than a day or two. Most, though not all, armies were small by modern-day standards since large armies could seldom be supplied and sustained for very long. Recall that William the Conqueror commanded a force that totaled only 7,000 soldiers at the Battle of Hastings. Many troops had already left William's army because of a shortage of supplies.

Typically, if the outcome of a battle was not decided quickly, the combatants were forced to return to their homes, perhaps hoping to renew hostilities at some future date when they might be able to rebuild their stores of supplies and arms. Only the greatest of the ancient empires—Egypt, China, Persia, Rome—had the capacity to provision sizeable armies for weeks or months in the field. And, even these forces relied upon their ability to purchase or, more often, to seize supplies and provisions from towns and settlements along their route of march. Alexander the Great, for example, was able to keep his army on the march by planning his line of advance to take advantage of the presence of cities from which supplies could be extorted.[13] Centuries later, Genghis Khan's Mongol armies excelled in the realm of logistics, often bringing enormous herds and flocks with them as they moved forward. The Mongols also organized huge camel caravans to carry supplies to their soldiers. Superior logistics was one of the keys to Mongol military prowess.[14] Nevertheless, Mongol armies in the field could by no means be fully provisioned from their home bases and depended upon their ability to capture food and other supplies along their route of conquest.

Indeed, theft from local granaries had always been an essential component of military tactics and remained so until the twentieth century. Armies led by such generals as Napoleon, Wallenstein, Gustavus Adolphus, Robert E. Lee, and, to some extent, even Moltke and Guderian depended upon food and supplies requisitioned, scavenged, and stolen from the country through which they passed. It was the problem of feeding soldiers in a poor and inhospitable land that led the ancient Greeks to develop and master their famous tactic of quick and decisive shock battle. Wars involving contending armies of Greek infantrymen, known as hoplites, were typically resolved in an hour or so of combat.[15]

Only with the development and elaboration of their bureaucratic "tails" could armies be substantially enlarged and freed from the need to end wars quickly or to find local supplies along their route of march. Part of the solution to this problem, of course, entailed the use of new modes of transportation such as railroads and, later, motor transport and aircraft, which increased the range and speed of movement of military forces and made it possible to bring large quantities of supplies to distant armies for long periods of time. The military potential of railroads, for instance, was initially suggested by the German economist Friedrich List in the 1830s and was quickly demonstrated by the Russians, Austrians, and French in the 1840s.[16] But rail transport technology alone did not change the character of warfare. It was the organization of bureaucratic entities able to make use of the rails that freed armies from their historic dependence upon local supplies and made it possible for them to fight for years in hostile lands. In the 1860s, for example, the Prussian army constructed an elaborate organization to take advantage of the possibilities manifested by the railroad system. By 1870, each Prussian army corps was served by a "train battalion," with 40 officers, 84 doctors, and 670 wagons, which carried the corps' provisions, food, ammunition, baggage, medical supplies, and a field bakery.[17] These helped to bring about the success of the Prussian military effort against France.

During the American Civil War, logistics, ordnance, and military engineering were raised to high arts, especially in the Union army under the leadership of Quartermaster General Montgomery Meigs, who supervised railroad construction and military contracting and procurement. Gen. U.S. Grant also took a special interest in these matters.[18] When on the offensive, Confederate armies adhered to the traditional tactic of seeking to capture food and other supplies along the route of march. The need to scavenge limited their mobility and the length of time Confederate forces could remain in the field, especially if their route of advance was blocked by Northern troops. The Union army, on the other hand, was the first in history to be fully supplied in battle over long distances and for long periods of time by railroad.[19] The Union army also developed a substantial Quartermaster's Department and detailed men from each line regiment to handle supply problems. By the end of the war, the Union Army's administrative and logistical tail had reached a nearly modern length and helped to bring about the North's victory in what became a long war of attrition in which supplies counted as much as fighting spirit and generalship.[20]

At the conclusion of the civil war the army was demobilized and its wartime capabilities soon lost. Six decades later, when the United States entered World War I, it had little or no capacity to equip or supply a large army for a protracted fight. To address this problem, the Wilson administration established the War Industries Board (WIB) to convert the nation's economy to war production. The WIB was mainly a failure, and the American Expeditionary Forces (AEF) was compelled to purchase virtually all of its equipment and supplies from the British and French. During the course of the war, the AEF bought from the French nearly 5,000 artillery pieces, 10,000 machine guns, 40,000 automatic rifles, millions of rounds of various sorts of ammunition, and more than 4,000 aircraft.[21] Perhaps overlooking the fact that no American horse soldiers had been dispatched to Europe, the WIB did see to it that more than three hundred thousand gas masks for horses would be shipped to the AEF.

At the beginning of World War II, the U.S. was better prepared. Between the wars, a joint board of army and navy war planners established a Joint Planning Committee, which engaged in strategic contingency planning for possible future wars against Japan and Germany. In addition, the 1920 National Defense Act had made the Secretary of War responsible for military procurement and supply policies. Successive secretaries issued orders detailing these functions and creating new agencies, such as the Munitions Board, a Procurement Division, a Planning Branch within the office of the Assistant Secretary of War, and the Army Industrial College (AIC) to ensure that the U.S. military would possess an adequate capacity for planning, procurement, and logistics in the event of a future war. Aircraft production was stepped up in 1939, and between 1940 and 1941, military budgets had been sharply increased, conscription had been instituted, and work had begun on aircraft carriers, tanks, and artillery in preparation for a war the Roosevelt administration thought almost inevitable.

The AIC, which included students and instructors from all services, was designed to train officers in all aspects of manpower mobilization, military procurement, supply of combat forces, logistics, and industrial organization for wartime needs as well as to provide planning in these realms.[22] By 1939, graduates of the AIC occupied important positions on the Munitions Board and in the Planning Branch, where they helped to manage military mobilization and industrial procurement. In addition, the individual services developed tactics, equipment, and organization designed to carry military forces and their equipment to distant battlefields and supply them for long periods of time. The Marine Corps, for example, developed tactics of amphibious warfare designed to land heavily armed troops on distant and hostile beaches along with logistical plans and personnel sufficient to supply those troops for years of fighting in regions where the time-honored military tactic of living off the land was not an option.

In the decades since World War II, of course, the United States has been at war on almost a continual basis. The nation has fought large engagements in Korea, Indochina, and the Middle East as well as numerous smaller conflicts throughout the world. For better or worse, America's prodigious military effort has been made possible by the enormous bureaucracies constructed to arm, feed, supply, and transport American troops to distant battlefields where they may spend months or years in combat. The high ratio of tail to teeth currently manifested by America's military forces—a ratio than does not even take into account the hundreds of thousands of employees of U.S. military contractors—is often taken to exemplify bureaucratic bloat and waste. What it actually exemplifies is the relationship between bureaucracy and violence. Anyone can be violent, but serious violence sustained over a long period of time requires bureaucracy.

BUREAUCRACY AND THE HUMAN LIMITS OF VIOLENCE

Left to itself, violence is limited not only in scope and duration but is also circumscribed by what might be called human limits. To put the matter simply, though violence is commonplace, most individuals are not especially violent nor are they particularly adept at the use of violence.[23] Most suffer from fear, uncertainty, and remorse when they engage in violence.[24] As sociologist Randall Collins concludes from his studies of fights and disturbances, most hostile confrontations between two or more individuals are characterized by "bluster and gesture" but generally do not lead to actual violence.[25] Collins attributes this outcome to what he terms "confrontational tension and fear." That is, faced with the possibility of engaging in or becoming the targets of violence, most individuals experience a high level of tension and often an overwhelming sense of trepidation that leads all sides to prefer face-saving or even humiliating ways of backing down and avoiding violence. Most police officers, for example, have never unholstered, much less fired, their weapons. Even in the case of military combat, moreover, a surprisingly high percentage of troops fail to use their weapons against the enemy. A famous study conducted by S. L. A. Marshall, the U.S. Army's chief combat historian during World War II, concluded that only about 15 percent of the army's front line troops had actually fired their guns in combat. Even face-to-face with enemy forces, the majority of soldiers took no hostile action whatsoever.[26] Studies of other armies and other wars seem to bear out Marshall's findings.

This same fear and tension also tends to render most of the participants in acts of violence incompetent if they are not actually able to retreat from the confrontation. In both small-group and individual fist fights, according to Collins's assessment, most individuals tend to become panicky, swing wildly, and often hit members of their own side.[27] In a similar vein, historian John Keegan estimates that 15 to 25 percent of all battle casualties are the result of accident and so-called "friendly fire."[28] And, about 10 percent of the individuals shot by the police during any given year are officers who fall victim to friendly fire from fellow officers. This figure does not include the bystanders injured every year by police gunfire or the accidents that result from more than a quarter of the car chases involving police officers and fleeing suspects.[29]

Of course, a small percentage of the populace, perhaps as little as 15 percent, characterized in one study as consisting of self-confident, physically strong extroverts, is less constrained by the tension and fear inherent in hostile confrontations.[30] Some subset of this group, perhaps the 2 percent that army psychiatrist David Grossman avers possess "aggressive psychopathic" tendencies, is less hampered by angst or timidity and is unusually competent in its use of violence.[31] In the 2005 motion picture *A History of Violence*, the central character, Tom Stall, played by Viggo Mortensen, exemplifies this type of individual. Stall prevails in a number of conflicts precisely because he has no fear of violence and no hesitance whatsoever about employing lethal violence against those who threaten him. Stall is apparently unaffected by the tension that discomfits and slows his nominally stronger opponents, leaving them vulnerable to his ferocious attacks.

A study of Los Angeles police department (LAPD) officers involved in the use of force found that 5 percent of the LAPD's officers accounted for 20 percent of the instances in which force was employed by the police, while 10 percent of the department's officers accounted for 33 percent of the use of force incidents.[32] In a similar vein, approximately 84 percent of all violent crimes committed in the United States are perpetrated by about 15 percent of the populace.[33] And, in the case of front-line soldiers, a small number of highly aggressive troops are typically responsible for much of the shooting and most of the effective shooting directed at the enemy in combat.[34] During World War II, the U.S. Army Air Corps discovered that 1 percent of its pilots accounted for 30 to 40 percent of all enemy fighters destroyed in the air. The majority of fighter pilots in combat never shot down an opposing aircraft nor actually tried to do so.[35]

Thus, all but a relatively small percentage of the populace generally seems to exhibit reluctance to engage in actual violence even when placed into confrontational situations. What Collins calls "confrontational tension" seems to have a substantial affect upon about 85 percent of the populace while the remaining 15 percent seem less hampered by such trepidation. These percentages roughly demarcate what might be called the human limits of violence. A variety of factors, including technology, can affect these human limits. For example, individuals far removed from the violence they perpetrate—say, those who fire a missile at a remote target—are less likely to feel the tension and fear normally associated with confrontational violence.[36] One of the most important instruments, however, through which the human limits of violence can be overcome is bureaucracy.

To begin with, bureaucratic organizations can provide indoctrination and training that help to inure their members to the fear of violence. One example is the case of contemporary modes of U.S. military training. Beginning in the Vietnam War, as Grossman reports, the U.S. military introduced major changes in its training methods designed to increase the number of soldiers who actually fired their weapons in combat. These changes included training that simulated actual combat situations, so that soldiers would be conditioned to reflexively fire their weapons. Rather than teach soldiers to shoot at stationary targets, soldiers today in such programs as Marine Corps Basic Warrior Training, are conditioned to fire reflexively and instantly at olive-drab, human-shaped targets that pop up randomly and unexpectedly on the training field.[37] If the target is hit, it falls, providing instantaneous positive feedback. Soldiers are rewarded for successfully "engaging" (a euphemism for killing) their targets and penalized for failing to do so.

The result of weeks of operant conditioning on the training field is that in actual combat soldiers react automatically as though they were still shooting at training targets. In the U.S. and other armies using such training methods, 90–95 percent of the soldiers fire their weapons, in contrast to the 15–20 percent who fired in earlier periods of history.[38] During the 1982 Falklands War, for example, British troops trained via conditioning faced much larger Argentinean forces trained using traditional methods. The result was an unequal contest in which almost all the British troops fired their weapons while most of the Argentineans did not.[39] One British veteran said he "thought of the enemy as nothing more or less than Figure II (man-shaped) targets."[40] Their high rate of fire is one reason American military forces have been so effective in recent decades. Indeed, in Iraq and Afghanistan U.S. casualties were mainly caused by improvised explosive devices (IEDs) or "booby traps" rather than exchanges of rifle fire from which American troops almost invariably emerge victorious.

Training effective soldiers is expensive and requires a substantial investment in facilities, a large staff, and a high level of organization. The U.S. Army's Training and Doctrine Command (TRADOC), charged with the training of the Army's troops, employs 27,000 military personnel and 11,000 civilians on its 32 training facilities. The Marine Corps, Navy, and Air Force each operates its own training programs and facilities. The Army requires each recruit to undergo nine weeks of basic training followed by specialized training. The Marines require thirteen weeks of basic training followed by four to eight weeks of specialized training. The marginal cost of basic military training in the U.S. is about $50,000 per infantry soldier. In sum, a very substantial bureaucracy is needed to train large numbers of individuals to employ violence effectively.

Bureaucracy is also a chief source of the leadership that can be a critical factor in overcoming the fear and tension that makes most individuals reluctant to engage in violence. The importance of leadership in this regard was firmly established in a series of famous experiments conducted by Yale psychologist Stanley Milgram in the 1960s. From his New Haven laboratory, Milgram recruited volunteers who were told they were participating in a study of learning. Ostensibly as part of the study, the volunteers were directed to pose a series of questions to subjects in the next room. When subjects answered questions incorrectly, the volunteers were told by the white-coated "doctor" directing the experiment to administer what they believed to be electric shocks of increasing severity using a switch attached to wires and a voltage meter. The volunteers could not see the subjects, to whom they were introduced at the beginning of the experiment, but they could hear them shouting and sometimes screaming in pain as the voltage level on the meter was increased to its maximum reading of 450 volts. In actuality, no electricity was used, the subjects were part of the ruse, and the screams were prerecorded. The volunteers, though, were unaware of the various deceptions.

A small number of volunteers had no difficulty administering shocks to the putative subjects. Most volunteers, however, became concerned, nervous, and even agitated as they delivered what they thought were severe electric shocks to other individuals. Varying with the precise conditions of the experiment, roughly 60 percent, however, continued to administer shocks up to the maximum voltage when ordered to do so by the white-coated and authoritative doctor standing behind them. If they hesitated, the doctor would say, "You have no other choice. You must go on." Milgram's interpretation of these results, presented in a number of papers and in his book *Obedience to Authority*, was that most individuals would allow commands from an authority figure to overcome their natural reluctance to inflict violence upon others.[41] Because the volunteers were willing to do harm while carrying out orders, Milgram's experiment is sometimes called the "Eichmann study."

Though Milgram's results have been questioned and the entire experiment sometimes viewed as unethical, his findings are consistent with those observed in a number of settings. For example, Christopher Browning carefully studied the men of German Police Battalion 101, a unit of the "Order Police" sent to Poland in 1942 where it was assigned to the task of capturing and killing Jews.[42] Among these Germans, a small number seemed enthusiastic about their task, while about 20 percent avoided direct participation in the killing. The majority carried out their orders, albeit without much enthusiasm. Members of this group, like Milgram's volunteers, became anxious and depressed and generally required direct supervision to carry out their assignments.[43]

Studies of military combat also indicate that leadership is a critical factor in determining whether soldiers will or will not engage their opponents. Like Milgram's volunteers, soldiers are likely to fight when given orders by a respected authority figure who is physically present to observe and encourage them. In the absence of authoritative leadership, soldiers will often find reason to avoid violent confrontations with their foes. Take, for example, the accounts compiled by Grossman of the *ad hoc* truces that sometimes developed between British and German soldiers facing one another during World War I. Out of sight of their officers, these nominal opponents might leave their trenches, play soccer with one another, and exchange Christmas gifts only to resume combat when officers intervened.[44]

Some famous military leaders, of course, have made it their business to inspire the troops by their personal presence on the battlefield—sometimes at the head of the front-line forces. Alexander the Great, for example, personally rode at the head of the elite Macedonian Companion Cavalry at Issus and Gaugamela. This sort of personal, charismatic leadership, however, has severe limitations. If the charismatic leader happened to be killed or incapacitated, the entire army could be thrown into disarray. For example, the death of Richard III during the Battle of Bosworth Field in 1485 led his army to quickly disintegrate and flee from their less numerous Tudor foes. Pre-modern military encounters, moreover, generally took place on relatively small battlefields where the presence of the leader could be felt by all the troops. Modern battles can, of course, be fought across hundreds of square miles of land and sea where no one general, however charismatic and energetic, can make his presence felt by the forces at his command.

Successful armies usually lessen their dependence upon the charismatic commander by developing cadres of lower-ranking leaders who can be suffused throughout the organization. The Roman legions, for example, depended heavily upon their centurions, a group of several thousand highly trained career soldiers who are the ancestors of today's NCOs. Centurions could be transferred from legion to legion as needed and generally served in the army for life. In battle, each centurion, wielding a distinctive staff, stood behind his 80 legionaries, watched and encouraged them, and, like the scientist in Milgram's experiment, ordered them to fight and kill their opponents.[45] If a centurion was himself killed or incapacitated, another would take his place. In essence, the Romans supplanted the individual charismatic leader with a bureaucratic organization. This bureaucratization of leadership gave the Roman legions a distinctive advantage over opponents led into battle by some individual king or chief. Even today, bureaucratically organized armies are seldom thwarted by the death of a senior officer while forces that depend upon individual charismatic commanders—say, an Osama bin Laden—can be thrown into disarray by their leader's demise.

When armies construct a bureaucratic leadership structure it is, of course, extremely important to invest subordinate officers with a considerable quantity of actual authority so that their troops will respect them as authentic leaders rather than view them as mere servants of higher commanders. This leadership style seems to be a characteristic of successful military forces. The Roman legions trained centurions to exercise a good deal of discretion. The German *Wehrmacht* gave its noncommissioned officers a great deal of authority.[46] And, in the U.S. Marine Corps, sergeants are given wide latitude to lead their troops in combat. This idea was dramatized in a 1986 Clint Eastwood film, *Heartbreak Ridge*. During the invasion of Grenada, the Eastwood character, Marine Gunnery Sergeant Thomas Highway, is threatened with disciplinary action by a somewhat pompous Marine major whose orders Highway has refused to follow. A Marine general who happens upon the scene severely castigates the officer for daring to interfere with the combat decisions of an experienced Marine sergeant. In the film, the Highway character seems to be the quintessential American hero, standing for the triumph of rugged individualism over societal strictures and bureaucratic formalities. Ironically, though, the empowerment of individuals like Tom Highway actually represents the bureaucratization of leadership to help enable armies to overcome the ordinary human limits of violence.

There is still another way in which bureaucracy circumvents the human limits of violent conduct. Bureaucracy allows individuals to participate in and contribute to violence without actually having to engage in violent conduct themselves. In cases of more or less spontaneous individual or even collective violence, those who are not involved in the fighting contribute little or nothing to its outcome. In the simplest case, two individuals engage in a brief and spontaneous fistfight while others observe or scurry out of the way. The course and result of the conflict are determined by the relative strength, skill, and ferocity of the two violent combatants. The fight may draw an audience, but however many bystanders watch the fracas, their impact upon the result is likely to be negligible. The outcome is decided by the fighters. If more individuals become involved and the two-person fight is transformed into a struggle among competing groups or gangs, the outcome may be affected, but, again, only those actually engaging in violent conduct will play a role in shaping the melee's course and conclusion.

When, however, violence is undertaken by bureaucratic organizations rather than by individuals or loosely organized groups, noncombatants can have a major impact upon the struggle, serving as what the military calls "force multipliers." Through bureaucratic organizations, the efforts and energies of large numbers of individuals who are not directly engaged and perhaps would not be willing to murder, maim, or assault anyone, can be employed to support and, perhaps, to amplify the endeavors of the usually much smaller number of individuals who do engage in violent conduct.

As an especially grim example of bureaucratic force multiplication, take the case of Nazi Germany. Between 1933 and 1945, Germans were responsible for the murder of more than six million Jews as well as the killing of millions of Russians, Poles, and others. The German population of that era, including Austria and the Sudetenland, which had been annexed to Germany, was slightly under 80 million. Of these Germans, according to Daniel Goldhagen, at least 100,000 participated directly in killing Jews, working as troopers in the SA or

SS, members of death squads, concentration camp personnel, and so forth.[47] Some fraction of these actually committed murders with their own hands. The three SS brigades, for example, that over a period of years murdered several million Jews in the Soviet Union consisted of a total of 25,000 men.[48] Many if not most of these men personally shot, beat, brutalized, and killed Jews. The same is likely true of the 6,000 members of the *Einsatzgruppen* operating in the Ukraine as well as many of the 19,000 men of the *Ordnungspolizei* tasked with killing Jews throughout Eastern Europe.[49]

Though their hands might not have been smeared with blood at the end of a work day, millions of other Germans worked in the various bureaucracies of the German state, the military and the Nazi Party that were involved with the murder of Jews. These might have included the train crews that transported Jews, the journalists and propagandists who sought to incite popular hatred of Jews, the administrators who wrote deportation orders, the church officials who verified that some of their congregants were converts of Jewish ancestry, the engineers, architects, carpenters, plumbers, electricians, painters, roofers, and other builders who constructed and maintained over 10,000 concentration camps as well as the infamous gas chambers, and the accountants and bookkeepers charged with documenting the disposition of confiscated Jewish property, the officials of firms that sold munitions and supplies to the SS and other actual killers, and so forth.[50] These individuals constituted the enormous bureaucratic tail that greatly multiplied the force of the relatively smaller group of individuals who actually engaged in killing Jews. In this way, bureaucracy helped to overcome the human limits of violence, allowing those who did not kill to contribute to the process of killing.

BUREAUCRACY AND THE MORAL LIMITS OF VIOLENCE

In addition to its natural and human limits, violence is also bounded by moral limits. The idea of human limits refers to the fear and tension that violent confrontations generally provoke. The notion of moral limits, on the other hand, refers to the idea that at least some individuals will view the prospect of doing harm to others as repugnant and contrary to their beliefs and convictions. Echoing Rousseau, Hannah Arendt said that all humans had a feeling of animal pity for the suffering of others. Perhaps Arendt was too optimistic and overlooked the fact that some individuals seem to have no moral compass: witness the 2012 shooting of moviegoers in Colorado, among other recent acts of random violence by seemingly remorseless killers. But most individuals do possess feelings of pity, and, indeed, in the Milgram experiment, a number of subjects found the instructions they were given morally objectionable and refused to carry them out on those grounds. One subject, declining to continue, said, "Surely you've considered the ethics of this thing."[51]

Bureaucracy undermines the moral limit of violence in at least three important ways. First, violence undertaken by bureaucratic organizations separates many of the actors from the ultimate act. Contractors and employees who labor in the weapons factories or offices of an army's extended tail, for example, do not directly confront whatever moral choices must be made by those in the front lines. As Zygmunt Bauman observes, such individuals seldom "face the moment of choice and face the consequences of their deeds."[52] Even if shown such consequences they can declare them to be unanticipated and unintended by them. Second, through the division of labor, bureaucratic organization breaks violent processes into small parts with each perpetrator undertaking only a fragment of the whole. The bureaucracy as a whole may be engaged in murder, but each individual, particularly those at a distance from the ultimate act, is responsible for only a portion of the task. One collects data, one works at a lathe, one repairs a generator. Taken by itself, each task is morally neutral. Finally, bureaucratic organization transfers moral responsibility from the actor to some abstract authority that absolves the actor of blameworthiness. A number of Nazi officials accused of war crimes famously declared that they were "just carrying out orders" (*Befehl ist Befehl*) and bore no personal moral responsibility for the actions mandated by those orders. For these several reasons, we can agree with Bauman that bureaucracies adiaphorize social action, seeming to make it neither good nor bad—thus effectively eliminating the moral limits of violence.[53]

Since the publication of Arendt's account of the trial of Adolf Eichmann, the issue of bureaucracy and morality has been much discussed. This discussion, however, is often freighted by the enormity of the Holocaust, which tends to become not only an example, but *the* example of the ways in which bureaucracies marginalize moral concerns and render them irrelevant to the operations of the organization. The danger of this focus on one powerful example is that the adiaphorous impact of bureaucracy on social action becomes conflated with Nazism and is accordingly viewed as an aberration rather than understood as a characteristic of all bureaucracies. I believe this is such an important point that I will devote much of the remainder of this chapter, relying mainly on court records and documents, to examining an American bureaucracy that today employs more than 500,000 Americans, not German Nazis. This bureaucracy, or complex of bureaucracies, is America's penal system, a set of institutions that typically houses more than two million individuals, mainly men, who have been sentenced for various crimes or are in jail awaiting a formal disposition of their cases.

While in the custody of America's prison bureaucracies many tens of thousands of the male inmates and a smaller number of women are subjected to violent, appalling, and disgusting treatment. In particular, many tens of thousands are sexually assaulted while incarcerated, usually by other inmates. Among the men, some are assaulted repeatedly, badly injured, and infected with the HIV virus—often a death sentence.

Of course, unlike the various German institutions dedicated to bringing about the Final Solution, America's carceral bureaucracies are not formally assigned to the task of promoting the rape of inmates. Indeed, neither the judges who sentence individuals to prison nor the guards and wardens who supervise them are usually the actual perpetrators of sexual assaults. Perhaps we should not consider them as blameworthy as the violent inmates who actually commit the bulk of the rapes. But if a man thoughtlessly and repeatedly pushes helpless individuals into cages containing savage beasts and carelessly locks the door and looks away, who is responsible for the result—the ravenous beasts or the indifferent man?

As we shall see below, when we examine a series of recent court cases, the law enforcement officials, judges, and jailers who control America's prisons usually commit no acts of violence themselves but do tolerate and seem indifferent to tens of thousands of cruel and violent acts committed in their institutions on a daily basis. Their indifference, moreover, exemplifies the three ways in which bureaucracy undermines the moral limits of violence. First, within the bureaucratic structure of the prison regime the various carceral officials are separated from the ultimate acts of violence their conduct promotes and can declare those acts to have been unanticipated and unintended by them. Second, the bureaucratic structure of the prison divides violent processes into small parts—the sentence, the transport, the cell assignment, the daily schedule, and so forth—each of which seems morally neutral. Finally, prison officials have no difficulty transferring moral responsibility for their actions elsewhere—lawmakers who enact sentencing laws and set prison funding levels, regulatory agencies that govern prison procedures, even the general public, some of whose members clamor for harsh sentences and respond favorably to late-night television comedians who joke about prison rape.[54]

If confronted in court with allegations that their conduct tolerated and permitted violent rape, prison officials customarily rely upon all three of these bureaucratic responses. And, to confirm the adiaphorous character of bureaucracy, America's courts generally accept their reasoning. The legal standard applied by the courts in cases of prison rape is known as "deliberate indifference." According to this standard, as we will see below, prison officials have liability for a rape committed in their institutions only if they knew that particular rape was likely to take place and, nevertheless, decided not to take action. Officials easily prevail in almost all cases by arguing that the particular rape in question was unanticipated; that each of their actions, viewed individually, was perfectly appropriate; and that they adhered fully to all prison rules and regulations. *Herr Oberst* Eichmann could not have presented a better statement of bureaucratic inculpability.

MALE PRISON RAPE

The general public has little interest in or sympathy for prison inmates, believing that if the conditions of incarceration are harsh, inmates deserve what they get.[55] One thing they get is rape. Precise numbers are not available, but according to some studies, as many as 20 percent of the male prisoners in America's penal institutions are the victims of sexual assault—many are repeatedly assaulted during their incarceration.[56] In a similar vein, a 1993 *New York Times* article estimated that more than 250,000 men are sexually assaulted in prison every year.[57] According to one commentator, prisons promote sexual terrorism.[58] Aggressive and strong inmates commonly exploit weaker inmates without much interference from prison authorities or, in some instances, with their collusion. A new inmate must either fight his attackers, seek segregation from the general prison population, or accept a position of subservience to another inmate or group of inmates capable of protecting him. While both the victims and assailants in cases of male prison rape are men, other inmates often redefine the victims as surrogate females, referring to them by derogatory terms for women such as "bitch" or "pussy" during and after the sexual assaults. If a man is successfully attacked once, he is likely to be seen as an easy target and to suffer additional attacks. Men who are raped in prison are, on average, raped nine times.[59] The

2003 federal Prison Rape Elimination Act (PREA), creating national standards, albeit weak ones, for inmate safety, was not actually implemented until 2012, and many of its provisions do not take effect until 2017, so its impact on prison rape remains unknown. Indeed, PREA's inmate safety standards are mandatory only within the federal prison system. In the state prisons, which hold the great majority of America's inmates, PREA offers financial incentives for compliance, but many authorities doubt these will have much effect.[60]

Rape can be humiliating and both psychologically and physically devastating for inmates, but beyond this, the effects of widespread prison rape reverberate through the larger society. The most obvious of these effects is related to AIDS. Thousands of prisoners are HIV positive or suffer from full-blown AIDS, and, between 1991 and 1995, one in every three deaths in prison resulted from AIDS infection. Accordingly, individuals raped in prison stand a good chance of contracting the AIDS virus. This not only represents a death sentence for the inmate but means that when that inmate is released he poses a risk to the larger community. Many experts believe that the high rate of new AIDS cases among black women is a result of the large number of black men who leave prison each year carrying the AIDS virus.[61] At the same time, inmates who have been raped may develop a sense of hostility and rage that translates into violent behavior after their release. It was, for example, widely reported that one of the three white men convicted in Texas in 1998 of attacking a randomly selected African American, James Byrd, tying him to a pickup truck, and dragging him to his death, had been recently released from prison. While imprisoned, this individual had allegedly been raped repeatedly by members of a black prison gang and subsequently vowed to kill the first black man he saw after his release. As he fulfilled that vow he was, in effect, bringing the consequences of prison rape into society at large.

Prison authorities are certainly aware of the prevalence of rape in their institutions. Many, however, have either felt powerless to deal with the problem or have been unwilling to treat rape prevention as an institutional priority. The United States currently houses approximately 2 million prisoners in facilities built to accommodate fewer than 1 million.[62] This severe overcrowding, coupled with understaffing, has made many prisons difficult to manage and reduces the ability of prison authorities to segregate prisoners who, by virtue of size, race, or sexual orientation, may be at special risk for sexual assault from prisoners with a history of or propensity for engaging in such assaults.

Beyond the obvious difficulties faced by authorities in attempting to maintain order within a prison, a number of studies indicate that prison officials often exhibit a callous disregard for the problem of sexual assault. Not unlike the public at large, guards and other officials sometimes believe that brutal conditions within the prison, including rape, function as a deterrent to crime and a just punishment for its commission.[63] "The guards just turn their backs," one inmate claimed. "Their mentality is the tougher, colder, and more cruel and inhuman a place is, the less chance a person will return."[64] In some instances, according to inmates' allegations, guards and prison officials use the threat of rape as an instrument of control, intimidating inmates by threatening to assign them to bunk with sexual predators, or even allowing violent or predatory individuals access to weaker inmates in exchange for their cooperation in maintaining order in the prison.[65] One inmate wrote, "The main reason why sexual assaults occur is because prison officials and staff promote them. It's their method of sacrificing the weak inmates to achieve and maintain control of the stronger, aggressive or violent inmates."[66] Another inmate said, "It seems that young men and gays and first timers are used as sacrificial lamb [sic]. The reason is to use these men as a way to keep the gangs and killers from turning on the system which created prison the Hell that it is."[67]

More generally, many guards reportedly view sexual assault prevention as the business of the individual prisoner rather than the responsibility of the institution. This harsh perspective is known colloquially as "fuck or fight" and is the dominant view in the institutional culture of many, if not all, correctional institutions.[68] For the most part, prison rapes are not investigated by the police, and their perpetrators are not prosecuted even when victims bring complaints. Prison administrators seldom collect physical evidence or interview witnesses to rapes in their institutions. The local prosecutors who would bear the responsibility for bringing charges typically do not see prison inmates as their constituents, nor do they see any political advantage to championing their cause.[69] To the extent that perpetrators are penalized at all, punishments generally take the form of minor administrative sanctions within the prison. Because their complaints are not taken seriously, many inmate rape victims do not report such assaults. They see little reason to bear public humiliation and possible reprisal when the authorities are unlikely to take any action against perpetrators. The advocacy group Human Rights Watch recently completed a study of 100 prison rapes and discovered that not a single one resulted in prosecution of the alleged perpetrators.[70]

CRUEL BUT NOT UNUSUAL

In principle, prison authorities bear some responsibility for protecting prisoners from sexual assault. The courts have held that this responsibility is derived from the Eighth Amendment's prohibition of cruel and unusual punishment. Traditionally, the Eighth Amendment was conceived to apply to punishments formally prescribed or meted out by the government, not to ills that might befall the inmate during the period of his confinement.[71] Beginning in the late 1980s, however, the Supreme Court began to rule that the conditions of a prisoner's confinement, even if not formally mandated by the government as an element of a prisoner's punishment, could be so execrable as to constitute cruel and unusual punishment in violation of the Eighth Amendment. Generally, these rulings came in response to suits challenging the severe overcrowding that plagues most penal systems, but other issues were also raised successfully. For example, in *Helling v. McKinney*, an inmate charged that his confinement in a cell with a prisoner who smoked as many as five packs of cigarettes a day constituted cruel and unusual punishment by subjecting him to a serious health risk.[72] The Supreme Court agreed. Similarly, in *Estelle v. Gamble*, the Court held that a prison's failure to provide adequate medical care for an inmate constituted a violation of his Eighth Amendment rights.[73] In *Wilson v. Seiter*, the Court affirmed that the reviewable conditions of a prisoner's confinement included the protection inmates received from harm inflicted by other inmates.[74] In that case an inmate had charged that his conditions of confinement, which included housing with dangerous and mentally ill inmates, constituted cruel and unusual punishment.

The specific question of protection from sexual violence was considered by the Court in the case of *Farmer v. Brennan*.[75] Brennan, a preoperative transsexual with feminine characteristics, alleged that federal prison authorities had placed him in the general population of a maximum-security facility where he was beaten and raped by other inmates. The Court held that prison officials, indeed, had a duty to protect inmates from sexual assault by other prisoners and that failure to carry out this duty could constitute cruel and unusual punishment.

A prisoner seeking to assert that his Eighth Amendment rights have been violated because of sexual assault or any other condition of confinement has a constitutionally guaranteed right to seek recourse in the federal court system.[76] Prisoners in state or municipal facilities usually bring suit under Title 42, Section

1983 of the *United States Code* (*U.S.C.*), which provides for redress in the federal courts for those injured by individuals acting under the color of state law. Section 1983 states: "Every person who, under color of any statute, ordinance, regulation . . . of an state . . . subjects, or causes to be subjected, any citizen of the United States . . . to the deprivation of any rights, privileges, or immunities secured by the Constitution and laws, shall be liable to the party injured in an action at law, suit in equity, or other proper proceeding for redress." Federal inmates, for their part, must generally bring a *Bivens* suit, so named because of the Supreme Court's decision in *Bivens v. Six Unknown Named Agents of Federal Bureau of Narcotics*, which essentially provides the same protection against misconduct by federal officials that Section 1983 provides against improper actions on the part of state officials.[77] Typically, such suits name individual prison officials or prison guards as defendants.

Practically speaking, bringing suit against prison officials is not an easy undertaking for the typical inmate. An inmate known to be contemplating or actually undertaking legal action against prison officials may become the target of intimidation and retaliation. Since 1996, moreover, congressionally mandated restrictions on prisoners' suits have placed a number of obstacles in the way of imprisoned victims of sexual assaults who seek redress in the courts. To begin with, Congress prohibited the Legal Services Corporation from providing funding to legal aid organizations that represent prison inmates. This reduced the number of lawyers available to litigate on behalf of prisoners and has meant that the majority of cases filed since 1996 involving the sexual abuse of inmates have been *pro se*. Inevitably, many of these *pro se* filings are dismissed in the early stages of litigation because of procedural errors.[78] In addition, the 1996 Prison Litigation Reform Act (PLRA) limited prisoners' access to the courts by requiring them to first exhaust all administrative remedies within the prison itself. The PLRA also increased filing fees for indigent prisoners and restricted court-awarded attorney's fees for successful suits. These restrictions help to explain why only a handful of sexual assault cases reach the courts even though many thousands of inmates are the victims of assault every year.

It must also be noted that federal judges are generally not sympathetic to prisoners' claims. Judges are often sympathetic to the problems faced by prison administrators and view prison violence as inevitable. In *Farmer v. Brennan*, Justice Clarence Thomas said in his concurring opinion, "Regrettably, some level of brutality and sexual aggression among [prisoners] is inevitable no matter what the guards do . . . unless all prisoners are locked in their cells 24 hours a day and sedated."[79]

THE DELIBERATE INDIFFERENCE STANDARD

Even those victims of sexual abuse behind bars whose cases are actually heard by the courts generally do not prevail. They must overcome what has been called the "nearly insurmountable burden" of the deliberate indifference standard enunciated by the Supreme Court in the *Farmer* case mentioned above.[80] The *Farmer* Court acknowledged that failure to protect inmates from sexual assault abridged their Eighth Amendment rights, a position consistent with prior Supreme Court and lower court decisions regarding the duty of prisons to protect inmates' health and safety.[81] In its decision, however, the Court developed a standard for determining the culpability of prison officials that is extraordinarily difficult to satisfy. Once the Court affirmed that prisons had a duty under the Constitution to protect inmates from sexual assault, the question was how to define the liability of prison officials who failed to carry out this duty. In prior cases involving injuries to prisoners, the circuits had split. Some circuits had applied the civil law concept of recklessness—failing to act in the face of an unjustifiably high risk of harm that is either known or so obvious that it should be known.[82] Other circuits had applied the criminal law definition of recklessness. The criminal law permits a finding of recklessness only when an individual disregards a risk of harm of which he is aware. In other words, a showing of intent is required, and, indeed, one circuit had come close to asserting that a prisoner plaintiff was required to show that guards and prison officials had wanted injury to come to him.[83]

Writing for the *Farmer* majority, Justice Souter said, "Deliberate indifference describes a state of mind more blameworthy than negligence."[84] He went on to equate deliberate indifference with the criminal law definition of recklessness and emphasized that the criminal law defined recklessness very differently from the civil law. By equating deliberate indifference with criminal law recklessness, Souter assigned plaintiffs the very high burden of proving subjective intent.

The deliberate indifference test, as developed in *Farmer*, consists of two parts. The first prong of the test requires that "the deprivation alleged, must be objectively and sufficiently serious."[85] Generally speaking, an allegation of rape almost automatically satisfies this requirement. Cases usually turn on the second prong, which requires that the prison official have a "sufficiently culpable state of mind."[86] Consistent with the criminal law's concept of recklessness, the Court defined "culpable state of mind" subjectively. To be culpable, the prison official must be aware that "a substantial risk of serious harm exists" and decide, never-theless, to disregard the risk. Given this standard, litigation generally centers on two questions: first, whether prison officials had knowledge that the inmate in question was at significant risk of rape; and, second, whether they took reason-able measures to abate the risk.

SPECIFIC NOTICE

As to the first question, the lower federal courts have held that defendants can acquire knowledge that an inmate is at risk of sexual assault by receiving "specific notice" of that fact. Officials are likely to be said to have possessed knowledge that an inmate was at risk if he previously complained to them about a specific threat to his safety that subsequently proved to be correct. In *Pope v. Shafer*, the court said, "A prisoner normally proves actual knowledge of impending harm by showing he complained to prison officials about a specific threat to his safety."[87] Similarly, a warning from one inmate about a specific threat to another is likely to constitute specific notice.[88] The most clear-cut evidence of specific notice is actual observation by a prison official of a sexual assault. In a case where a guard stood aside while an inmate was assaulted by other prisoners, the court found that the guard clearly had knowledge that the plaintiff was at risk.[89]

REASONABLE MEASURES

The second issue surrounding culpability is whether, upon receiving notice of risk, prison officials took reasonable measures to protect the plaintiff from sexual assault. Deliberate indifference is most clear-cut when guards or other officials witness a sexual assault but fail to intervene. For example, in *Walker v. Norris*, the court held in favor of a deceased prisoner's administratrix in a case involving prison guards' failure to intervene in an assault.[90] One prisoner, wielding a knife, chased another inmate into the yard of the Tennessee State Prison. There, in full view of guards, he stabbed the victim to death. Apparently the guards had several chances to intervene but failed to do so. The court described the guards' conduct as "deliberate indifference."[91]

Similarly, in *Solesbee v. Witkowski*, correctional officers were held to have exhibited deliberate indifference when they stood aside for several minutes while an inmate was being assaulted.[92] Unfortunately, such cases are not rare. Typically, the defendants plead that they were unable to take action because of concern for their own safety. Moreover, courts have held that officials have no duty to intervene if they reasonably fear that intervention may cause them serious injury.[93]

Prison authorities may also be deemed culpable for failing to separate especially vulnerable inmates from likely aggressors. In *Doe v. Lally*, the court said, "The state should make every effort to identify victims of homosexual assaults early in the initial classification process."[94] Failure to do so can constitute deliberate indifference, especially if the prison is one deemed to exhibit a pervasive risk of harm. One area of considerable controversy is the question of racial segregation in prison housing. A number of studies of prison rape have found that the majority of cases involve black assailants and white victims. One study, for example, found that 75 percent of the sexual assaults perpetrated in Rhode Island prisons involved black perpetrators and white victims.[95] In *Lee v. Washington*, however, the Supreme Court prohibited racial segregation in prison housing except under extraordinary circumstances.[96]

Prison authorities are also required to investigate reported rapes and to refer them for prosecution if appropriate. In *LaMarca v. Turner*, the court indicated that failing to investigate an allegation of rape including failing to collect medical evidence or to take statements from victims and witnesses led to "an atmosphere of tolerance of rape which enhanced the risk that incidents would occur."[97] In *Vosburg v. Solem*, the Eighth Circuit Court of Appeals held that failure to refer cases of rape for prosecution amounted to deliberate indifference on the part of prison authorities.[98] In that case, an inmate had been raped four times, but none of the assailants had been referred for prosecution. In fact, the court found that during a four-year period, some 140 assaults had occurred at the South Dakota State Penitentiary without a single prosecution resulting. In neighboring North Dakota, by contrast, every suspected assault during the same time period had been investigated and referred to state prosecutors for action.

DELIBERATE INDIFFERENCE: PRINCIPLES AND REALITIES

Each of the foregoing principles represented a victory for one or more inmate plaintiffs. Yet, despite these principles, the overall record indicates that the inmate who becomes the victim of sexual assault is, in reality, extremely unlikely to prevail in litigation against prison authorities, however compelling his case seems to be. In practice, the federal courts are inclined to show considerable deference to prison authorities.[99] Judges believe that prison guards and administrators have extremely difficult jobs and must be given considerable latitude in managing often violent facilities and dangerous inmates. These points are made in case after case. "Federal courts ought to afford appropriate deference and flexibility to state officials trying to manage a volatile environment."[100] "The court should have accorded wide ranging deference in the adoption and execution of policies and practices that in [prison officials'] judgment are needed to preserve internal order and discipline and to maintain institutional security."[101]

Against the backdrop of judicial deference to prison authorities, it becomes extremely difficult for an inmate-plaintiff to meet the burden of the deliberate indifference standard. Since the authorities are presumed to be acting properly, only the most blatant disregard for inmates placed in dangerous situations and only the most egregious failure to act are likely to be seen as deliberate indifference, and even in these extreme situations most inmates can almost certainly not count on prevailing. Take, for example, the 2001 case of *Doe v. Bowles*, illustrating the minimal action by prison authorities deemed to demonstrate the absence of "indifference."[102] Jane Doe, the pseudonym of a transgendered inmate at an Ohio state facility, had been placed into a protective custody unit to protect him from other inmates. While in the unit, Doe was punched and threatened by another prisoner, Hiawatha Frezzell, who was also housed there. Doe reported the incident to the guards, who decided that there was no reason to separate the two prisoners, but later Frezzell attacked Doe again and threatened to kill him. Authorities now planned to isolate Frezzell, but, in the meantime, Frezzell was allowed to leave his cell. He took advantage of this opportunity to enter Doe's cell again and sexually assault him with a mop handle. In this case, authorities knew that Doe was at particular risk to be victimized, knew that Frezzell had assaulted Doe twice and threatened further harm, and yet, despite very specific notice, had failed to take effective action to protect Doe. Nevertheless, the Sixth Circuit found that the authorities were not guilty of deliberate indifference because, after all, they had made plans to move Frezzell. Though the plans were unconsummated, this good intention was deemed adequate to show that the authorities were not indifferent.

In the 1996 case of *Langston v. Peters*, it was not poor planning but ignorance that was deemed to protect prison guards against a charge of deliberate indifference.[103] Eugene Langston, a convicted murderer, was placed in a Joliet prison cell with Eric Rayfield, another convicted murderer. Several days later, Rayfield raped Langston. Langston told a guard that he had been raped and requested medical attention. Initially, he was denied treatment, but several hours later he was taken to the infirmary where he was treated for rectal bleeding. Langston sued a number of prison officials, claiming that his Eighth Amendment rights had been violated when the authorities failed to protect him from being raped by another inmate and when he was denied medical attention. The Seventh Circuit, however, found that all defendants were entitled to summary judgment. Rayfield had a history of committing sexual assaults, which, as Langston was able to show, was known to prison authorities. However, the court ruled that Langston had not proven that the particular official who decided to place Rayfield in his cell knew of Rayfield's past record at the time of the cell assignment.[104] Given the obvious fact that the prison is a huge bureaucracy, requiring the plaintiff to prove that each and every bureaucrat knew a particular fact creates an almost impossible burden for the plaintiff. As for the delay in obtaining medical care, this was held not to have produced any actual harm to the plaintiff. The amount of blood found in Langston's rectum when he was finally examined was deemed by the court to have been "microscopic."[105]

In the 2001 cases of *Hedrick v. Roberts* and *Jones v. Roberts*, a court again showed deference to prison authorities and sympathy for their administrative problems in denying an inmate's claim.[106] In each case, the absence of any action was held not to show indifference to an inmate's plight. Both Hedrick and Jones had been arrested and were being held in the Hampton County, Virginia, jail awaiting trial. The two men were white, and one was a former local police officer. At one point both men were placed in a holding cell with a group of mainly black inmates. Both Hedrick and Jones were assaulted, and their screams for help were unanswered by guards for a period of twenty minutes. Hedrick was taken to the hospital immediately, but Jones was not sent for medical care until twelve hours later. He needed emergency surgery, lost his spleen, and was hospitalized for nearly a month. Hedrick and Jones both brought suit against the county sheriff, alleging that their Eighth Amendment rights had been violated.

The court held in favor of the defendant, Sheriff Roberts, ruling that although Roberts might have known that the plaintiffs were at risk for assault, his ability to respond reasonably to the risk was limited by the physical characteristics of the jail. Though built to hold only 146 inmates, the jail housed 350 prisoners and lacked adequate facilities for the classification and segregation of inmates. The court took note of the fact that the sheriff had launched a campaign to alleviate overcrowding at the jail, including implementing work release and diversion programs, filing suit against the State Department of Corrections to force the state to accept prisoners, and pleading with the state legislature and the Hampton City Council for additional funding. The sheriff's efforts had, thus far, been unsuccessful. However, the court found precedent supporting the idea that the sheriff should not be held liable so long as he could show that he had taken reasonable steps to alleviate overcrowding and thereby reduce the risk of assault.[107] The fact that these efforts failed could not be held against the sheriff. "Under the circumstances," said the court, the defendant's actions were "reasonable and not made with deliberate indifference to their safety."[108] It would appear, in other words, that given the conditions of this jail, no actions on the part of the jail authorities could reach the level of deliberate indifference. Such indifference was inherent in the situation.

In addition, the court attributed the sheriff's failure to send the seriously injured Jones to the hospital until twelve hours after the assault to poor judgment rather than deliberate indifference. The court found that the defendant "acted reasonably" with regard to providing medical treatment. "There is no question that [Jones] was eventually transported to the hospital. The fact that Jones was not immediately transported to the hospital . . . does not show deliberate indifference but rather, at most, poor judgment."[109]

A fourth case that reveals the extreme difficulty faced by a prisoner-plaintiff in meeting the deliberate indifference standard is *Lewis v. Richards*, where rather foolish actions by the authorities were held to show that they were not indifferent.[110] In this case, inmate Tommy Lewis was allegedly raped by two members of a prison gang. He reported the rape to prison officials but recanted his account when threatened by a large group of gang members. Several months later, he told officials his story again and was transferred to another prison dormitory. After his transfer, members of the same gang raped Lewis again. He reported the rape and was placed in protective custody. Subsequently, Lewis was raped again by three gang members. Most of Lewis's allegations were accepted by the court, but in dismissing his complaint, the Seventh Circuit held that prison authorities had not been deliberately indifferent to his plight. Indeed, authorities had responded to Lewis's original complaint by moving him to another part of the prison. As was generally known in the institution, members of the same gang were housed in that part of the prison as well, and Lewis was subsequently sexually assaulted in his new housing unit. Was failure to foresee the obvious an example of deliberate indifference? Not at all. At worst, said the court, the prison's authorities had used poor judgment in their handling of the case. And, said the court, "exercising poor judgment falls short of meeting the standard of consciously disregarding a known risk to safety."[111]

Another case worth reviewing is the Fifth Circuit's 2004 decision in *Johnson v. Johnson*, which reveals how difficult it is for an inmate to even gain access to the courts.[112] The plaintiff, Roderick Johnson, described as a homosexual with an effeminate manner, was serving a Texas sentence for burglary. After being told by prison authorities, "We don't protect punks on this farm," Johnson was housed in the general population. Almost immediately, a gang leader named Hernandez asserted "ownership" over Johnson and forced him to become his sexual servant. Johnson informed the assistant warden and guards of his plight and requested medical attention. According to Johnson's affidavit, he was told by these officials that medical care was available only for emergencies and that he should file a written request for medical attention.[113] Over the next several months, Hernandez allegedly beat and raped Johnson repeatedly and forced him to submit to sexual relations with other inmates as well. Medical personnel documented instances of bruising and swelling on Johnson's face. Later, Hernandez sold Johnson to another prison gang, and, over the ensuing months, Johnson was raped and owned by a number of individuals in several different prison buildings.

Johnson repeatedly sought help from prison authorities. He filed numerous "life endangerment" forms, wrote to prison administrators, and requested protective custody or transfer to a different prison. Johnson made numerous appearances before the prison's Unit Classification Committee (UCC) to request alternative housing, but these requests were denied. Johnson several times also made use of the prison's formal grievance procedure. Prison officers who investigated Johnson's complaints, however, averred that they could not be substantiated. Officials did not interview any of the inmates mentioned in Johnson's complaints, claiming that such interviews would "undermine the integrity of the investigation" or place Johnson in danger.[114] Prison authorities took no action against Johnson's alleged assailants, allegedly telling Johnson, "You need to get down there and fight or get you a man" and "There's no reason why black punks can't fight and survive in general population if they don't want to f***." Another official allegedly told Johnson that since he was a homosexual he probably enjoyed the assaults to which he was subjected. Johnson was also told that his complaints were invalid because the UCC had already rejected them when denying his request for alternative housing arrangements.[115]

After he contacted the American Civil Liberties Union, Johnson was placed in protective custody in another unit of the prison. In 2002, Johnson brought suit against more than two dozen prison employees charging, among other things, that his Eighth Amendment rights had been violated by officials who failed to protect him from harm. Though elements of Johnson's case continue to be litigated, he has already suffered a number of legal setbacks. Johnson's case against most of the prison supervisors whom he named in his suit was dismissed. The Fifth Circuit held that supervisory personnel had in every instance responded to Johnson's letters and grievances by referring the matter for further investigation to lower-level personnel. Prison supervisors, said the court, "cannot be expected to intervene personally in response to every inmate letter they receive. The record in this case shows that they responded to Johnson's complaints by referring the matter for further investigation or taking similar administrative steps."[116]

As to the non-supervisory personnel, the court found that in most instances Johnson had failed to exhaust the prison's institutional grievance mechanisms. To be sure, Johnson had filed numerous formal grievances, but he had not always fully complied with the complex rules governing these grievance procedures. The court found that under the 1996 Prison Litigation Reform Act, Johnson was required to fully exhaust his administrative remedies before he was entitled to bring a Section 1983 Action. The court ruled that he had not done so in every instance. Prison rules required that a grievance be filed within 15 days of the complained-of event. Johnson had filed a number of grievances, but in some instances he had missed the deadline or filed a grievance regarding multiple events, some of which had occurred more than 15 days earlier. Thus, in the case of many of the assaults to which Johnson had been subjected, he had not exhausted all administrative remedies as required by the law. This finding led to a dismissal of his complaints against several other defendants. Portions of the overall case continue to be heard, but most of the defendants who ignored or laughed at Johnson's brutalization for nearly two years will face no sanctions.

Johnson sought help before and after he was raped. *Perkins v. Grimes* tells the story of an inmate who unsuccessfully sought help from prison guards while he was being raped.[117] Kenneth Perkins was arrested for public intoxication and jailed in the Sebastian County, Arkansas, adult detention center. At the jail, he was placed in a cell with R. B. Wilson. Wilson assaulted Perkins, who banged on the cell door for help. When a guard looked in the door's window, Perkins mouthed the word "Help," but the guard ignored him. Perkins was then raped by Wilson. Afterward, a guard opened the door and allegedly asked Wilson if he was "getting some." On a subsequent day, Wilson raped Perkins again. After an investigation, Wilson was prosecuted and ultimately convicted of both rapes.

Perkins charged that jail employees had violated his Eighth Amendment rights by failing to protect him from Wilson and failing to come to his assistance when he begged for help. The court found, however, that guards had no *a priori* reason to suspect that Wilson might be a threat to Perkins. Jailers testified that Wilson had been incarcerated in the facility many times and had never been a threat to anyone unless they "mouthed off."[118] Guards denied that Perkins had asked for help during the first assault, and, of course, Perkins had no way to corroborate his claim. This, of course, is a common problem faced by prisoners making allegations against guards and other officials. It is often the inmate's word against that of the guards. In the absence of compelling reasons to the contrary, courts are virtually certain to accept the latter.

Finally, consider the case of *Spruce v. Sargent*, which reveals that when officials do not know what they obviously should know, their actions cannot be said to be deliberate.[119] Spruce, an Arkansas prisoner, was raped repeatedly in 1991 by at least twenty different fellow inmates. During the course of this ordeal, Spruce was infected with the HIV virus. Spruce brought suit against a number of prison officials including the Assistant Director of the Arkansas Department of Corrections, Larry Norris. Spruce had sent a grievance form to Norris indicating that he had been threatened and assaulted by other inmates and feared further assaults. Norris signed the form, proving that he had received it, but he testified that he had not realized the seriousness of the situation. The Eighth Circuit accepted Norris's claim as showing lack of deliberation. In its opinion, the court said, "An official's failure to alleviate a significant risk that he should have perceived but did not, while no cause for commendation, is not deliberate indifference to an inmate's health or safety and therefore not a violation of the Eighth Amendment.[120]

These cases, drawn from several dozen heard by the federal courts in recent years, illustrate the difficulty of meeting the Supreme Court's deliberate indifference standard. If prison authorities are unaware of a problem, their actions cannot be deemed to be deliberate even if they should have been aware of the problem. So long as authorities make some gesture in the direction of dealing with the problem, however minimal or even foolish that gesture might be, they have not been indifferent. If officials do nothing, but doing something might have been difficult, they were not indifferent. If officials make no effort at all to respond to an inmate's complaints but the inmate failed to comply with the institution's complex grievance procedures, officials might have been indifferent but probably have no liability. One would be compelled to conclude from the cases that an inmate victimized by sexual predators has little recourse in the court system and should probably follow the brutal admonition to learn to fight if he hopes not to be forced to f***.

Many commentators and some jurists, to be sure, have been critical of the deliberate indifference standard and have suggested alternatives.[121] For my present purposes, however, the question of hypothetical alternatives is less relevant than the fact that the current standard underscores the adiaphorous character of bureaucracy. Be they German or American, bureaucracies have no remorse and no pity. As institutions, they erode the moral limits of violence.

CHAPTER 3
FORCE AND GOVERNANCE

It is sometimes claimed that governments cannot rely exclusively upon force or the threat of force to retain their power, and there is some truth to this idea. While some regimes, say, the Democratic People's Republic of Korea, appear to be able to hang on, decade after decade, mainly by cowing or killing all their opponents, most ultra-repressive regimes are short-lived, succumbing to coups and revolts or collapsing under the weight of their economic incompetence.

The problem with force as a mechanism of rule is that it produces sullen and sometimes rebellious subjects who do the minimum to get by and avoid the government's wrath. A popular saying in the old Soviet Union was "The government pretends to pay us and we pretend to work." Unbridled force also requires the maintenance of powerful security forces that can themselves be a source of plots and coups and, in an infinite regress, must be watched by other security forces.

Successful governments obviously do not dispense with the use of force. Every regime depends upon its military and police forces to deal with external foes and internal threats. On any given day, thousands of American troops are in combat and America's jails and prisons house more than two million of the nation's citizens. Successful governments, however, have learned to transform and refine brute force so that it becomes a more effective instrument of governance. Domestically, they have refined force by establishing the rule of law and by legitimating their power through such instruments as political participation. In the international realm, governments employ what Joseph Nye termed "soft power" as an adjunct to, or cloak for, military might or political pressure. These instruments—law, legitimacy, soft power—are sometimes seen as alternatives to violence. This, however, is a misperception. These instruments are the handmaidens of violence, not alternatives. In military parlance, they might be termed "force multipliers."

No doubt, citizens are better off when their rulers rely more upon refined force and less upon brute force. Yet, refined force should not be mistaken for the absence of force. And when refinement fails to produce the desired results, even liberal regimes are only too ready to drop their velvet gloves and bring out their waterboards.

THE RULE OF LAW

One important instrument used to refine force is legalism or the rule of law. The rule of law means that governments' actions cannot be arbitrary but must, instead, be based upon published, clearly stated, and prospective statutes that are binding upon government officials as well as citizens. Of course, the rule of law is generally seen as a safeguard for citizens, protecting them from arbitrary action by government officials, and that is certainly among its functions. However, at the same time the rule of law has beneficial implications for citizens, it also serves the interests of the state.

If a government is arbitrary and capricious in its conduct, citizens may feel fear—even terror—but they may not know what to do to please their rulers. The arbitrary exercise of power may produce trepidation but does not offer direction or promote obedience. A small example illustrates the point. Residents of Washington, D.C., are familiar with the often capricious character of parking enforcement in the nation's capital. Fines for illegal parking in the District of Columbia are quite high, often $75 or $100, and vehicles deemed to be illegally parked are frequently towed by the authorities. To make matters worse, the District sometimes fails to keep records of which vehicles it has towed and the precise location to which towed vehicles have been taken, which can lead to days of fruitless searching for the missing vehicle. Accordingly, motorists familiar with the District are fearful of the parking authorities and anxious to avoid their wrath. This understandable fear and anxiety, however, does not promote lawful conduct.

To begin with, many of the signs that ostensibly indicate whether or not parking is allowed in a particular area are self-contradictory and, in some cases, totally incomprehensible. One of the local radio stations often delights in conducting interviews with the chief of police in which the chief is shown a photo of a District of Columbia parking sign and asked whether the sign indicates that parking is allowed or is not allowed. The chief usually concludes that it is impossible to tell from the language of the sign. Moreover, the District's traffic enforcement officials are notoriously capricious. I was once cited for having parked front-first on a block where vertical parking was mandated. I intercepted the enforcement official and asked what I had done wrong. She replied that I should have backed into the space. When I protested indignantly that there was no sign with such an instruction and pointed out that many other vehicles had parked exactly as I had, the officer shrugged, informed me that I should have known, and walked on.

The upshot of erratic parking enforcement is that many motorists believe that it makes little difference whether they endeavor to obey the District's parking regulations or not. The rules are vague and their enforcement arbitrary. Cars parked in what seem to be legal spaces are as likely to be ticketed as those parked in what seem to be illegal spaces. Many motorists park their cars wherever they see an empty spot and hope for the best. Absent the rule of law, the District of Columbia's parking authorities inspire fear among motorists but do not compel obedience.

Parking enforcement in the District of Columbia is a small and, perhaps, insignificant example of a more general problem. Absent the rule of law, governments can inspire fear but cannot elicit compliance. Barrington Moore's well-known account of the effects of state terror in Stalin's Soviet Union tells the same story in a more significant setting. During Stalin's thirty-year reign, Soviet citizens were subject to arbitrary arrest, incarceration, torture, and murder by the regime's security services. In some instances, their offense might consist of deviating by word or deed from the ever-changing party line. Actions that were encouraged and applauded one day might result in arrest and punishment the next. What was and was not permissible became difficult to understand and predict. While this regime of terror inspired widespread fear, it turned out to be counterproductive and self-defeating. Fear by itself could not produce obedience. "The subordinate," Moore observed, "will not obey his superior if he is made to feel that this obedience will soon be held against him."[1] The Soviet experience, said Moore, showed that a measure of legality was necessary even to the most despotic state.

Historically, the idea of the rule of law in the West was often espoused by those who sought to protect citizens' liberties from the actions of despotic rulers. Yet, not all the proponents of legalism were oblivious to its importance as an instrument of governance. The framers of the American Constitution, for example, feared arbitrary rule as much because it undermined governance as because it threatened citizens' liberties. James Madison's views, expressed in the *Federalist 62*, are instructive in this regard. Madison writes, "It will be of little avail to the people that the laws are made by men of their own choice if the laws be so voluminous that they cannot be read, or so incoherent that they cannot be understood; if they be repealed or revised before they are promulgated, or undergo such incessant changes that no man, who knows what the law is today, can guess what it will be tomorrow." Such a state of affairs, according to Madison, reduces popular respect for government and undermines economic development. "What prudent merchant will hazard his fortunes in any new branch of commerce when he knows not but that his plans may be rendered unlawful before they can be executed?"[2]

Similar concerns have inspired a number of regimes, including such authoritarian states as the Chinese People's Republic and Russia to endeavor to strengthen the rule of law in their domains. The Chinese leadership has viewed the rule of law as essential to economic development, and, in Russia, Prime Minister Dmitry Medvedev recently said, "Shortcomings in implementing laws . . . are basically macro-economic factors which restrain the growth of national prosperity."[3]

In many instances, the power of a regime will be increased if the arbitrary power of rulers and officials is reduced. James Madison understood this principle, but it is one that many rulers, jealous of their personal powers and prerogatives, fail to grasp. In China, for example, the central government's efforts to promote legalism as a spur to economic development are often thwarted by local officials accustomed to exercising discretionary power—and securing bribes.[4] Even in the United States, as we shall see in chapter 5, officials often find reason to behave quite arbitrarily. Americans are strongly encouraged to believe in a law of law that is sometimes more mythological than true.

The rule of law is not a substitute for force. It is a refinement and enhancement of force. It serves citizens by protecting them from arbitrary actions by officials. At the same time, however, it enhances the power of the state. This trade-off is not necessarily beneficent. The rule of law may not be arbitrary, but it can be harsh. Indeed, in recent years federal criminal law in the United States has become increasingly draconian.[5] The rule of law may protect citizens from arbitrary actions but not from harsh treatment. It is not an instrument for reducing the state's power. It serves, instead, to make government less arbitrary and, as a result, *more* powerful.

LEGITIMATION

The second key instrument through which governments refine force is legitimation. It is often claimed that governments must possess a measure of legitimacy in the eyes of their subjects to retain their power. James Madison, for example, declared that "public opinion sets bounds to every government."[6] And Hannah Arendt said that force was actually the opposite of true power. Reliance on violence, according to Arendt, usually reflected a desperate and unpopular regime's weakness rather than its strength.[7]

Though so frequently repeated that they have become truisms, such views seem just a bit idealistic. Obviously, as events in Egypt and Tunisia in 2011 indicate, unpopular regimes can occasionally be toppled by their disgruntled citizens. Indeed, such regimes sometimes seem to have so little support that they appear to collapse quickly in response to popular protests. The overnight collapse of a feared regime, though, usually requires not only popular pressure and discontent but also depends upon a decision by the military and other security forces to abandon the government to its fate or, in such cases as the Bolshevik revolution, a decision by many soldiers in the capital to throw their support to the insurrectionists. As Leon Trotsky observed, "There is no doubt that the fate of every revolution at a certain point is decided by a break in the disposition of the army. Against a numerous, disciplined, well-armed and ably led military force, unarmed or almost unarmed masses of the people cannot possibly gain a victory."[8]

Often, a government can survive for quite a long time on a narrow base of support so long as its military and security forces are adequately staffed and remain loyal. Indeed, fearing popular reprisals if the regime falls, its security services may fight with special ferocity to prevent a hated government's overthrow. East Germany's *Stasi*, Romania's *Securitate*, and Haiti's *Tonton Macoutes* are a few of many examples of police forces that kept detested but feared regimes in power for decades through the continual application of intimidation and terror. At its peak, the *Stasi* employed 91,000 full-time officers and 173,000 informants. This amounted to one police officer for every 180 East German citizens and roughly one informant for every 76 adults.[9] The feared prewar Gestapo, by contrast, employed only some 7,000 agents to watch a much larger populace. Though the German Democratic Republic (DDR) had little popular support, its citizens were generally among the most obedient in the Soviet satellite empire until a change of policy in Moscow condemned the DDR to oblivion.

At any rate, Arendt to the contrary notwithstanding, violence and legitimacy should not be understood as polar opposites. Rather, they are closely connected. Perhaps some citizens may be disinclined to flout what they conceive to be legitimate authority.[10] But however legitimate it might be, no government can completely eschew the threat or use of force. Governments, as Max Weber pointed out, claim the legitimate use of force, not legitimacy without force. Perhaps in the Kingdom of Heaven citizens cheerfully pay their taxes and dutifully obey every law, but in earthly kingdoms they generally need a bit of encouragement. Popular support and legitimacy do not obviate the need for force. Instead, they facilitate the use of force by reducing popular resistance to its application. Thus, for example, in the United States riots and disturbances have occasionally broken out in response to police encounters with suspects in impoverished black communities, as they have in the heavily Muslim Parisian *banlieues*, where support for the authorities is generally low and the police are sometimes seen as an illegitimate occupation army. In more affluent neighborhoods where political and social institutions are generally held in higher esteem, law enforcement officials do not expect to encounter community resistance to their efforts.

Legitimacy not only makes it easier for governments to use force against their own citizens; it also helps them to secure the support of those selfsame citizens—mobilized as citizen soldiers—for the use of force against others. The modern era of the citizen soldier began at the end of the eighteenth century. Before that time, wars were typically fought by armies of professional warriors who campaigned for pay and booty. Armies were small by contemporary standards. The eighteenth-century Prussian army, for example, one of the most powerful in Europe, consisted of only 80,000 men.[11] For major campaigns, kings commonly filled out their forces by recruiting mercenary troops. But mercenaries were mere hirelings. Occasionally loyal to their entrepreneurial captains, but seldom to the regime that employed them, they sometimes switched sides in the middle of campaigns. Their commanders tended to regard battle casualties as a capital loss inconsistent with good business practice, a policy powerfully supported by their troops.

These military practices were defeated in battle by the *Levée en masse* of the French Revolution. In 1793 it produced 300,000 volunteers and conscripts to defend France and the Revolution. Though scarcely trained and poorly equipped, many of the French troops fought with an ardor born of devotion to a cause. Under Napoleon, the French nation's call to its people produced an army of 1.3 million. Its battlefield triumphs converted France from a kingdom to an empire and demonstrated that popular support could be transformed into military power.

For the rest of the nineteenth century, other European governments tried to convince their own subjects to emulate the *élan* and self-sacrifice of the French troops. Universal military service became European norm, along with nationalist indoctrination, which was soon extended from soldiers to children by universal compulsory schooling. In time, the expansion of military service led to the development of national pension systems, initially introduced to reward former soldiers and their immediate dependents. And finally there was the right to vote. Proponents of suffrage expansion argued that the franchise would give subjects a sense of ownership in the state and inspire them to fight for their country.

Legitimacy and force are related in another way, as well. When they use force to protect their citizens from threats to their security and well-being, governments generally enhance their own legitimacy. In some instances, indeed, rulers can find it expedient to invent enemies and threats whose defeat can unite the populace behind the regime.[12] This is popularly known as the "wag the dog" tactic—a term derived from a 1997 film in which a fictional president invents a foreign threat to divert attention from his own misdeeds. In a similar vein, the late political sociologist Charles Tilly famously characterized government as a "protection racket," often protecting citizens against imaginary threats or from the government's own actions.[13]

Thus, far from being polar opposites, force and legitimacy are often intertwined in what, from a government's perspective, can constitute a virtuous cycle. Governments seek legitimacy in order to facilitate their use of force. In turn, the successful use of force can enhance a regime's legitimacy by demonstrating its power and offering the citizenry protection from real or imagined threats. Of course, regimes unsure of their ability to establish their right to rule in an existing society may decide that a measure of social engineering—which could include political murder, ethnic cleansing, and so forth—might provide them with a more favorable social foundation. In this way, not only are force and legitimacy intertwined, but more than one regime has begun its search for legitimacy from the crest of a mountain of corpses.

THE PROCESS OF LEGITIMATION

Issues of statehood, territoriality, and power are generally decided by force. Once the smoke of violent struggle begins to clear, however, the victors frequently seek to validate their success and persuade both internal and external audiences of the finality and legitimacy of the outcome. This process of legitimation typically has three stages. The first, which might be called the smashing of idols, consists of the destruction of institutions and symbols associated with the defeated forces or regime and the erection, in their place, of symbols designed to call attention to the power and virtue of the victors. Soon after they captured Iraq's capital in 2003, for example, American troops made a point of smashing the enormous statue of the late Iraqi president, Saddam Hussein, which had dominated central Baghdad's Firdos Square. Televised around the world, the toppling of the statue symbolized American military might and Hussein's overthrow, and was followed by the introduction of a new Iraqi flag and other symbols of post–Saddam statehood.

In a similar vein, after destroying the military power of the Aztec and Inca empires, Spanish *conquistadors* made a determined effort to suppress the religious institutions and beliefs that played central roles in the lives of their new subjects. The elimination of indigenous religious practices and the forcible conversion of native populations to Roman Catholicism were viewed by the Spaniards as important steps in the pacification of their new possessions. By destroying the natives' holy places and religious symbols and replacing them with their own churches, priests, and icons, the Spaniards sought to affirm the moral superiority of European civilization as well as to deprive their new subjects of a potential rallying point for continued resistance.

In the case of the Incas, resistance continued for many years after Pizarro hanged the Inca emperor Atahualpa and attempted to install a puppet regime through which the Spaniards hoped to govern the empire. As an important element of their resistance to Spanish rule, members of the Inca nobility, or *panaqa*, endeavored to protect their empire's most important religious symbols, particularly including the mummified remains of former emperors, widely venerated as sacred objects. Members of the *panaqa* endured death by torture at the hands of the Spaniards to prevent these sacred mummies from falling into Spanish hands.[14] The Spaniards, for their part, viewed the mummies as a threat to their own power and hunted for them for nearly three decades before finding and destroying them.

Significantly, after taking the Inca emperor prisoner, Pizarro organized a mock trial for Atahualpa. The Spaniards accused their captive of a number of crimes, including idolatry, polygamy, and the murder of his brother, Huáscar. The trial was, of course, a sham conducted to further demonstrate the power of the Spaniards and to demoralize the Incas by subjecting their ruler to public indignities. Prior to his execution, Atahualpa was coerced into accepting baptism into the Catholic faith, which, of course, amounted to a public declaration by the Aztec emperor that Spanish culture was superior to that of his own people.

These sorts of mock or "show" trials are commonly a second phase in the process of legitimating the outcome of a violent struggle. The victors often employ a quasi-legal process to demonstrate that the leaders of the vanquished nation or group were little better than common criminals who misled their followers and lacked any real claim to authority. The victors, of course, hope to wrap themselves in the mantle of law, affirming to one and all that they represent justice and morality, not merely the spirit of conquest. Thus, not only did American forces topple Saddam's statue, but in 2003 they took Saddam and many of his lieutenants into custody, eventually handing them over to be tried for a variety of offenses by the Iraqi Interim Government that had been established under the protection of the United States. In the proceedings that began in 2005, a good deal of evidence was presented demonstrating Saddam's brutality. He was accused of committing genocide against the Kurds, of launching bloody reprisals against those he believed to have been associated with a 1982 assassination attempt, of a murderous campaign against Iraqi Shiites in 1991 and 1999, and various other crimes. Saddam was found guilty of most charges and was sentenced to death and hanged in 2006.

There can be little doubt that Saddam was a ruthless tyrant. The United States, however, maintains cordial relations with quite a number of more or less equally tyrannical rulers. The point of the proceedings initiated against Saddam was less to secure redress for his victims than to discredit his defeated regime and to bolster the moral authority of the American-backed Iraqi government that had been created to take its place. Legitimation, not justice, was the goal of the proceedings.

A similar point might be made with regard to the 1945–46 Nuremberg Trials. These were a series of military tribunals organized by the main victors of World War II for the purpose of prosecuting the former rulers of the now-defeated Nazi Germany. Several of the major Nazi leaders such as Heinrich Himmler, Joseph Goebbels and Adolf Hitler had committed suicide at the end of the war. However, hundreds of other important officials were in Allied custody along with many lesser figures. The major Nazi leaders, including Hermann Göring and several important military officers, were charged with war crimes and crimes against humanity. Several were ultimately sentenced to the gallows. Several lesser officials of the Nazi regime, including concentration camp personnel, corporate chieftains who abused slave laborers, and physicians who had engaged in medical experiments on concentration camp prisoners, were sentenced—some to death—in subsequent trials.

There can certainly be little doubt that the Nazi government was among the most murderous in modern times and that its leaders committed the various atrocities of which they were accused. Nevertheless, like the trial of Saddam Hussein, the Nuremberg tribunals were designed more to legitimate the outcome of the war than to secure justice for the victims of Nazism. In point of fact, tens of thousands of Germans had been willing participants in the most heinous crimes of the Nazi era, serving as concentration camp guards, as members of the mobile killing squads known as *Einsatzgruppen*, and as agents of the SS, the SD, and the Gestapo. Not only were most of these individuals unmolested after the war but some, including a number of infamous Gestapo and SS officers, such as Klaus Barbie, were recruited by American and other intelligence agencies that saw them as potentially useful Cold War assets. Thus, a small number of high-ranking Nazis were, with great fanfare, tried and punished in order to assert the criminality of the Nazi regime and the moral superiority of the victorious allies. Thousands of other Nazis, among them the perpetrators of vicious and brutal acts, were ignored or put to work for those same allies. Legitimation required the punishment of fewer perpetrators than actual justice might have demanded.

A contemporary variant of the show trial is the "truth and reconciliation commission." A number of these commissions have been established in recent years in the wake of wars, civil wars, and revolutions to investigate wrongdoing on the part of the defeated side. Truth commissions operated in recent years in South Africa, Argentina, Chile, Peru, and a number of other nations. Rather than seek punishment for those who committed criminal acts—who were usually granted amnesty—the function of these commissions was to bring about some degree of rapprochement between the victims and perpetrators of past acts of violence.

To this end, commissions heard testimony, sought to establish facts, endeavored to reassure victims that their plight was recognized, and, in some instances, elicited expressions of regret and apology from those guilty of wrongdoing. The commissions' proceedings were designed to increase the likelihood that previously warring sides would begin to coexist. Generally speaking, truth and reconciliation commissions, rather than criminal tribunals, are established when the side that has been defeated in a violent conflict retains sufficient power to persuade the victors of the expedience of seeking its cooperation.[15] Through the truth and reconciliation commission, the victors can affirm their moral superiority while offering an olive branch to those whom they have vanquished.

The destruction of idols and the organization of show trials are generally early steps in the process of legitimation. Over longer periods of time, regimes will seek to legitimate their rule by creating positive beliefs about the new regime and its leaders. Governments employ a variety of instruments for this purpose. Among the most important are nationalism, participation, religion, and ideology. Nationalism or patriotism is the idea that those occupying a particular territory have something in common that makes them distinct from and superior to other people. Generally, nationalism is built upon myths about the common origins and history of a people, as well as their exploits and suffering as a nation, their heroes and their mission in the world. Such myths are often grounded in historic truths, but they usually do not depend for their acceptance on whether they are true or false.

Among the most common of the myths associated with nationalism is the idea that nations create states. From this perspective, the state is viewed as an outgrowth of the nation, established to promote the nation's interests and to protect its people. In point of fact, however, nations are more often created by states than the contrary. Almost every nation owes its historic existence to the efforts of some set of rulers to gain the support of the inhabitants of whatever territory they have acquired. Take France, for example. Most of the individuals living within the borders of the state of France consider themselves members of the French nation. However, France was not created by the French nation. Instead, successive Parisian governments worked for several centuries to imbue the inhabitants of the territories they conquered with a sense of national identity and patriotism that would make them more amenable to being governed. As recently as the early nineteenth century, many if not most of those living within the borders of France identified more with their regions—Brittany, Normandy, Franche-Comté and so forth—than with France. Indeed, many spoke little or no French, preferring to converse in Norman, Languedocian, Limousin, Provençal, or any of a number of regional tongues. Even as recently as the 1870s, French was a foreign language for half the citizens of France.[16]

Beginning at the time of the Revolution, though, successive French regimes worked to transform the miscellaneous inhabitants of France into Frenchmen— citizens who identified with the nation and spoke its language and would fight in its armies and accept the authority of the state. One of the main instruments in this process was the common school, an institution that, by 1882, all children were required to attend. Here, successive generations of students studied French language and culture as well as a glorified and romanticized version of French history designed to instill in them a sense of national honor and pride.

A similar process is evident in the United States. After the American Revolution, few inhabitants of the thirteen former British colonies regarded themselves as Americans. Most identified with their states. They were citizens of Virginia, Massachusetts, New York, and so forth. For many, the state remained the primary focus of identification well into the nineteenth century; witness the many tens of thousands who fought for their states against the United States government during the Civil War.

American patriotism grew slowly, encouraged by the government's creation of national symbols. As in France, a spirit of patriotism was promoted by an educational system that glorified American history, presented the nation's leaders as heroic figures, and encouraged children to develop a strong sense of attachment to the nation. The schools also imposed the English language and American culture upon the children of immigrants and upon the Spanish-speaking residents of the vast territories seized from Mexico in 1848. As in France and elsewhere, citizens were gradually created by the government—not the reverse.

A second commonly used instrument of legitimation is participation. A good deal of evidence suggests that an opportunity to participate in the decision-making processes of the institutions that rule them affords many individuals enormous psychic gratification that is not dependent upon their approval of the specific decisions that ultimately result.[17] This is true so long as the process is not seen as a complete sham, as in the case of, say, elections in the former Soviet Union. Thus, for example, employees are known to derive satisfaction from being consulted about company policies. From management's perspective, such consultation is a means of inducing employees to be more cooperative and to work harder.[18] Virtually everyone has encountered this management tactic at one time or another.

Governments, for their part, have long been aware of the potential benefits of popular participation though, to be sure, many national leaders have not been sufficiently enlightened or self-confident to risk their own defeat at the polls for the larger good of the regime. One group of notably enlightened statesmen, however, assembled in Philadelphia in 1787 to draft the American Constitution. A number of the framers seemed clearly to understand that the new government they were proposing would be strengthened if ordinary citizens were allowed to participate in its affairs. James Wilson of Pennsylvania, for instance, said he supported the idea of popular election of the members of the House of Representatives because this would increase the new government's power. Wilson averred that he favored "raising the federal pyramid to a considerable altitude" and therefore wished to give it "as broad a base as possible."[19] Even delegates who feared excessive citizen influence agreed that election of at least some national officials would enhance the power and stability of the proposed new government by enhancing the popular "confidence" it was likely to inspire.[20]

Most often, governments need popular support during times of war and national emergency, and, as a result, war, like civil disorder, has been a great incubator of voting rights. In the United States, both the Revolutionary War and the War of 1812 prompted state authorities to lower the barriers to voting in order to increase the martial enthusiasm of the militiamen upon whom the American military effort depended.[21] World War I was associated with suffrage expansion in both the U.S. and Europe. Indeed, the introduction of women's suffrage in the United States, Britain, and Canada was prompted mainly by these governments' desires to secure women's support for the war effort.[22] The relationship between war and voting rights is perfectly captured by the nineteenth-century Swedish slogan "One man, one vote, one gun." In recent years, of course, this slogan has been abbreviated and its original meaning nearly forgotten.

The benefits they hope to derive from popular voting, coupled with their desire to avoid more disturbing forms of popular political action, has impelled many governments and national political elites to encourage citizens to vote while discouraging them from engaging in other forms of political activity. Their goal is not to stimulate participation per se. It is, rather, to make certain that those who are moved to participate are channeled into the electoral arena. In the United States, the virtues of voting are taught in the schools, promoted by the mass media, and touted by a host of civic institutions and foundations. And, every year, state and local governments spend hundreds of millions of dollars to operate the nation's electoral machinery. Voting is the only form of popular political activity that receives this type of governmental subsidy. Those who wish to lobby or litigate must foot the bill themselves. And those who endeavor to express their views via protests, sit-ins, or demonstrations are likely to incur the displeasure of the authorities.

A third instrument of legitimation is religion. Many regimes and political leaders endeavor to wrap themselves in a godly mantle and to convince their citizens that support for the state is divinely sanctioned. A small number of contemporary regimes—Iran for example—are actual theocracies, ruled by members of the clergy or leaders approved by the clergy. But even the leaders of secular states often find it expedient to claim that they and the regime, more generally, are blessed and guided by God. President George W. Bush claimed to be a "born again" Christian and courted the support of evangelical Protestants and other religious groups. For his part, President Barack Obama declared at the February 2011 National Prayer Breakfast, "When I wake in the morning, I wait on the Lord, and I ask Him to give me the strength to do right by our country and its people. And when I go to bed at night, I wait on the Lord, and I ask Him to forgive me my sins, and look after my family and the American people, and make me an instrument of His will."[23]

Beyond this sort of rhetoric by politicians, many secular governments offer considerable financial and institutional support to religious institutions. Several Western European states provide financial subsidies to officially recognized religious denominations and subsidize religious education. A number of nominally secular regimes also pay the salaries of members of the recognized clergy. In the Czech Republic, for example, in 2010 members of the clergy were paid 16,800 crowns per month and were exempted from the 10 percent wage cut that affected other state workers.[24]

In the United States, most property owned by religious institutions is exempt from local property taxes, and contributions to religious organizations are tax deductible. These two tax benefits amount to a multi-billion-dollar governmental subsidy for religious entities. In addition, a number of religious organizations are currently the recipients of federal grants and contracts to operate a variety of social service programs—another subsidy to religious institutions worth as much as $2 billion every year.

In exchange for these and other forms of support, governments expect established religious entities to urge their adherents to back the regime and its leaders and, in effect, to tell the faithful that God wants them to obey secular authority. The bargain is usually kept. In the United States, many religious services include prayers and blessings for our nation and its leaders, religious figures give their blessings to sessions of Congress, church groups provide chaplains for the military services, and so forth. It is no accident that many of America's most religious groups are also among its most patriotic. In particular, white Protestant evangelicals are both among the most pious and the most nationalistic groups in America. Many believe that America has a special role to play in the world and that the nation has received special protection from God for much of its history.[25] In recent years, white Protestant evangelicals have been among the strongest supporters of the wars in Iraq and Afghanistan and have generally been staunch advocates of American military dominance in the world. Many evangelicals believe they have a duty to send their sons and daughters to defend the nation. As one pastor said, "sacrificial patriotism" is a high value in the evangelical community.[26]

A similar pattern of church-state relations is evident in other nations as well. In Russia, for example, the collapse of Communism along with the Soviet empire left the regime without any particular claim upon citizens' loyalties. Accordingly, Russian leaders turned to religion as an important instrument of legitimation. Prime Minister Vladimir Putin makes sure to wear a cross, attends church regularly, makes well-publicized visits to holy places, and frequently affirms the "special role" of the Russian Orthodox Church.

The church, for its part, regularly gives the regime its blessing. Priests have gone so far as to sprinkle holy water on Russian weapons systems. Indeed, the head of the church, Patriarch Alexy II, recently blessed the briefcase carrying Russia's secret nuclear codes. "The state supports the church and the church supports the state," said Russian human-rights activist Sergei Kovalyov.[27]

Finally, there is the matter of secular ideology. A number of regimes have sought to foster beliefs that have the character of secular religions, substituting a particular leader or dogma for the deity. In recent decades, the most prominent of these beliefs has been Communism, though Nazism was also important for a brief period in the mid-twentieth century. Communism, derived from the nineteenth-century writings of Karl Marx, Friedrich Engels, and others, calls for the creation of a classless society in which productive resources, including land, are owned by individuals in common. Though Communism also predicts the emergence of a stateless society, it became the official ideology of a very powerful state, the Union of Soviet Socialist Republics (USSR), its satellite empire, and, in its Maoist form, of the People's Republic of China. Successive leaders of the USSR as well as China's Mao Zedong averred that their repressive internal programs and often aggressive external policies were needed to promote and defend their utopian ideals.

It is difficult to know what percentage of the Soviet or Chinese populace actually subscribed to their regimes' official ideologies. At one time or another, however, tens of millions of individuals found inspiration in the Communist creed and were prepared to overlook their regimes' sometimes murderous acts.[28] Such individuals gave the Soviet and Chinese regimes support both inside and outside their borders. Foreign Communists, generally motivated by commitment to the regime's ideology, provided the Soviet Union, in particular, with extremely important intelligence, propaganda, and espionage services from the time of the Bolshevik revolution through the end of the Cold War. The collapse of the Soviet Union and China's shift to a market-driven economy after Mao's death, however, eroded much of the ideological appeal of Communism as an ideology.

By contrast with religious doctrines, which usually promise the faithful a heavenly reward in the next life, secular creeds assert the possibility of an earthly utopia—a worker's paradise for loyal Communists, or an Aryan utopia for faithful Nazis and their descendants. The price of admission to these secular heavens is generally obedience to the directives of the regime and, in the cases of Soviet Communism, Maoism, and Nazism, strict obedience to the will of the Supreme Leader.

Secular ideologies can often generate enormous initial enthusiasm, inspiring millions of individuals to march, work, fight, kill, and be killed for a leader or cause. During the heyday of Communism, political zealots sometimes asked to be buried with their beloved copy of the *Communist Manifesto* much as religious zealots might seek to be buried with sacred symbols, such as famous "tickets to heaven" issued to young Iranian soldiers by the Ayatollah Khomeini, to ease their souls' journey to the next world. The life expectancy, however, of secular dogmas is generally much shorter than that of religious creeds. Communism was important for less than a century, and Nazism lasted barely twenty years. The general problem faced by secular creeds is that they tend to be falsifiable. If the earthly paradise is not achieved or its prophets defeated, the enthusiasm of the creed's supporters is likely to wane as quickly as it once waxed. Though millions of Germans were fervent Nazis in the 1930s, by 1946 few had much allegiance to National Socialism beliefs or the party's defunct leadership. In a similar vein, several decades of poverty and privation left few Soviet or Chinese citizens with much faith in Communism. The claims made by religious faiths or even national myths, by contrast, are not falsifiable. The gods may allow the faithful to suffer in this world but redemption is certain—perhaps all the more certain—to come in the next. Once established, religious faiths can persist for millennia, exerting pressure upon the faithful to obey despite empirical indications of heavenly indifference.

FORCE AND LEGITIMACY

Once established, legitimacy facilitates the use of force by governments against their citizens as well as the mobilization of those citizens for the use of force against others. This relationship between force and legitimacy is particularly evident in the case of military conscription. Since the late eighteenth century, conscription, or the draft, has been one of the chief means by which nation states have recruited the soldiers needed to fill the ranks of their military forces. The origins of conscription are popularly associated with the French *Levée en masse* of 1793, a draft of all male citizens ordered by the new Republic to protect France from invasion by its various European adversaries. The 1793 *Levée* produced, as we saw above, a force of some 300,000 men, and the routine system of conscription introduced after 1798 provided France with more than two million troops—an enormous number in the context of the time.[29] In response to its defeats at the hands of the French, Prussia introduced a comprehensive system of conscription via the Boyen Law of 1814, and other European powers followed suit with their own more or less universal programs of compulsory military service.

As to the United States, during America's Revolutionary War, the Continental Congress authorized the states to draft citizens for the Continental army, but this conscription program was short-lived.[30] During its first decades as an independent nation, the geographically isolated United States found that a small quasi-professional army of volunteers, augmented during actual conflicts by state militia forces also composed of volunteers, was more than adequate to meet its limited military needs.[31] During the Civil War, however, enormous manpower needs led both the Confederacy and the Union to institute military conscription. The Confederacy began drafting men in 1862, and the federal government followed suit in March 1863 with the passage of the Enrollment Act, which provided for a military draft and established a new federal agency, the Bureau of the Provost Marshal General, to supervise the military conscription system.[32]

There may, at first glance, appear to be a substantial difference between conscription and voluntary military enlistment. The former is, after all, compulsory while the latter is a matter of free individual choice. The distinction, however, between the two forms of military recruitment is not as substantial as might seem to be the case. Though nominally compulsory, an effective system of conscription requires a fairly substantial level of popular support for the regime that is ordering its citizens to serve and general acceptance of the need for the risk and sacrifice associated with military service. Efforts to conscript members of an unwilling or hostile populace are likely to be met with evasion, resistance, and even violence. A typical example is that of early nineteenth-century Egypt. Here, Mehmed Ali sought to conscript peasants into his new national army without making much of a prior effort to inculcate in his prospective soldiers any sense of national obligation or loyalty. The result was a high level of popular resistance. To escape recruitment officers, families abandoned their homes and villages while entire regions rebelled against the regime. When these methods failed, prospective conscripts resorted to self-mutilation. Thousand gouged out eyes or amputated limbs so as to be unfit for military service.[33]

During the American Civil War, opposition to conscription was widespread, especially in areas of the Union where there was considerable sympathy for the Confederacy and areas of the Confederacy where unionist sentiment was strong. In the North alone, hundreds of thousands of men failed to report when called, particularly in the closing years of the war.[34] And in numerous instances, efforts to conscript less-than-enthusiastic soldiers led to violence against conscription officials and even large-scale riots. The best known is, of course, the New York City draft riot of 1863 in which draft offices and other public buildings were destroyed and more than one hundred lives lost before regular army troops restored order.[35] Of course, a century later, resistance to the Vietnam-era war draft manifested itself in demonstrations, thousands of court cases, and various other forms of resistance to service in an unpopular war.

On the other hand, where there is substantial support for the government, and the populace accepts the need for military service, conscription is likely to proceed smoothly and efficiently and to produce an army of citizen soldiers prepared to fight and sacrifice for their nation. Thus, France's 1793 *Levée* produced an enormous army of citizen soldiers whose enthusiasm for the cause more than compensated for their lack of training and equipment. And, of course, during World War II more than ten million Americans were drafted. With the Pearl Harbor attack bringing about virtually universal acceptance of the need to fight, draft resistance was almost nonexistent during the war.[36] Neither post-

Revolutionary France nor World War II–era America could have relied upon legitimacy as a substitute for force. Instead, their legitimacy lessened popular resistance to compulsory modes of troop recruitment.

FORCE AS AN INSTRUMENT OF LEGITIMATION

However successful a regime may be in promoting a sense of nationalism or religious or ideological attachments, a persistent failure to protect its citizens from internal or external threats to their security will almost certainly lead to a decline in support for the government or at least for the politicians thought to be responsible for such failures. In the United States, politicians who are labeled as being "soft on crime" or inattentive to the nation's military defense are almost certainly doomed to defeat at the polls. Today, the governments of Mexico and Guatemala, among others, seem unable to cope with criminal violence and have, as a result, lost considerable support among their citizens. Many citizens of these states demand that their governments develop a greater capacity for violence to counter the criminals.[37] Thus, far from serving as a substitute for force, the maintenance of political legitimacy and popular support requires governments to be able to make effective use of force.

SOFT POWER

The rule of law and programs of legitimation are important instruments of governance in the domestic arena. Governments make use of analogous force multipliers in the international realm, as well. Collectively, these are sometimes described as mechanisms of "soft power" and include such instruments as cultural diplomacy, political propaganda, and humanitarian aid designed to enhance what Joseph Nye characterizes as a state's "attractiveness" in the international arena.[38] Attractiveness refers to the ability to elicit the support and cooperation of other states and their citizens by virtue of their admiration for a given state's goals, values, culture, and ideology. It was often said, for example, that America's values and institutions generated much goodwill throughout the world, which, in turn, helped the U.S. win support for its political goals.

Soft power is sometimes incorrectly seen as a substitute for the use of force in international affairs. In fact, like law and legitimacy in domestic governance, instruments of soft power should be understood as the handmaidens of force. Indeed, soft power is often used in coordination or conjunction with military might or economic pressure to achieve a regime's international objectives. As Joseph Nye wrote, "Hard and soft power are related because they are both aspects of the ability to achieve one's purpose by affecting the behavior of others."[39] Typically, indeed, instruments of soft power serve as force multipliers, helping a state to persuade other states or their citizens to cooperate with its efforts so that it can achieve its international goals with a smaller expenditure of force than might otherwise have been needed.

For example, for decades the Soviet Union sponsored the Communist International and a variety of cultural and political institutions designed to promote Communist ideology and the idea of the USSR as a utopian society deserving of respect and support throughout the world. This effort was enormously successful for a number of decades. Everywhere in the world, dedicated Communists worked vigorously to promote the interests of the Soviet Union, in some cases committing acts of espionage and treason against their own nations for what they saw as a higher purpose. Soviet soft power translated directly into hard power when, for example, dedicated American Communists transferred the secret of the atomic bomb to the USSR. The hard power generated by its soft power made the USSR America's most formidable military foe for a half century. Today, of course, the Muslim religion is a major source of soft power for anti-American forces in the Middle East. Shiite Islam, for example, serves as an important source of soft power for Iran in its effort to establish regional hegemony in the region. As in the Soviet case, its soft power helps Iran win support for its efforts to expand its hard power through its nuclear weapons and other military programs. A variety of Islamic terrorist groups also make use of religious appeals to attract supporters and adherents who, in turn, provide the money and manpower that enhance the groups' military effectiveness.

POWER WITHOUT FORCE?

Governments often prefer not to rule by force alone—whether at home or in the international arena. The techniques they use, however, should not be seen as peaceful alternatives to force. Instead, they are force multipliers, usually used to enhance governmental power at home and abroad. The rule of law refines force and makes it a more effective instrument of governance. Legitimacy renders citizens more amenable to the threat or use of force against them. Soft power helps state and, sometimes, non-state actors achieve more in the international realm than they might have through force alone. Indeed, as the Soviet example suggests, soft power can become a source of hard power. These assorted instruments of governance are refinements and sometimes cloaks for violence, but not its substitutes.

CHAPTER 4

AMERICA

A TOUGH NATION

Violence is ubiquitous, but, at any given time, some states are more violent than others. Indeed, any given state's level of bellicosity, particularly in the international realm, can vary enormously over time. Winston Churchill once quipped that, historically, the Germans could sometimes be found at their neighbors' feet and other times at their throats.[1]

In the international realm, any number of factors can induce aggressive conduct on the part of a given state—ideology, hope for material gain, fear of aggression by others, and so forth. Indeed, at some point in time almost any state may find reason to consider hostile action against its neighbors. In 1948 even the usually placid and pastoral Netherlands launched a brutal military offensive against its former colony, the newly formed and internationally recognized Republic of Indonesia. Perhaps, consistent with this apparent rebirth of the Dutch martial spirit, thought to have been lost in the seventeenth century, the Netherlands contributed very accurate and lethal bombs to NATO's air campaign against Libya in 2011. We should probably acknowledge, though, that the bombs were not actually used by Dutch forces. They were, instead, dropped on Libyan government troops by warplanes flying under NATO auspices and emblazoned with the emblem of another infamous rogue state—the Kingdom of Denmark.

Violence among nations is so commonplace and its causes so diverse that the question we should ask is not why states engage in violence but, rather, what factors might place limits upon violent conduct and possibly induce a regime to favor peaceful modes of action even if it has the capacity to choose violence. The answer to this question is often political. The most important limits on violence are frequently political constraints imposed by political groups or social forces that view foreign adventures as a diversion of national attention from pressing domestic problems and, perhaps, a form of policy that gives their domestic political foes command of the state and its resources. Take the case of a famous call to arms in the ancient world—Cato's cry for the eradication of Rome's long-time rival, Carthage. "*Carthago delenda est*," or "Carthage must be destroyed," was a slogan Cato repeated continually in the Roman Senate and other public forums. Cato's call to battle, though, was for years opposed by a powerful political faction led by the consul Publius Cornelius Scipio Nasica. Cato was a so-called "new man" of plebeian origin and a foe of Rome's great patrician families. Scipio Nasica, on the other hand, was the political leader and spokesperson for those selfsame families and feared that another war with Carthage would harm the trade interests and political power of his class. Though eventually Cato prevailed, Scipio Nasica and his political followers were able to avert war for many years, frequently declaring that the continued existence of Carthage as a rival helped to ensure Rome's greatness by serving as a check on the "licentiousness" of the multitude.[2]

In the modern Western world opposition to militarism and the use of military force was initially associated with Labor, Social Democratic, and other "progressive" political forces. During the nineteenth and early twentieth centuries, Socialists viewed war and militarism as programs that strengthened the aristocratic forces that generally controlled the military as well as the capitalists and industrialists who were seen as profiting from military contracts and construction. In essence, socialists favored peace because they believed that war strengthened their political foes and enhanced their opponents' control of the state. In both Europe and the United States, Socialists and their allies were at the forefront of the ultimately futile opposition to the First World War, leading anti-war and anti-draft movements both before and during the conflict.[3]

In Europe today, defenders of the welfare state have been successful in convincing their countrymen that more guns inevitably meant less butter on the table. This accomplished what the Socialists could not—the effective demilitarization of Western Europe. The same argument in the United States, however, met with far less success. During the Vietnam War, to be sure, liberal Democrats, seeking to protect "Great Society" programs, asserted that funds spent on weapons and the war could be better used to meet pressing domestic needs. For a time, this argument seemed to prevail. The war was brought to a close, and defense spending as a percentage of gross national product (GNP) dropped sharply through the 1970s.[4] This victory, however, was short-lived. After 1980, the new Reagan administration had no difficulty making the case that America's security interests required a massive military buildup regardless of domestic concerns. As Daniel Wirls has shown, in the American context politicians defending butter are seldom a match for those arguing in favor of more guns.[5] Indeed, even the budget and debt crises of 2011 produced more pressure for cuts in social spending than major reductions in defense programs. And even the end of the Iraq War brought plans for only relatively small cuts in U.S. defense spending. In January 2012 the Obama administration proposed a cut in the defense budget of 8 percent to be introduced over the next ten years. This rather modest proposal was greeted with howls of protest from the various proponents of defense spending. The military hardly bothered to object, believing that the proposed cuts were not likely to materialize.

By 2013, of course, budget deficits and the ongoing sequestration of previously authorized expenditures led to somewhat greater reductions in military spending, but America's military was hardly starved for funds. Under the terms of President Obama's proposed 2014 budget, military spending would be cut by 1.6 percent, not including war costs or nuclear weapons activities.

As we shall see, for the past century and a half, contrary to the image most Americans have of their own land, the United States has been a tough nation, often employing a good deal of violence against its own citizens and against other states, as well. Because the U.S. was a tough nation it built a carceral state rather than a welfare state to deal with its social problems. America's weak welfare state, in turn, lacked and continues to lack the capacity of its politically more robust European counterparts to constrain military spending. America has spent its money on guns rather than butter, building the world's most powerful national security state. National security is certainly important, but the United States tends to be too tough, expending its blood and treasure in pointless exercises like the nine-year-long war in Iraq because there are too few voices saying no when America's Catos call for military action. Today, America's carceral and national security states reinforce and learn from one another, as America's war on crime and war on terror mimic one another's methods in a reciprocal relationship that promises to make the U.S. an ever tougher nation.

TOUGH ENOUGH?

Within its borders, the U.S. has constructed a considerably more harsh criminal justice system than any of its advanced industrial counterparts. In 2009,

America's prisons and jails held more than 1 percent of the nation's adults—2.3 million people—with five million more on parole, probation, or temporarily free on bail awaiting trial. In Western Europe, by contrast, fewer than two-tenths of 1 percent of the adult populace is behind bars.[6] This 400 percent discrepancy in incarceration rates is more a function of the relative severity of America's criminal laws than differences between Europe and the U.S. in the actual incidence of serious crime.[7] And, of course, while Western European nations no longer execute convicted criminals, the U.S. remains committed to the use of capital punishment.

This pattern of harsh treatment of U.S. citizens also extends to political dissidents. Despite constitutional protections, the U.S. can be tough on political dissent. During many periods of American history constitutional principles were circumvented or ignored as the federal and state governments moved to stifle opposition and protest. In the nineteenth century, radical labor movements were the targets of violent repression by local and state governments assisted by federal troops.[8] In the decades preceding the First World War, suspected Communists and Anarchists were often subject to arrest and imprisonment without much in the way of legal process. In 1903, when told his troops' roundup of radicals violated the U.S. Constitution, one Colorado militia officer proclaimed, "To hell with the constitution, we aren't going by the constitution."[9] During World War I, opposition to American participation in the fighting was ruthlessly suppressed by state and federal authorities. After the war, suspected Communists were arrested and deported in what came to be known as the Great Red Scare. In the 1940s and 1950s, individuals believed to harbor left-wing sympathies were hounded by the authorities. In the 1960s and 1970s, outspoken anti-war and civil rights activists were the targets of government surveillance and, occasionally, violence. Today, under the auspices of "war on terror" legislation, the federal government engages in surveillance, warrantless searches, lengthy detentions, and deportations of individuals deemed to show excessive sympathy for Islamic fundamentalism.[10]

In terms of its external conduct, as well, judged by its history rather than its rhetoric, the U.S. is among the most bellicose nations on the face of the earth. Since the Civil War, American forces have been deployed abroad on hundreds of occasions for major conflicts as well as minor skirmishes. Writing in 1989, historian Geoffrey Perret commented that no other nation "has had as much experience of war as the United States."[11] America has not become less warlike in the years since Perret published his observation. Between 1989 and the present, American forces have fought two wars in the Persian Gulf and a war in Afghanistan, while engaging in lesser military actions in Panama, Kosovo, Somalia, and elsewhere. Every year, of course, America's military arsenal and defense budget dwarf those of other nations. America currently spends more than $600 billion per year on its military and weapons programs—a figure that represents more than one-third of the world's total military budgets and nearly ten times the amount spent by the Chinese People's Republic, the nation that currently ranks second to the U.S. in overall military outlays.

America's internal and external "toughness" are related through a set of historic choices. The first choice involved the question of how to maintain order and social peace at home. In this realm, while Europe chose the welfare state, America chose the carceral state. This choice about modes of internal governance eventually had implications for America's choices about its relationship with the outside world, as well.

THE CARROT OR THE STICK

There are, to state the matter simply, two ways in which governments can endeavor to keep the peace within their borders. These are the carrot of social programs and the stick of police and punishment. The carrot consists of public welfare, employment, education, health care, and other redistributive programs. These are designed to maintain public order by offering those on the lowest rungs of the social and economic ladder—the stratum historically associated with the bulk of violent crime and civil unrest—a sense of connection to society, hope for the future, and, of course, an opportunity to deal with their immediate economic needs without being compelled to resort to criminality. Piven and Cloward refer to this tactic as "regulating the poor" and argue that it is the main function of public welfare policy.[12] The stick, of course, consists of the use of incarceration and other forms of punishment designed to keep order by isolating or otherwise disabling known recreants while intimidating others who might be tempted to make trouble. Neither welfare programs nor the threat of punishment guarantees a halt to crime and disorder. Yet a considerable body of evidence suggests that both sorts of programs can have an impact upon criminality.[13]

Of course, every government employs a mix of carrots and sticks, but the precise ratio of one to the other varies with time and place. For much of Western history, governments relied mainly upon the stick in the form of the frequent use of extremely severe punishment to keep order.[14] In Western Europe, commonly used criminal sanctions included public flogging, branding, mutilation, and dismemberment as well as cruel and degrading forms of execution.[15] Severe corporal punishments including public hangings were also common in the American colonies and, after independence, were not immediately ended by the Eighth Amendment's prohibition of cruel and unusual forms of punishment—a prohibition that applied only to the federal government and not to the states until 1962.

In the later decades of the nineteenth century, though, Western European regimes gradually reduced the severity of many criminal penalties, along with the frequency of their application and, at the same time, began the creation of today's welfare states, introducing a variety of social insurance and employment programs. By the second half of the twentieth century, the welfare state had become the major focus of government spending in every Western European nation, drawing resources away from all other state functions and serving, particularly, as an increasingly powerful brake on its main budgetary rival, military spending, which came more and more to be ignored or left to the Americans. Today, the politicians and bureaucrats who derive power from their control of the institutions of the welfare state, as well as the welfare state's tens of millions of beneficiaries, form an almost impregnable political bulwark against significant cuts in social services. Military spending, on the other hand, has become a small and vulnerable fraction of every European budget, constantly threatened with further reductions when more funds are required to maintain high levels of social support in hard economic times.[16] Butter has taken precedence over guns everywhere in Western Europe as symbolized in 2011 by the once-proud Royal Navy's consignment of its last aircraft carrier to the scrap yard—for budgetary reasons.

One important Western government that lagged in the construction of a welfare state was, of course, the United States of America. American "exceptionalism" in this realm is an issue that has engaged the interest of many distinguished historians and sociologists including Louis Hartz, Daniel Boorstin, and Seymour Martin Lipset.[17] Briefly stated, America's Lockeian liberal tradition has meant that Americans, more than almost any other people, have subscribed to what Louis Hartz termed the "Horatio Alger myth" of individual self-help and personal responsibility. From their school books and the media, Americans absorb a success narrative in which every individual, however poor or humble their origins, can rise from rags to fame and riches through pluck and hard work. Conversely, failure is thought to be a reflection of an individual's shortcomings.

If any worthy individual can succeed, those who fail must be unworthy. This historically ingrained perspective has led many Americans to view social programs as unjustified sops to undeserving idlers—a view that has been reinforced by racism and ethnic prejudice.[18]

Thus, while Western Europe was devising social programs to quiet crime and disorder, America's state and federal authorities continued to rely upon the police baton and the prison to maintain social order—building a carceral regime of relatively inexpensive law enforcement and penal institutions organized primarily at the state level. These address the nation's social problems through the stick of punishment rather than the carrot of social services and are the institutions that make the U.S. such a tough nation internally.

Local programs of poor relief, to be sure, existed even in nineteenth-century America, but these efforts were sketchy and sporadic.[19] Until the aftermath of the Civil War, such assistance as was offered to the poor was given grudgingly and sparingly. Following the Civil War, the U.S. established a large-scale pension system for the benefit of Union veterans and their survivors. By the end of the century, millions of individuals were receiving regular pensions, mainly funded by revenues from the federal tariff.

This pension system differed substantially from the welfare states being established in Europe during the same period. Under the pension law, only those who could claim service on the Northern side in the Civil War, and their survivors, were eligible for pensions. Claimants' current needs and means were irrelevant.[20] Thus, the Civil War pension was designed not as a system of poor relief but as a reward to those who had served their nation on the battlefield. Even in the federal budget, the pension was classified as a military expenditure rather than as a form of social spending.[21] Millions of impoverished Americans who were not Union army veterans or veterans' survivors were ineligible to receive pensions. Proposals for more general old-age pensions, health and unemployment insurance like those emerging in Europe in the latter decades of the nineteenth century were, with the exception of several programs aimed at helping mothers and children, soundly rejected in turn-of-the-century America as inconsistent with national values.

During the New Deal era, of course, the Roosevelt administration introduced a number of social programs, including old-age pensions and Aid to Dependent Children (ADC), which was later renamed Aid to Families with Dependent Children (AFDC). Both programs were included in the 1935 Social Security Act. Because of intense opposition to "welfare" programs, even during the Great Depression, Roosevelt rebuffed calls for the creation of a federal health care program and agreed that ADC eligibility requirements would be set at the state, rather than the national, level. This allowed locally powerful conservative forces in a number of states to limit access to the welfare rolls. This was especially important in the South, where most needy African Americans were denied federal assistance during the initial decades of the program.[22] At the same time, the most important New Deal social program, the system of old-age pensions that survives to this day as Social Security, was designed to resemble a contributory insurance scheme rather than a welfare program so that Roosevelt could deny assertions that he had built a socialistic welfare state.

In later decades, the U.S. introduced a number of other social programs including Medicare and Medicaid—"Great Society" programs developed during the administration of President Lyndon Johnson. Medicare provided health care subsidies for pensioners while Medicaid provided subsidized health care for the indigent. Johnson also reintroduced the so-called Food Stamp program, an effort first introduced on a temporary basis by Roosevelt to provide food assistance to the working poor while helping farmers by reducing agricultural surpluses. Other post–New Deal social programs include the Earned Income Tax Credit (EITC) to provide a modest wage supplement for the working poor, as well as a variety of education, training, and housing programs. Most recently, the Obama administration succeeded in bringing about the enactment of a modest national health care program, though its ultimate fate is far from certain.

As has often been noted, though, most of America's social spending is aimed at assisting the elderly and the middle class rather the nonworking or marginally employed poor. The major program aimed at providing assistance to this latter group, AFDC, was constantly criticized for allegedly subsidizing lazy and undeserving "welfare queens" from minority communities.[23] In 1996, Congress terminated AFDC and replaced it with a new program, Temporary Assistance for Needy Families (TANF), which restricted welfare recipients to a lifetime limit of five years of benefits. The TANF program was an expression of America's historic hostility to the idea of a welfare state. The spirit of the nineteenth century's mythical hero, Horatio Alger, seems to live on in twenty-first-century America. So deeply ingrained is America's historic distrust of the welfare state that many Americans believe that welfare is a cause of, rather than a cure for, crime. While Europeans have generally viewed social programs as potential antidotes to criminality, many Americans have readily accepted the assertions of conservative social theorists that welfare programs tend to increase crime rates, allegedly by promoting a growth in the number of single-parent families whose undisciplined offspring are likely to exhibit antisocial behavior.[24]

Though the economic and social role of the national government has, of course, increased substantially in the past several decades, to this day, levels of social spending in the U.S. are substantially less than those of Europe's social democracies. Indeed, as a percentage of the gross domestic product (GDP), the U.S. barely spends half as much on social services as its Western European counterparts. And recent debates over health care reveal that millions of Americans continue to be reluctant to expand the scope of the nation's social programs. Carrots continue to be unpopular on the American dining table.

The weakness of America's welfare state has meant, in turn, that the institutions and political forces that inhibit military spending in Europe have had far less political clout in the U.S., leaving the way open for America's more bellicose international impulses to be translated into action—as they once were in Europe. In essence, America's nineteenth-century choice of the stick over the carrot to deal with its social problems is an important reason that American governments can continue choosing guns over butter today.

THE WARFARE STATE

While Europeans were expanding their welfare states, the United States built the world's largest and most powerful warfare state. During the 1940s and 1950s, the United States constructed, as President Eisenhower observed, "an immense military establishment" linked to a "permanent armaments industry of vast proportions," which wielded "economic, political and even spiritual" influence that reached into "every city, every statehouse, every office of the federal government."[25]

The U.S. could build a warfare state because the proponents of spending on guns faced only weak opposition from those who demanded more spending on butter. And, once the warfare state came into being, it generated a powerful "iron triangle" of supporting interests that made it as impregnable as the welfare state became in Europe. Members of Congress received access to a huge pork barrel, which incumbents could use to enhance their political security.[26] The warfare state made it possible for public expenditures to be maintained at a level that kept labor reasonably happy. Moreover, through the procurement of weapons and supplies, major elements of the business community profited from and became dependent upon the defense establishment.

The foundations of America's warfare state were laid by the 1947 National Security Act. The Act had three major parts. First, it reorganized the military services by separating the Air Force from the Army and abolishing the historic division between the War Department and the Navy Department. All three military branches were now placed within a single National Military Establishment, later renamed the Department of Defense (DoD), under the leadership of a civilian cabinet officer—the Secretary of Defense. Second, the Act created the Central Intelligence Agency (CIA) to coordinate the government's activities in the realms of information gathering, espionage, and covert operations. Finally, the Act established the National Security Council (NSC), chaired by the president and including the major cabinet secretaries, the chairman of the Joint Chiefs of Staff (JCS), the three service secretaries, and a number of other high-ranking officials. The NSC was to assist the president in coordinating national security planning and decision making. Taken together, these provisions created the basis for a warfare state led by what later critics would call the "imperial presidency."

PRESIDENTIAL CONTROL OF THE MILITARY

To begin with, the 1947 Act represented a further step in the professionalization of the military services and their subjection to presidential control. America's military effort had historically depended upon state militias that often answered as much to governors, senators, and members of Congress as to the president. During the Civil War, for example, many politicians secured gubernatorial commissions in state militia units, and through them, as well as through the state governors, Congress frequently sought to interfere with Lincoln's military plans. Presidential control of the military was enhanced at the beginning of the Spanish-American War when Congress passed the 1898 Volunteer Act. Under its terms, the general officers and their staffs of all state militia units, now renamed the National Guard, were to be appointed by the president rather than the state governors. The 1903 Dick Act further increased presidential control of the nation's military forces by authorizing the president to dissolve state guard units into the regular army in times of emergency, while the 1916 National Defense Act gave the president authority to appoint all commissioned and noncommissioned Guard officers in time of war. The 1916 Act also began the creation of the national military reserves, which eventually supplanted the state units as the force employed to fill out the military's ranks in time of emergency.[27]

While these pieces of legislation gradually gave the president and the military brass in Washington fuller control over what originally had been primarily state forces, the long-standing division of the military into two cabinet departments—War (Army) and Navy—also undermined presidential control. Historically, each of the services, as well as branches within the services, most notably the Marine Corps and, more recently, the Army Air Corps, had their own ties to supporters in the Congress, and they used these to circumvent their nominal superiors. For example, during the First World War, the Marines mobilized their allies in Congress to induce the president to accept their participation in the American Expeditionary Forces over the objections of the secretary of war, the secretary of the navy, and General Pershing, the force's commander.[28] In a similar vein, between the wars, some lawmakers became enchanted with the idea of military aviation and supported General Billy Mitchell's quixotic crusade against the War and Navy departments. Over the objections of the president and the secretary of war, Congress enacted the 1926 Air Corps Act, which made the Air Corps a virtually autonomous entity within the Army.[29] Even more important, the War Department and the Navy Department presented Congress with separate budgets and competing visions of the nation's military needs and priorities. The annual struggle for funding between the two service branches, complete with competing testimony by the nation's foremost military authorities, opened the way for increased congressional intervention into military decision making.

The 1947 National Security Act created a single defense secretary responsible for all defense planning and the overall military budget. As amended in 1949, the Act diminished the status of the individual service secretaries, who were no longer to be members of the president's cabinet or the National Security Council. Instead, the individual service secretaries were to focus on manpower and procurement issues and to report to the secretary of defense and his assistant secretaries. To further centralize military planning, the 1949 amendments created the position of chairman of the Joint Chiefs of Staff to denote the officer who was to serve as the principal military advisor to the defense secretary and the president. By creating a more unified military chain of command and a single defense budget, the National Security Act diminished Congress's ability to intervene in military planning and decision making and increased the president's control over the armed services and national security policy. In 1948, under the auspices of the first defense secretary, James Forrestal, the chiefs of the three military services met at Key West and negotiated a set of agreements on missions and weapons that were expected to mute inter-service squabbles and the congressional intervention that inevitably ensued.

During this period, the U.S. also began the creation of an enormous standing army. Historically, the United States had built large armies in wartime and quickly disbanded them at the war's end. Opposition to maintaining standing armies in peacetime predated even the birth of the Republic. To meet Korean War needs, Truman was forced to halt the force reductions that had been under way since the end of World War II. By 1951, Truman and his advisors, however, were concerned with more than America's immediate military needs. The president had concluded that American security required the construction of a permanent military force capable of deterring military attack from the Soviet Union and its allies anywhere on the globe. This had been the conclusion reached in a planning document known as NSC-68, drafted primarily by Paul Nitze and the State Department's policy planning staff and presented to the National Security Council in April 1950. This document, which became a cornerstone of American security policy, asserted that the principal goal of Soviet policy was the subversion or destruction of the United States. Preventing the Soviet leadership from achieving this goal would require a long-term commitment on the part of the United States to the "containment" of its adversary. This would require the development of enormous military forces—forces so powerful that the Soviets would be deterred from committing acts of aggression against the United States and its allies by the knowledge that the U.S. had the capacity to retaliate with overwhelming force. In short, the United States must commit itself, for the first time in its history, to the maintenance of powerful peacetime military forces.

Truman did not act on the recommendation of NSC-68 until the next year, when he called for expanded military spending and American rearmament to meet long-term challenges.[30] By 1952, the U.S. had tripled its military spending, expanded its nuclear weapons programs, begun the deployment of a fleet of heavy bombers capable of attacking the Soviet Union, doubled the size of the Army and Marine Corps, and increased rather than diminished the size of its naval forces. To make certain that sufficient manpower would be available to meet military needs, Congress enacted the Universal Military Training and Service Act of 1951 and the Armed Forces Reserve Act of 1952. The first of these pieces of legislation expanded the military draft, which had already been reinstated under the 1948 Selective Service Act. In principle, all 18-year-old men would now be required to undertake military training. However, to mute political opposition, the law allowed the Selective Service System to provide for educational and occupational deferments. In practice, these deferments, like the Civil War commutation fee, which had allowed men to pay $300 in lieu of conscription, permitted individuals wealthy enough to remain in school or puissant enough to secure occupational deferments from local draft boards to avoid service. Labor leaders like Walter Reuther and African American leaders like A. Philip Randolph objected to the elitist character of the draft.[31] The system of deferments and exemptions, however, helped to forestall objections from the nation's more influential strata. As Selective Service System director Lewis Hershey warned, if any effort was made to eliminate the deferments, "all hell will break loose.[32] Those who did serve in the military, whether as conscripts or volunteers, were required under the Reserve Act to remain in the ready reserves, available for call-up in the event of emergency. By 1953, nearly 4 million Americans were on active military, backed by sizeable National Guard and reserve forces.[33]

To make certain that the nation's military forces had adequate matériel and equipment, Congress enacted the 1950 Defense Production Act, which gave the president authority to purchase strategic materials and order industries to give priority to military needs. Three years earlier, the 1947 National Security Act had provided for the creation of a National Security Resources Board to help the president coordinate military and industrial planning in wartime.[34] Rather than attempt to command industry to meet military needs, however, the president opted to expand and institutionalize the World War II contracting system. At the beginning of the Second World War, Secretary of War Henry Stimson had advised Roosevelt to "hire" industrialists by providing them with lucrative military contracts. "If you are going to try to go to war, or to prepare for war, in a capitalist country, you have got to let business make money out of the process or business won't work," Stimson said.[35] During the Truman era, this hiring of industrialists became a permanent feature of the American industrial and political landscape. Hundreds of firms received contracts for military equipment ranging from meals, uniforms, and vehicles through missiles, aircraft, and naval vessels. Most major contracts required subcontracting, so that thousands of firms, throughout the nation, profited from defense work. For some, like Lockheed Martin˙, Northrup Grumman˙, and other aviation companies, military undertakings became the principal focus of their business. These contractors made themselves virtual arms of the military, usually working closely, if not exclusively, with one particular service branch that, always arguing that the maintenance of a secure industrial base was necessary to promote the nation's security, made certain that its contractors always received a share of military business. The firms' executive ranks, filled with retired admirals, generals, captains, and colonels who now sold weapons to their former services, came to resemble officers' clubs.[36] Where existing enterprises did not meet the government's needs, it sponsored the creation of new ones. One of the most important was the RAND Corporation sponsored by the U.S. Air Force. Formally known as a Federally Funded Research and Development Center or FFRDC, RAND and a number of other corporations were established with the support of the military to engage in weapons research and operational planning.[37] As noted above, the various corporations linked to the military and dependent upon military contracts, and situated in virtually every state and congressional district, but particularly in the South and Southwest, became a powerful constituency for maintaining high levels of military preparedness—and spending—in the years to come.[38] The intense political support of thousands of firms and their unionized workers helped successive administrations ensure that the president would always have at his disposal an enormous and powerful military machine.

INTELLIGENCE AND PLANNING

In addition to centralizing military decision making, the 1947 National Security Act increased America's capacity for foreign policy and security planning, intelligence gathering and evaluation, and covert intelligence operations. The first of these results stemmed from the creation of the National Security Council. The Council itself was never more than a loose-knit presidential advisory body and seldom had any independent influence. Beginning during the Kennedy presidency, however, the NSC staff became an important presidential instrument. Truman and Eisenhower relied upon the State Department's policy planning staff and the JCS for policy analysis and advice. These groups, however, did not work directly for the president and had other institutional loyalties. Kennedy expanded the NSC staff and designated McGeorge Bundy, an Ivy Leaguer and former intelligence officer, to serve as his special assistant for national security affairs and as head of the NSC staff. During subsequent presidencies, the NSC staff, eventually consisting of nearly two hundred professional employees organized in regional and functional offices, along with the national security assistant, became important forces in the shaping of foreign and security policy, often eclipsing the State Department and its leadership. For example, when he served as Richard Nixon's national security assistant, Henry Kissinger effectively excluded the secretary of state, William Rogers, from most foreign policy decision making. Similarly, during the Carter administration, the president allowed his national security assistant Zbigniew Brzezinski to marginalize Secretary of State Cyrus Vance. Both Rogers and Vance eventually resigned.[39]

The construction of a national security bureaucracy within the executive office of the president made possible the enormous postwar expansion of presidential unilateralism in the realm of security and foreign policy. Beginning with Truman, presidents would conduct foreign and security policy through executive agreements and executive orders and seldom negotiate formal treaties requiring Senate ratification. Presidents before Truman—even Franklin D. Roosevelt—had generally submitted important accords between the United States and foreign powers to the Senate for ratification and had sometimes seen their goals stymied by senatorial opposition. Not only did the Constitution require senatorial confirmation of treaties but, before Truman, presidents had lacked the administrative resources to systematically conduct an independent foreign policy. It was not by accident that most of the agreements—particularly the secret agreements—negotiated by FDR concerned military matters where the president could rely upon the administrative capacities of the War and Navy departments.[40]

The State Department's policy planning staff and, especially, the NSC staff created the institutional foundations and capabilities upon which Truman and his successors could rely to conduct and administer the nation's foreign and security policies directly from the Oval Office. For example, American participation in the International Trade Organization (ITO), one of the cornerstones of U.S. postwar trade policy, was based on a sole executive agreement, the GATT Provisional Protocol, signed by President Truman after Congress delayed action and ultimately failed to approve the ITO charter.[41] Truman signed some 1,300 executive agreements, and Eisenhower another 1,800, in some cases requesting congressional approval and in other instances ignoring the Congress. Executive agreements take two forms: congressional-executive agreements and sole executive agreements. In the former case, the president submits the agreement to both houses of Congress as he would any other piece of legislation, with a majority vote in both houses required for passage. This is generally a lower hurdle than the two-thirds vote required for Senate ratification of a treaty. A sole executive agreement is not sent to the Congress at all. The president generally has discretion over which avenue to pursue. All treaties and executive agreements have the power of law, though a sole executive agreement cannot contravene an existing statute.[42] During the Truman and Eisenhower presidencies, barely two hundred treaties were submitted to the Senate as stipulated by Article II of the Constitution.[43] The same pattern has continued to the present time. Indeed, two of the most important recent international agreements entered into by the United States, the North American Free Trade Agreement and the World Trade Organization agreement, were confirmed by congressional executive agreement, not by treaty.[44]

In a similar vein, the policy planning staff and NSC opened the way for policy making by executive order in the areas of security and foreign policy. Executive orders issued to implement presidents' military foreign policy goals have been variously called National Security Presidential Directives (NSPD) and National Security Decision Directives (NSDD) but are most commonly known as National Security Directives or NSDs. These, like other executive orders, are commands from the president to an executive agency.[45] Most NSDs are classified, and presidents have consistently refused even to inform Congress of their existence, much less their content. Generally, NSDs are drafted by the NSC staff at the president's behest. Some NSDs have involved mundane matters, but others have established America's most significant foreign policies and security postures. As mentioned above, NSC-68, developed by the State Department's policy planning staff prior to the creation of an NSC staff, set forward the basic principles of containment upon which American Cold War policy came to be based. A series of Kennedy NSDs established the basic principles of American policy toward a number of world trouble spots.[46] Ronald Reagan's NSD 12 launched the president's massive military buildup and force modernization program, while his NSD 172 began the development of anti-missile programs. President Bush issued a number of NSDs authorizing domestic eavesdropping. President Obama continued this practice, though calling his directives Presidential Policy Directives or PPDs. Obama has issued PPDs regarding terrorism, biological threats, and national preparedness. Thus, the creation of new administrative capabilities gave presidents the tools through which to dominate foreign and security policy and to dispense with Congress and its "incompetent obstructionists."

The warfare state was further augmented in the 1947 Act by the creation of the CIA, which became a centrally important presidential foreign policy tool. The CIA gave the president the capacity to intervene in the affairs of other nations without informing Congress or the public. At the president's behest, the CIA undertook numerous covert operations and clandestine interventions in

foreign countries during the Cold War and afterward. The agency's covert operations branch was established by a top-secret presidential order, NSC 10-2, issued
in June 1948. These operations were to include propaganda, economic warfare,
sabotage, subversion, and assistance to underground movements. The U.S. government was to be able to "plausibly disclaim responsibility" for all covert operations.[47] Carrying out successive secret presidential orders, usually framed as
NSDs, the CIA overthrew the Iranian government in 1953 and installed the
shah, who ruled Iran for the next quarter century. During the 1950s, the CIA
also overthrew governments in Guatemala, Egypt, and Laos, which were deemed
to be unfriendly to the U.S.[48] The CIA helped organize and, for a number of years,
subsidized anti-Communist politicians and political parties in Western Europe.
In some instances, of course, CIA operations resulted in embarrassing failures
such as the abortive Bay of Pigs invasion of Cuba in 1961. Nevertheless, covert
CIA operations have been used by presidents to advance American interests in
virtually every corner of the globe—literally from Afghanistan to Zaire. For the
most part, the nation's new intelligence capabilities were directed outside its own
borders. Truman hoped to avoid infringements on the civil liberties of Americans
and opposed Director J. Edgar Hoover's efforts to expand the domestic intelligence activities of the FBI.[49] By executive order, however, Truman created a
Loyalty Review Board that brought together a number of World War II programs designed to screen prospective government employees and to investigate
charges of treasonable or disloyal conduct. Individual agencies were authorized to
develop their own loyalty programs.[50] Truman also issued a number of executive
orders establishing a classification system for government secrets that ultimately
led to the classification of millions of pages of documents and allowed the president and the various federal agencies to stamp as "secret" almost any information
they chose not to reveal to the public and the Congress.[51]

REVENUE EXTRACTION

The construction of America's new standing army and other national security
institutions would require the nation to bear, on a permanent basis, levels of
military spending previously seen only during wartime emergencies. Stated in
constant dollars, President Truman's 1952 defense budget of more than $46
billion represented a 20-fold increase over America's defense spending in 1940
and approached World War II spending levels. And, the nation was expected to

sustain these outlays into the indefinite future. To accomplish this Herculean task, however, Truman could rely upon the tremendous extractive capabilities of the federal tax system developed by the Roosevelt administration during World War II. The Second World War marked a watershed in U.S. government finance. First, the Revenue Act of 1942 substantially broadened the nation's tax base, increasing the number of households subject to the income tax from 13 million to 28 million. By 1944, tax rates began at 3 percent on incomes between $500 and $2,000, rose to 20 percent for incomes above $2,000, and climbed steeply to reach a nominal rate of 91 percent on income over $200,000.[52] The second important innovation associated with the war was the enactment of the Current Tax Payment Act of 1943. Before 1943, federal income taxes were to be paid quarterly in the year after the income was received. This system depended heavily upon the honesty, goodwill, and foresight of individual taxpayers. Under the terms of the 1943 Act, however, employers were required to withhold 20 percent of wages and salaries and to remit these to the government as the income was earned. The 1943 Current Tax Payment Act partially freed the government from its historic dependence upon the support and integrity of the individual taxpayer. It made the collection of income taxes automatic and involuntary from the perspective of the taxpayer and, together with higher rates, increased federal income tax revenues from slightly more than $1 billion in 1940 to more than $45 billion by 1945. At the end of World War II, of course, there was considerable political pressure to cut taxes, and Congress did enact a tax cut over the president's veto in 1948.[53] The outbreak of the Korean War, however, produced a series of temporary tax increases that, in many instances, became permanent, leading to $65 billion in revenues in 1955 and beginning the march toward today's $2 trillion in federal income tax receipts.

To make this tax burden more palatable to millions of ordinary Americans, the government relied upon the principle of progressivity. Progressivity, enshrined in American tax law since the Revenue Act of 1862, was a concession to the popular sense of justice. According to tax historian Sidney Ratner, progressivity accompanied the extension of new and relative high rates of taxation to citizens with small incomes.[54] In principle, at least, the handful of wealthy Americans had to be taxed at even higher rates in order to convince tens of millions of their less prosperous fellow citizens that the tax system was fair and that they should comply with its demands. At the same time, however, to prevent those very same wealthy and powerful Americans from mobilizing to block the imposition of high tax rates, Congress filled the income tax with numerous "loopholes" mainly designed to reduce the tax burdens of upper-income wage earners, investors, and business owners.[55] As in the case of "universal" military conscription, those with sufficient influence to make trouble were bought off.

In addition to taxes, the White House sought to generate financial support for an expanded military effort from two other sources. One was the sale of arms and military equipment to friendly and neutral nations. Allowing American military contractors to sell arms to other countries helped increase the production runs and, hence, to reduce the unit costs to the American military of expensive weapons, as well as to bring the armies of foreign countries into the American military orbit.[56] At the same time, arms sales would help maintain the vitality of the American arms industry, the so-called "defense industrial base," and its contribution to the nation's security.[57] Today, some $40 billion worth of American military hardware is sold abroad every year.

A second and more important source of financial support for America's military effort was "burden sharing." America expected its allies to share the costs of defense either by contributing financially or by contributing troops and equipment in time of need. Burden sharing was certainly not a novel idea. As long ago as 430 BCE, Periclean Athens supported its fleet by creating the Delian League and requiring the islands of Chios, Lesbos, and Samos to make financial contributions for the maintenance of Athenian military and naval forces.[58] At the end of the Second World War, to be sure, America's chief allies were financially exhausted. Therefore, to ensure that the Western European democracies would possess the means to resist Communism and to bolster America's own security, the U.S. undertook major programs to promote European economic recovery, including the 1948 Marshall Plan.[59] The success of these efforts, in turn, made the Europeans worthwhile alliance partners. The British, in particular, were expected to contribute significantly to the American defense burden and were, in return, given privileged access to U.S. decision making.[60]

In the 1950s, the United States built a number of military alliances, most notably the North Atlantic Treaty Organization (NATO), which required participants to shoulder a portion of America's military costs. During the 1950s, NATO added some twenty divisions of British, German, and other European troops along with thousands of aircraft and tanks to the six American divisions defending Western Europe.[61] Other American military agreements ultimately involved more than fifty nations in Europe and the Pacific region.[62] Military burden sharing continues to the present day but in diminished form as Western Europe continues to reduce its military expenditures.

In addition to defraying America's military expenses, treaties and defense pacts served presidential interests in another way as well. Presidents could use the cover of one of America's thousands of treaty obligations to undertake actions, especially in the military realm, that faced significant opposition in the Congress. International commitments became a presidential trump card to be used against the Congress even as more and more of these commitments were based on executive agreements made by the president without congressional consultation. Early in the Vietnam War, for example, Secretary of State Dean Rusk explained to the Senate Foreign Relations Committee that American assistance to Vietnam was required under the terms of bilateral assistance agreements. It turned out that all of these agreements, which the administration now cited as American obligations, had been entered into by the White House without the knowledge of Congress. Upon further inquiry, the Foreign Relations Committee uncovered hundreds of American international obligations, negotiated by presidents, without congressional sanction.[63]

Winning authorization from the United Nations Security Council has been a particularly important presidential ploy. President Truman sought and received Security Council approval to intervene against North Korea before even consulting with congressional leaders and then cited the UN resolution rather than congressional approval as the basis for going to war.[64] In a similar vein, President George H. W. Bush used UN Security Council Resolution 678 authorizing the use of force against Iraq to bring pressure on a reluctant Congress to approve the deployment of American forces in the Persian Gulf in preparation for the 1990 war.[65] Indeed, on numerous occasions, presidents have ordered American forces on UN "peacekeeping" missions without seeking any endorsement at all from the Congress.[66]

Thus, in the early years of the Cold War, President Truman built a huge, permanent military establishment and solidified the principle of centralized presidential control over the military. The president also laid the foundations for funding this military machine and began to assemble a political constituency that would support high levels of military spending. While levels of military spending would fluctuate with international events and political currents over the next several decades, the maintenance of a huge standing army, once unthinkable, had now become a matter of course. Truman, moreover, established a national security staff within the executive office and began the construction of an intelligence service capable of covert operations around the globe. These, in turn, helped Truman and subsequent presidents circumvent Congress and engage in unilateral management of the nation's foreign and security policies. Possession of institutional capacity does not guarantee its use, but it certainly makes its use possible, and the White House emerged from the Truman era with what Schlesinger and others called "Imperial" capabilities.

FROM THE KOREAN WAR TO THE WAR ON TERRORISM

The Imperial Presidency overcame challenges from Congress and from members of its own military, notably General MacArthur, to strengthen its power during the Korean War. In June 1950, when North Korean forces invaded South Korea, President Truman and his advisors believed that if they failed to respond forcefully, they would encourage Soviet aggression throughout Europe and Asia. Uncertain about Congress's mood, rather than turn directly to Capitol Hill, as noted above, the president first secured a UN Security Council resolution authorizing military intervention. He then met with a bipartisan group of congressional leaders, informed them of the UN resolution, and received their support. Congressional leaders expected Truman to ask for a formal resolution approving the use of force, if not for a full-blown declaration of war. Truman, however, influenced by the views of Secretary of State Dean Acheson, decided he would not ask for a congressional vote. Instead, Truman accepted Acheson's view that his constitutional powers as commander in chief, coupled with America's obligation to enforce the UN's resolution, were adequate grounds for ordering American forces into combat. By deploying massive forces without asking congressional approval, even though he had been assured that approval was forthcoming, Truman sought to assert the principle that the president, not Congress, could decide whether and when to go to war. Congress complained, but given the growing sense of national emergency, acquiesced by voting appropriations and extending the draft.[67] A fundamental principle had been established. In the future, even when presidents sought congressional assent to the use of force, there was a tendency to view this as a courtesy rather than a constitutional requirement.

Over the next two years, the war became unpopular as the fighting dragged on inconclusively. The new powers of the presidency, however, proved equal to the task of fighting a war and resisting efforts by the Congress and others to interfere with presidential prerogatives. Two factors worked in Truman's favor, the economy and the draft. To begin with, Truman chose to finance the war chiefly through increases in federal income tax rates. Though higher taxes are never popular, the early 1950s were a period of economic growth in the U.S. and higher taxes were more than offset by rising incomes.

The next two presidents made ample use of the capabilities forged by Truman. Eisenhower further centralized presidential control over the military establishment and continued the Truman-era loyalty program. In 1955 and 1956, President Eisenhower, in effect, demanded a blank check from Congress for possible military action in the Taiwan Straits and the Middle East and, in 1958, sent 14,000 marines into Lebanon without asking Congress for authorization. Eisenhower issued numerous NSDs and made ample use of the CIA's covert capabilities. In 1954, Eisenhower made his own contribution to the enhancement of presidential power when he made a virtually absolute claim of executive privilege in refusing to turn over records to the Congress.[68] John F. Kennedy, for his part, seemed cut from the same mold. Kennedy expanded the executive's capacity for covert operations by creating the Special Forces, an elite military corps reporting more fully to the president than to the regular Army command, and sent Special Forces and other American military elements to assist the South Vietnamese without consulting the Congress. By the Kennedy era, these sorts of actions on the part of the president were more or less taken for granted by Congress, by the public, and by most scholars.[69]

The end of the Vietnam War represented not only a military defeat for the United States but also a defeat for the presidency and the warfare state more generally. In the aftermath of the war and, in particular, after the disintegration and eventual collapse of the Nixon administration, Congress seized the opportunity to enact a number of pieces of legislation designed to curb presidential power in the foreign policy and security domains. These included the 1972 War Powers Resolution to limit presidential control over the deployment of American military forces; the 1973 Case-Zablocki Act, requiring that Congress be informed of all executive agreements; the 1974 Hughes-Ryan Amendments to regulate foreign military assistance; the 1977 International Emergency Economic Powers Act (IEEPA) to regulate the exercise of presidential emergency economic power; the Foreign Intelligence Surveillance Act of 1978; the Intelligence Oversight Act of 1980 to provide for congressional oversight of intelligence operations; and the 1976 Arms Export Control Act to limit presidential use of proxy forces. Congress also created intelligence oversight committees to monitor the president's use of the nation's intelligence agencies.

The post-Vietnam retrogression of presidential power and the government's capacity to wage war, however, proved to be short-lived. Johnson's successors took a number of steps that, within less than two decades after the last American troops were evacuated from Saigon, had more than restored presidential power in war and foreign relations. The first of these steps involved the recruitment and internal structure of the military and its relationship to American society. For two centuries, America had relied upon citizen soldiers to fill the ranks of its armed forces and spurned the idea of a professional army as being inconsistent with democratic values. In the wake of the Vietnam War, however, presidents and military planners realized that dependence upon citizen soldiers could impose serious constraints upon the use of military forces. The risks facing citizen soldiers provided opponents of the use of military force on any given occasion with a potent issue to use against the government. The casualties and hardships borne by citizen soldiers, moreover, reverberated through the society and might, as the Vietnam case illustrated, fuel antiwar movements and resistance to military conscription. University of Chicago economist Milton Friedman, who served as a member of the Gates Commission, created by President Nixon to examine the elimination of military conscription, argued that three-fourths of the opposition to the Vietnam War was generated by the draft.[70] Citizen soldiers might be appropriate for a national war in which America was attacked and domestic opposition driven to the margins. Anti-Vietnam war protests, however, convinced President Richard Nixon and his successors that an army composed of professional soldiers would give them greater flexibility to use military power when they deemed it necessary.[71] As Andrew Bacevich put it some years later, "The so-called all-volunteer force," provides the government "with an instrument well suited to the pursuit of imperial ambitions."[72]

Accordingly, Nixon ended the draft in 1973 and began conversion of the military into an all-volunteer force of professional soldiers. The presumption was that sending military professionals into battle would spawn less popular and political resistance than deploying reluctant conscripts, and this supposition seems to have been borne out. Indeed, in 2002, some opponents of President George W. Bush's buildup of American forces for an attack against Iraq argued for a renewal of conscription precisely because they believed that the president would be constrained from going to war if the military consisted of draftees.[73] Members of this new professional force, moreover, especially those recruited for its elite combat units, receive extensive training and indoctrination designed to separate them from civilian society, to imbue them with a warrior ethic emphasizing loyalty to the group and organization as primary values, and to reduce their level of integration into the larger society.[74] This training is designed to immunize the military against possible contagion from antiwar and defeatist sentiment that may spring up in civilian America, and it appears to have produced a military, especially an officer, corps that views itself as a distinct caste.[75] To a significant extent, the current military lives as a state within a state, subject to its own rules, norms, and governance.[76] Many are recruited from families with a strong military tradition and from areas of the country, primarily the South and West, where conservative politics and support for the military are widespread.[77] This is a military better prepared for the idea that war is a normal state of affairs and whose members are less likely to complain to the media and members of Congress about the hardships they may endure in their nation's service.

To be sure, the active-duty, all-volunteer force is backed by approximately one million reservists and National Guard troops who train on a regular basis but are only called into service when needed. Reservists make up a large percentage of troops trained in a number of support specialties—such as water supply, medical specialties, and chemical warfare—that are usually needed only in actual combat situations.[78] Tens of thousands of reservists were mobilized during the 1990 Persian Gulf War for the various military operations conducted during the Clinton years and, again, in 2002–2003 in preparation for a second war with Iraq. Though the reservists are volunteers and many are veterans of the regular military, calling them up for service can disrupt the civilian economy and society and sometimes produces hardship and resentment among the reservists, their families, and their employers. During the Vietnam War, both Lyndon Johnson and Richard Nixon refrained from calling up the reserves, believing that such an order would intensify political opposition to the war. Because of these problems, in 2003 Defense Secretary Donald Rumsfeld ordered military planners to find ways of diminishing or even eliminating the armed forces' reliance upon reserve troops. This was likely to entail some expansion of the size of the active-duty military as well as training regular forces to take over the specialties currently dominated by reservists.[79] Though both steps would add to defense costs, lessening the government's dependence upon the last of its citizen soldiers would create a military force even more readily available for use whenever and wherever it was deemed to be needed. Consistent with Rumsfeld's wishes, defense budgets since 2004 have been providing for the conversion of thousands of civil affairs, psychological operations, and special operations slots from reserve to active-duty forces.[80]

In the aftermath of Vietnam, the military was not only professionalized; it was also further centralized. The 1986 Defense Reorganization Act (Goldwater-Nichols) significantly increased the power of the JCS chairman, the defense secretary, and the president to determine military missions and set procurement policies.[81] This change not only promised to improve military effectiveness but also further reduced the opportunity for the individual services to publicly air their squabbles and open the way for congressional intervention. This had been a continuing, albeit muted problem since the struggles of the Truman era and had broken out anew during the Vietnam War when the Army publicly accused the Air Force of failing to provide adequate close air support for its ground combat troops.[82]

While a more professional and centralized military might diminish the political constraints on presidential war making, it could not fully eliminate them. Many Americans might be willing to accept the idea of sending professional soldiers into harm's way, especially if their own children were not subject to conscription. But even professional soldiers are Americans with home towns, parents, relatives, and friends, and the Vietnam conflict had demonstrated that American casualties could become a political liability and, ultimately, a constraint on the use of military force. This problem was one of the factors that led successive administrations to search for means of waging warfare that would minimize American casualties. After the carnage of the Civil War, American military doctrine had already begun to emphasize technology and maximum firepower in order to keep casualties low and maintain public support.[83] In the years after the Vietnam War, the military services invested tens of billions of dollars in the development of cruise missiles, drone aircraft, precision-guided munitions, and a multitude of other advanced weapons systems capable of disabling or destroying America's opponents while reducing the risks to which American troops were exposed.[84] Thus, in the 1990 Persian Gulf War and, even more so, in the 2001–2002 Afghan campaign, precision-guided weapons inflicted enormous damage on enemy forces and gave U.S. troops all but bloodless victories. In the 2003 Iraq War, pilotless aircraft, precision-guided munitions, battlefield computers, and new command-and-control technology helped bring about a rapid victory over substantial Iraqi forces with what once might have been seen as impossibly low casualties.[85]

By 2011, various "unmanned aerial vehicles" (UAVs) controlled by the Air Force and the CIA were conducting numerous operations on a daily basis against Taliban forces in Afghanistan and militants in Pakistan and Somalia.

In a much-publicized operation conducted in August 2011, a CIA-controlled UAV, firing missiles, killed al-Qaeda's number-two leader in Pakistan. Today, the Air Force actually trains more UAV operators than pilots, and all the military services are seeking to develop robotic warriors to undertake land and undersea missions as well as missions in the air.[86] Military analysts have pointed to these developments—sometimes called a revolution in military affairs—as indicative of a technological revolution in the conduct of war. Like past transformations in military tactics, however, this one has been caused as much by political as technological or exclusively military factors.[87] At any rate, to the extent that U.S. casualties can be limited to smart bombs and pilotless aircraft, popular opposition to the use of military force is less likely to become a political problem. After one *Predator* drone aircraft was downed in 2002, an Air Force officer involved in the program said, "It was on page six of the *Washington Post*. If that had been a [manned] F-16, it would have been page one."[88] While the destruction of Iraqi military forces was accomplished with few American casualties, Iraqi resistance to the subsequent American occupation produced a steady stream of casualties over the next several years. Opponents of the president's policies pointed to American deaths as a reason for withdrawing U.S. forces. Presidents and the military, however, had learned many valuable lessons from the Vietnam War. Some of these lessons concerned media and money. Most military officers and defense officials were convinced that negative media coverage played an important role in the waning of popular support for America's intervention in Southeast Asia. Stories of atrocities and casualties and a steady diet of media accounts questioning or contradicting official views of the war undoubtedly played a role in turning public opinion against the war during the mid-1960s.[89] After the war, all the services sought to devise procedures and tactics designed to prevent negative media coverage in future conflicts.

On the one hand, the services developed rules restricting media access to combat theaters. In the Persian Gulf, Grenada, Panama, Afghanistan, and the other regions in which American forces were sent into battle, reporters were restricted to pool coverage and were strictly prohibited from making unescorted visits to war zones. In general, the press was only able to show what the military wanted the public to see. At the same time, defense brass made a major effort to cultivate reporters and media personalities and assigned only the most articulate military and media-savvy civilian defense officials—Generals Colin Powell and Norman Schwarzkopf in 1990 and Defense Secretary Donald Rumsfeld in 2001—to brief the media and answer questions.

In preparation for an attack on Iraq in 2003, reporters were sent to military "boot camps" where they were prepared for the rigors of combat and given a chance to absorb military perspectives. Some reporters were attached to particular combat units in the hope that they would file favorable stories about the soldiers with whom they lived and worked on a daily basis. One journalist observed that the purpose of this practice was to induce reporters "to bond, to feel part of a unit and to get the military good press."[90] This program of "embedding" reporters with military units was extremely successful. Many journalists clearly identified with their units and typically used the pronoun "we" when describing military actions undertaken by those units. Such press criticism as was heard during the war generally came from reporters far from the front or from military analysts in New York and Washington. These critics, however, could not compete with the enthusiastic "embeds" who provided dramatic real-time combat photos and coverage via satellite.

Simultaneously, experienced and able White House communications staffers, like Deputy Communications Director James Wilkinson, were temporarily assigned to serve as information managers for senior military officers.[91] This was to prevent generals who might lack communications skills from making statements that were inconsistent with White House views or that might be deemed politically incorrect. The combination of restriction and astute public relations had a generally positive effect on the tenor of media coverage of U.S. military action. The networks themselves, to be sure, engaged in a good deal of self-censorship. Stung by Republican charges that they lacked patriotism, the major news networks generally made a point of treating Americans to favorable coverage of America's war effort. CNN went so far as to assign a more upbeat anchor team for its domestic broadcasts than for its international service. International audiences heard critical coverage from a team consisting of Jim Clancy, Michael Holmes, and Becky Anderson, who consistently questioned the claims of American officials. American viewers, by contrast, saw the team of Paula Zahn, Aaron Brown, and Wolf Blitzer, who seemed to find considerably more to praise than to question in their review of America's military effort.[92]

As to money, the U.S. government had learned in Vietnam that waging war with funds extracted from its own taxpayers could be politically harmful. Taxpayers might grow restive, and Congress might employ its power of the purse to interfere with military operations. During the course of American history, Congress has seldom refused to provide funding for military action when asked to do so by the president. In 1973, however, Congress voted to cut off funding for combat operations in Cambodia, a move that hastened the end of the Vietnam War.[93] Two years later, moreover, Congress voted to block the use of any funds for U.S. military intervention in Angola.[94] In order to make themselves less dependent upon taxpayers and the Congress, post-Vietnam presidents redoubled their efforts to induce American allies and others to share the military burden. This tactic first became apparent during the Reagan administration, when the White House solicited funds from the Sultan of Brunei to pay for military aid to the Nicaraguan Contras. Apparently, the funds were placed in the wrong Swiss bank account and never actually reached the Contras.[95] Despite this fiasco, the ploy of turning to foreigners to fund America's military efforts has been increasing in importance. In the 1990 Persian Gulf War, for example, the Bush administration made much of the fact that the United States had organized a coalition of nations to liberate Kuwait. But, with the exception of Great Britain, which contributed valuable combat forces, America's coalition partners provided only token military units. Instead, members of the coalition were expected to contribute financially to the American military effort. Thus, Saudi Arabia, Kuwait, the United Arab Emirates (UAE), Germany, Japan, and France—nations threatened by Iraq or dependent upon Middle Eastern oil— collectively paid the United States some $54 billion as their contribution to the war effort. This sum was actually slightly more than the final cost of the war.[96]

The president had wanted the payments to be tendered as "gifts" directly to the Defense Department, which could then spend the money as the administration saw fit. Congress, however, insisted that the funds be paid to the Treasury, where any subsequent disbursements would require a congressional appropriation.[97] The importance of fiscal considerations in the Persian Gulf War is one reason the U.S. was anxious to keep in its coalition nations like Saudi Arabia and the UAE, which had money but virtually no military prowess, but kept out of its coalition militarily potent but impecunious nations like Israel. The U.S. had enough firepower; it needed cash.

Several years later, the wars in Afghanistan and Iraq were financed almost entirely through government borrowing. Not only were taxpayers not asked for more money, but the administration actually cut taxes while stepping up military spending.[98] This policy helped to bring about a fiscal crisis in 2011, but for several years it muted opposition to the nation's war policies.

FROM VIETNAM TO AFGHANISTAN AND BEYOND

The lessons of Vietnam having been learned, albeit not the lessons that antiwar protestors of the 1960s had hoped, successive presidents, most notably Ronald Reagan and George H. W. Bush, worked to break the legal fetters through which Congress had sought to constrain presidential war making. Some of these fetters proved illusory. For example, the 1980 Intelligence Oversight Act lacked sanctions or penalties and seemed to assume that the president would cooperate with Congress.[99] No subsequent president, however, showed any intention of cooperating, and, indeed, beginning with President Reagan, the White House interpreted the Act as authorizing the executive to conduct covert operations.[100]

Other fetters were removed by the courts. For example, Congress drafted IEEPA to narrow the president's emergency powers and attached a legislative veto provision to ensure its ability to control presidential actions under the Act. The U.S. Supreme Court, however, in the 1981 case of *Dames & Moore* v *Regan*, stemming from President Carter's handling of the Iranian hostage crisis, construed the president's emergency powers broadly.[101] And in the 1983 case of *INS v. Chadha*, the Court invalidated legislative veto provisions like those in IEEPA.[102] The result was to leave the president with broader emergency economic powers and less congressional control than he had before Congress attempted to limit executive discretion.[103] The *Chadha* case also undermined the 1976 National Emergencies Act, which had provided that an emergency declared by the president could be terminated by a congressional resolution. As a result, an emergency today can only be ended by a joint resolution, which is, of course, subject to presidential veto.[104] The president is still required under the Act to notify Congress every six months of the continuation of an emergency situation once it has been declared, but this reporting requirement is hardly a limit on the president's power.

A third presidential fetter was broken by aggressive presidential action beginning in the early Reagan years. The 1973 War Powers Resolution provided that presidents could not use military forces for more than ninety days without securing congressional authorization. Many in Congress saw this time limit as a restraint on presidential action, though, as has often been observed, it gave the president more discretion than had been provided by the framers of the Constitution. President Gerald Ford had carefully followed the letter of the law when organizing a military effort to rescue American sailors held by North

Korea. But this was the first and last time that the War Powers Act was fully observed.[105] The demise of the Act began during the Reagan administration. President Reagan and his advisors were determined to eliminate this restriction, however negligible, on presidential war power.[106] Accordingly, between 1982 and 1986, Reagan presented Congress with a set of military *faits accomplis* that undermined the War Powers Act and, in effect, asserted a doctrine of sole presidential authority in the security realm. In August 1982, Reagan sent U.S. forces to Lebanon, claiming a constitutional authority to do so.[107] After terrorist attacks killed a number of Marines, Congress pressed Reagan to withdraw American forces. To underscore its displeasure, Congress activated the 60-day War Powers clock, but after the administration accused lawmakers of undermining America's military efforts, Congress extended the president's authority to deploy troops to Lebanon for another 18 months.

The president essentially ignored Congress but withdrew American forces in February after further casualties and no prospect for success. In October 1983, while American forces were still in Lebanon, President Reagan ordered an invasion of the Caribbean island of Grenada after a coup had led to the installation of a pro-Cuban government on the island. Once again, the president claimed that his position as commander in chief gave him the power to initiate military action on a unilateral basis. Congress threatened to invoke the War Powers Act, but Reagan withdrew American troops before the Senate acted. The invasion of Grenada was quick, virtually without casualties, and quite popular, especially after the president claimed to have rescued a group of American medical students attending classes on the island. Also generating considerable popular approval was the 1986 bombing of Libya in response to a terrorist attack in Berlin, which the administration blamed on Libyan agents. Again, Reagan acted without consulting Congress and claimed that his authority had come directly from the Constitution. President Reagan was, thus, able to use American military forces on three separate occasions while denying that he was required to seek congressional authorization for his actions. Congress threatened and grumbled but, in each instance, was outmaneuvered by the president. Of course, in 1987, several of the president's aides were prosecuted for violations of federal law when it was revealed that the administration had transferred arms to Nicaraguan Contra guerillas then fighting against the *Sandinista* regime in that nation, despite specific congressional prohibitions. Nevertheless, Reagan's successor, George H. W. Bush, resumed using American military forces on his authority as commander in chief. In December 1989, Bush ordered an invasion of Panama designed to oust Panamanian strongman General Manuel Noriega. Bush claimed that American citizens living in the Canal Zone were in danger and charged that Noriega had become involved in drug trafficking. Since drugs are shipped to the United States from many nations, often with the connivance of high-ranking officials, this seemed a rather flimsy pretext. Congress, nevertheless, made no official response to the invasion. A nonbinding House resolution expressed its approval of the president's actions but urged Bush not to use drug smuggling as a reason to invade Mexico or the remainder of Latin America.[108]

In 1990–91, of course, the Bush administration sent a huge American military force into the Persian Gulf in response to Iraq's invasion and occupation of Kuwait, actions that posed a substantial threat to American economic and political interests. Consistent with the tactics devised by Harry Truman, the administration quickly secured a UN Security Council Resolution authorizing member states to use "all necessary means," i.e., military force, to compel Iraq to restore Kuwaiti independence. The president's spokesmen, Defense Secretary Richard Cheney, in particular, asserted that the UN resolution was a sufficient legal basis for American military action against Iraq. Given the UN resolution, said Cheney, no congressional authorization was required.[109] After House Democrats expressed strong opposition to unilateral action by the president, Bush asked Congress for legislation supporting the UN resolution. Both houses of Congress voted to authorize military action against Iraq—the Senate by the narrowest of margins—but the president made it clear that he did not feel bound by any congressional declaration and was prepared to go to war with or without Congress's assent. Indeed, the president later pointed out that he had specifically avoided asking Capitol Hill for "authorization" since such a request might improperly imply that Congress "had the final say in . . . an executive decision.[110] President Clinton continued the Truman and Bush practice of securing authorization to use military force from a compliant international body and then presenting Congress with a *fait accompli*. Thus, in 1994, Clinton planned an invasion of Haiti under the cover of a UN Security Council resolution. The president hoped to oust the military dictatorship that had seized power in a coup and to reinstall President Jean-Bertrand Aristide. Congress expressed strong opposition to Clinton's plans, but he pressed forward nonetheless, claiming that he did not need congressional approval. The invasion was called off when the Haitian junta stepped down, but Clinton sent ten thousand American troops to occupy the island and help Aristide secure power. Congress was not consulted about the matter. In a similar vein, between 1994 and 1998, claiming to act under UN and NATO auspices, the administration undertook a variety of military actions in the former Yugoslavia, including an intensive bombing campaign directed against Serbian forces and installations, without formal congressional authorization. The air campaign lasted some seventy-nine days, involved more than 30,000 American troops and more than 800 aircraft and was conducted exclusively on the president's own authority.[111] The War Powers Resolution seemed to have entered the same legal limbo as state laws prohibiting lascivious carriage, a commonly used nineteenth-century catch-all charge that still appears in some state statute books but is never used today.

By the end of the Clinton administration, it was no longer clear what war powers, if any, remained in the hands of the Congress. Ronald Reagan, George H. W. Bush, and Bill Clinton had all ordered American forces into combat on their own authority, outmaneuvered, bullied, or ignored the Congress and repeatedly asserted the principle that the president controlled security policy and, especially, the use of military force. Early in the administration of President George W. Bush, Islamic terrorists destroyed the World Trade Center and damaged the Pentagon. The president organized a major military campaign designed to eliminate terrorist bases in Afghanistan and to depose the Taliban regime that sheltered the terrorists. Congress, for its part, quickly authorized the president to use America's armed forces to prevent future acts of terrorism. The congressional resolution was little more than a blank check, barely mentioned by the press and ignored by the public. Both were, by now, fully aware that, whatever its rhetoric, Congress had very little real control over the use of American military might. Subsequently, President Bush issued a variety of executive orders establishing military tribunals to try suspected terrorists, freezing the assets of those suspected of assisting terrorists and expanding the authority of the CIA and other intelligence agencies. National Security Directives were issued authorizing the use of "enhanced interrogation techniques." America's allies were also asked to contribute matériel and financial support for the endeavor, though only Great Britain made a substantial contribution.

Congress was not completely quiescent. Within a month of the terrorist attacks, the White House had drafted and Congress had quickly enacted the USA Patriot Act, expanding the power of government agencies to engage in domestic surveillance activities, including electronic surveillance, and restricted judicial review of such efforts. The Act also gave the attorney general greater authority to detain and deport aliens suspected of having terrorist affiliations.[112] The following year, Congress created the Department of Homeland Security, combining offices from 22 federal agencies into one huge new cabinet department that would be responsible for protecting the nation from further acts of terrorism. The new agency, with a tentative budget of $40 billion, was to include the Coast Guard, Transportation Safety Administration, Federal Emergency Management Administration, Immigration and Naturalization Services, and offices from the departments of Agriculture, Energy, Transportation, Justice, Health and Human Services, Commerce, and the General Services Administration. The actual reorganization plan was drafted by the White House, but Congress weighed in to make certain that the new agency's workers would enjoy civil service and union protections. In 2004, Congress enacted the Intelligence Reform and Terrorist Prevention Act in an attempt to centralize and streamline intelligence collection and analysis.

It should also be mentioned that in October 2002, Congress voted to authorize the president to attack Iraq, which the administration accused of supporting terrorism and constructing weapons of mass destruction. As had become customary, the congressional resolution gave the president complete discretion, and the president, while welcoming congressional support, asserted that he had full power to use force with or without Congress's blessing. Only the late Senator Byrd even bothered to object to the now obvious political if not constitutional truth of Bush's claim.

In 2008, of course, a new Democratic president, Barack Obama, entered the White House promising to change his predecessors' policies and approaches to the world. By 2011, however, the president had authorized sending 30,000 more troops to Afghanistan as a "surge" to defeat the Taliban. The president had also intensified the use of "Special Operations," including the raid that resulted in the death of Osama bin Laden. The president did not immediately hasten planned troop withdrawals from Iraq though; after a dispute with the Iraqi regime, Obama announced that all American forces would be withdrawn from that nation by 2012, and they were. The president, without consulting Congress, also authorized the use of force against the Libyan regime. In short, Obama had done little to distinguish his policies from those of his predecessors, except, perhaps, limiting the use of torture in interrogations.[113]

What explains the metamorphosis of a candidate who promised change into another Imperial President? One answer is that America's warfare state has succeeded—through its infiltration of the economy and the media and by exempting the well-to-do from fighting—in muting opposition and forging the lenses through which we view the world. Americans see the world in terms of security threats. As former Defense Secretary Donald Rumsfeld once observed, we must fear both the "known unknowns" and the "unknown unknowns." In this nightmare world, only the warfare state speaks with clarity and reassurance. This is the "spiritual influence" to which Eisenhower referred. Louis Hartz once argued that Lockeian liberalism was so pervasive in America that its truth was beyond argument. It was simply a given. Ironically, the givenness of liberalism played a role in the creation of the carceral state and the weakness of the welfare state in America. This, in turn, paved the way for a new given—the warfare state. One small step from Horatio Alger to Curtis LeMay.

Yet this step is not the last. The carceral state helped pave the way for the warfare state, but the warfare state also contributes to the strengthening and expansion of the carceral state. Indeed, the two reinforce one another on an ongoing basis. As James Foreman has argued, America's carceral state, fighting its war on crime, contributed mightily to the war on terror. Harsh treatment of prisoners, assaults on judicial authority, and efforts to limit the role of defense attorneys, all hallmarks of the war on terror, began with the war on crime of recent decades.[114] At the same time, tactics devised to fight the war on terror have found their way into the law enforcement methods used for more mundane matters. These include the use of delayed-notice search warrants, electronic surveillance, intelligence-led policing, and the militarization of police forces.[115] Indeed, local police forces are beginning to deploy their own UAVs, so far only for surveillance, but can the armed county police drone be far off?[116] America is a very tough nation—and is becoming tougher.

CHAPTER 5

MORALITY AND VIOLENCE

iscussions of violence can hardly avoid addressing moral issues and concerns. Though commonplace, violence is terrible, and an enormous body of philosophical and religious literature is concerned with the conditions under which individuals, groups, and nations may or may not justifiably brutalize, maim, and kill others. Of course, those who actually initiate acts of violence seldom read this literature. Or, if they do claim some moral basis for their actions, the principles adduced often seem to be more or less thinly disguised justifications for actions undertaken for possibly less noble reasons than those given.[1] Governments seem especially adept in this realm, frequently employing huge dollops of moralistic and patriotic propaganda to convince the citizenry to part with its taxes and blood in military adventures.[2]

Violence of course takes many forms—domestic violence, workplace violence, criminal violence, and so forth. Some acts of violence are committed by individuals or groups against one another for personal, pecuniary, and, sometimes, political reasons. Other violent acts are committed by states against rival states or by so-called non-state actors, such as terrorist groups, against foreign states and even their fellow citizens.

Of the many forms of violence, among the most troublesome from a moral perspective are those stemming from confrontations between governments and their own citizens. Of course, every form of violence raises serious moral questions. For example, issues surrounding acts committed in the course of interstate conflicts have given rise to an enormous body of "just war" theory.[3] Indeed, virtually all nations and even some non-state actors purport to recognize limits on violence. In principle, hardly anyone rejects such ideas as right intention, last resort, and proportionality. Practice, of course, is often another matter.

Yet violence committed by governments against their own citizens or by citizens against their own governments raises particularly perplexing issues. Citizens are often said to owe their own governments special obligations.[4]

Socrates famously chose to drink the poison hemlock rather than allow his supporters to arrange for his escape. He tells Crito that it would be wrong to disobey the laws of the city in which he was born and which had nurtured him.[5] Many, albeit not all, contemporary philosophers agree that those who live in a polity participate in its affairs and benefit from its institutions have a general obligation to obey its laws.[6] At the same time, governments can be said to have special obligations toward their own citizens. The signers of America's Declaration of Independence, for example, declared that governments were established in order to more firmly secure citizens' natural rights, i.e., "Life, Liberty and the Pursuit of Happiness," and deserved to be altered or abolished if they failed to fulfill this obligation. Every American has read the words of the Declaration, but few see their actual relevance to the United States. Most assume that unlike such dictatorships as North Korea or Syria, the U.S. boasts a political process and an independent judiciary that provide the citizenry with some means of compelling the government to fulfill its obligations. And perhaps they are correct in this assumption.

But we might find it instructive, nonetheless, to focus our attention on the case of the United States. Unfortunately, we shall see that in the U.S. as elsewhere, while citizens and the state may have obligations to one another, there is an imbalance or asymmetry in the relationship. Even in the United States, to say nothing of North Korea, citizens are held to much stricter account than the government for failure to fulfill civic obligations. Thus, members of the public who fail to pay their taxes or fail to obey any of thousands of statutes and ordinances may be fined or, in the U.S., join their 2.5 million fellow citizens in jail or prison. Many of these individuals are incarcerated for crimes such as drug possession that lack a discrete victim. These, as noted above, are essentially crimes against the state.

The government, on the other hand, gives itself a great deal of leeway in living up to its end of the bargain. The government does not actually obligate itself to fulfill the nominal obligations that the authors of the Declaration of Independence thought were so important. Take, for example, the often-cited case of *Bowers v. DeVito*.[7] A young woman called the police many times to beg them to protect her from her boyfriend, who, as she learned, had previously killed another woman. The police became annoyed and threatened to arrest her if she did not stop bothering them. The boyfriend came to the young woman's door and shot her through the head. In response to a suit subsequently filed against the police department, the U.S. Circuit Court said, "There is no constitutional right to be protected by the state against being murdered by criminals or madmen." So much for securing "Life." When citizens misbehave, they are subject to arrest. But when the state misbehaves, even egregiously, its liability is limited. In the United States, the doctrine of sovereign immunity gives the federal and state governments a considerable measure of protection from being sued—unless they consent.[8] In a similar vein, individuals whose legal and constitutional rights have been abridged by the actions of law enforcement officials generally find it extremely difficult to find a legal remedy.[9] Indeed, even when law enforcement officials use deadly force against citizens under questionable circumstances, the nation's courts usually defer to the police and offer the victims' survivors little recourse.[10] Even the five New Orleans police officers who callously gunned down several unarmed individuals who were seeking safety from flooding on the Danziger Bridge in 2005 were found guilty only of assorted civil rights violations six years after the shootings.[11]

Americans, to be sure, have sometimes responded to perceived injustices with actions outside the nation's legal framework—with civil disobedience, demonstrations, riots, and violence of many sorts.[12] During the 1850s, mobs of abolitionists used violence to protest the fugitive slave law and attempt to free slaves captured in the North before they could be returned to the South. During the late nineteenth century, militant labor groups such as the Molly Maguires, the Western Federation of Miners, and others fought pitched battles against the police, the state militias, and the U.S. Army to secure rights for industrial workers. In the 1960s civil rights protestors and rioters attacked and undermined America's *apartheid* system. In retrospect, at least, there seems to be general agreement that citizen violence, though regrettable, was appropriate in these instances given the magnitude of the injustice and the absence of alternative means through which to bring it to an end.

Slavery, the oppression of workers and racial segregation were society-wide injustices, depriving large classes of persons of human and civil rights. The scope of the injustice helped to produce the remedy: large-scale collective action. Most injustices, though, are discrete rather than collective. They emerge from confrontations between individuals and the government that are not readily aggregated to form a basis for collective action.

Every day, indeed, thousands of confrontations arise between governments and their citizens. Police officers tell groups of individuals loitering on a street corner to move along, or they halt a motorist for a traffic infraction. Health or safety inspectors order a business to shut its doors. Private land is seized from its unwilling owner for a road project under the government's right of eminent domain. In the United States, in 2009, more than 13 million persons—nearly 5 percent of the nation's population—were arrested by law enforcement officials. Every year, American police officers also issue citizens millions of traffic and parking tickets, while tens of thousands of citizens are handed citations or served with judicial and administrative summonses compelling them to appear before magistrates, judges, or administrative agencies to answer the government's questions about their activities.

In such confrontations, it often seems that citizens have many obligations while the state has mainly power. A police officer who makes a false arrest, for example, generally has qualified immunity from subsequent liability. A citizen, on the other hand, who resists or flees a false arrest is not likely to fare well in the police station, the courts, or, in some instances, the hospital.[13] The truth of the matter is that ordinary citizens, even middle-class citizens, are regularly subjected to harsh, unjust, and even violent treatment by various government agencies for which they have only limited recourse within America's legal system and political process. What then? Many examples of what might be called "everyday injustice" in the United States, such as the infamous Rodney King beating, have come to light in recent years because of the ubiquity of cell phone and surveillance cameras and the casual presumption of police, prosecutors, and other government officials that they are beyond the reach of the legal system.

Take the well-publicized recent case of New York City police officer Patrick Pogan, who, on July 25, 2008, attacked a cyclist riding through Times Square with a group of "Critical Mass" activists who frequently stage bike rides on behalf of environmental and other causes. Unaware that a tourist was photographing the event, Pogan strode several feet to intercept the passing cyclist, Christopher Long, who swerved away in an effort to avoid a collision. Seemingly without provocation, Pogan shoved Long to the ground and then handcuffed and arrested him, charging the cyclist with assault, disorderly conduct, and resisting arrest. Unfortunately for Pogan, a tourist who happened to video the confrontation posted the clip on YouTube, where it was viewed several million times. This widespread publicity compelled the district attorney to take action. In 2010, Pogan was found guilty of making false statements when he filed his criminal complaint against Long. Pogan, though, was acquitted of several other charges and given a conditional discharge.[14]

In a similar vein, four Florida police officers were caught on camera conspiring to bring a false DUI charge against a motorist whose car had been hit by one of the officers at a stoplight. While the motorist was handcuffed in the backseat of one of the squad cars, the officers discussed their story. "I don't lie and make things up ever because it's wrong," said one officer whose voice is quite audible on the tape, "but if I need to bend it a little to protect a cop, I'll do it." The officers rehearsed their story before driving the motorist to the city lockup.[15]

Or, take the case of a Denver man, John Heaney, who rode his bicycle past three undercover Denver police detectives outside Coors Field on the Colorado Rockies' opening day, April 4, 2008. For reasons that are not entirely clear, the three officers attacked Heaney, knocked him to the ground, slammed his head into the pavement, and allegedly broke several of his teeth. The officers then arrested Heaney and charged him with assaulting a police officer and with criminal mischief (for allegedly breaking one officer's sunglasses during the melee). The assault charge potentially carried a three-year prison term. The detectives alleged that Heaney attacked them and hit one in the face and chest as they sought to subdue him. They denied slamming Heaney's face into the ground or breaking his teeth. Unfortunately for the police, a local television crew was in the vicinity taping the Rockies' opening-day festivities. The crew turned its camera on the arrest and shot tape clearly contradicting the story told by the detectives.[16] Charges against Heaney were dropped, and one of the three detectives was charged with assaulting the cyclist but was later acquitted when jurors found that the video showed the officers shaking Heaney's head near the pavement but did not show his head actually striking the pavement. Heaney's civil suit has not yet been resolved.

In 2010, in Maryland, a group of five Prince George's County police officers confronted a crowd of rambunctious students who were noisily celebrating the Maryland basketball team's victory over archrival Duke. The officers arrested one of the students, Jack McKenna, and charged him with assault and resisting arrest, claiming that he attacked them and fought when they sought to detain him. Several students who witnessed the event had cell phone cameras and shot videos, which they posted on the Internet. The videos show the officers launching an unprovoked attack against McKenna, whom they threw against a wall and beat with their batons. When the videos aired on national television news, charges against the student were dropped and the police officers were suspended.[17]

In 2011, seven New York City narcotics detectives were convicted of planting drugs on innocent individuals to meet their arrest quotas. Eight other New York officers were charged with smuggling guns into the state. Another officer was accused of making a false arrest as a favor for his cousin, and three more officers were convicted of robbing a warehouse. In none of these instances had the official Internal Affairs Bureau of the police department taken any action.[18]

Of course, law enforcement officials—who generally know better—assert for the record that these cases are isolated and unusual events. It seems more likely, though, that what makes these cases unusual is that the events in question were filmed so that conduct normally hidden from the public's view came into the open. There are many reasons to believe that police abuse of ordinary citizens is commonplace. One recent study indicates that between April 2009 and June 2010, the national news media reported 5,986 instances of police misconduct.[19] In a study published in 2008, University of Chicago law professor Craig Futterman found that between 2002 and 2004 more than 10,000 complaints of police brutality were filed by the citizens of Chicago alone. In 85 percent of the cases, the police department cleared the accused officers without bothering to interview them. Only nineteen complaints resulted in any disciplinary action.[20] Chicago, remember, is the same city where in 2010 a top police commander was sent to prison on charges stemming from his involvement in the torture of hundreds of suspects held by the police over more than a decade.[21] A good deal of police misconduct, of course, is never reported. A study conducted by the Justice Department's Bureau of Justice Statistics indicated that only 10 percent of the citizens who believed that they were victims of police brutality bothered to file formal reports. Most were afraid to make complaints or believed that their reports were unlikely to result in any action.[22]

And, as to those pesky videos, several police departments have harassed and, in some cases, arrested individuals spotted photographing problematic police activities. For example, in 2009 in Oakland, California, a police officer, Johannes Mehserle, firing at point-blank range, shot and killed a 21-year-old black man who had been pulled from a BART train. The unarmed man was lying on his stomach and offering no resistance. Dozens of frightened commuters photographed the killing on their cell phones. Police officers fanned through the crowd of onlookers attempting to confiscate the phones and, at one point, chased an uncooperative cell phone owner onto a subway car.[23] Despite these police efforts, several photos of the shooting were posted on the Internet, leading to riots in Oakland and forcing the local authorities to take action. The officer was charged with manslaughter and served eleven months in prison.[24]

In several states, such as Maryland, Pennsylvania, and Illinois, statutes stipulate that individuals cannot be recorded without their consent. The police maintain that this prohibits citizens from taping or filming their activities, though no court has ever upheld the idea that such a statute can apply to the police or other public officials performing their duties, especially in a public setting where there is no expectation of privacy. Nevertheless, police departments have arrested a number of individuals and charged them with violating anti-taping or wiretapping statutes. Thus, Chicago police arrested a woman who recorded efforts by internal affairs officers to discourage her from filing a complaint against a police officer who she says groped her breast.[25] Maryland and Pennsylvania police have brought charges against a number of persons who sought to make a record of their confrontations with police officers.

By preventing photos and videos, of course, the police hope to prevent incontrovertible evidence of their misconduct from becoming a matter of general knowledge. From their perspective the problem is not misconduct but the public perception that misconduct is widespread. Without the photos, police denials seem plausible, as do claims that inappropriate and violent action on the part of officers is aberrational rather than commonplace.

The problem of ordinary injustice goes beyond abusive police action, manifesting itself in three main forms—laws that entrap innocent individuals, deliberately abusive action by ambitious prosecutors and other public officials, and the special problem of bureaucratic injustice and indifference. Let us examine each in turn and then consider the implications for citizens' obligations to the state.

UNJUST LAWS

Because of America's troubled racial history, we instantly tend to equate unjust law with racial discrimination or other forms of state action that invidiously discriminate against particular classes of citizens. Blatant discrimination, however, is only one form of injustice. Unjust law today is more subtle and is to be found mainly in the growing body of federal criminal law. Historically, in the United States, criminal law was the province of the states rather than the national government. In recent decades, though, members of Congress have been eager to demonstrate their commitment to dealing with such public concerns as law and order and national security and have enacted more than a thousand new federal criminal statutes, bringing the total to about 4,500.[26] We should recall that the U.S. Constitution itself listed only three federal crimes—treason, piracy, and counterfeiting.

Some of the new federal statutes are outgrowths of the "war on crime," "war on drugs," and "war on terror." Others are results of recent campaigns to rein in corporate malefactors or to protect the environment. Thus, liberal politicians and conservative politicians, albeit with different agendas, have both contributed to the expansion of the federal government's powers in the realm of criminal law.

The expansion of federal criminal law has contributed to a 300 percent increase in federal criminal prosecutions from slightly more than 20,000 in 1980 to more than 80,000 in 2009 and an eightfold increase in the federal prison population during the same period.[27] Accompanying the expansion of federal criminal law has been an enormous increase in the number of federal criminal investigators. Some 4,000 are currently employed by agencies such as the Environmental Protection Agency, the Labor Department, the Department of Education, and the National Oceanic and Atmospheric Administration (NOAA), agencies not usually seen as having involvement in criminal matters. Increasingly, however, these regulatory and service agencies are mandated to enforce the growing number of federal criminal statutes and to employ armed agents to do so. In 2008, for example, a group of NOAA agents, armed with assault rifles, raided a Miami business suspected of having violated a federal regulation prohibiting trading in coral. It turned out that the coral had been properly obtained but the business owner had failed to complete some of the necessary forms. She was fined $500 and sentenced to one year's probation for the record-keeping error.[28] This result could probably have been achieved without the assault rifles.

The idea of NOAA agents armed with assault rifles may seem to be a bit outlandish. Unfortunately, however, the smaller federal agencies not traditionally associated with law enforcement have been bulking up and expanding their police and, sometimes, paramilitary forces, which number in the thousands. And they do not hesitate to use their agents and arsenals against the citizenry. In August 2011, heavily armed Fish and Wildlife Service agents armed with the now-ubiquitous assault rifles raided the Nashville office of the Gibson Guitar Corporation. The agents seized a half million dollars in wood that Gibson had imported from India, claiming that Gibson had used an inappropriate tariff code when importing the wood. After nearly a year, the government concluded that it lacked evidence for criminal charges. Gibson agreed to pay a fine and make a "community service payment" of $50,000 to the National Fish and Wildlife Foundation, an entity sponsored by the Fish and Wildlife Service that conducted the original raid.[29] Who says crime doesn't pay?

If more examples are needed, another egregious case involved the tiny Custer Battlefield Museum in Garryowen, Montana. In 2008, according to court filings, a group of 24 federal agents armed with, of course, assault rifles, burst into the museum threatening its founder, Christopher Kortlander, and pushing one of the museum's interns to the ground. The agents were drawn from several federal organizations, including the Fish and Wildlife Service, the Bureau of Land Management, and the National Park Service. The agents claimed that the museum was selling artifacts under false pretenses as historical items found at Little Bighorn, site of "Custer's Last Stand." No such artifacts were found, so another raid was conducted several months later. This time agents alleged that Kortlander was in illegal possession of eagle feathers. No feathers were found and no charges were ever brought in connection with the raids. However, in the second raid, Bureau of Land Management agents confiscated several Cheyenne bonnets on display in the museum. The agency never alleged that there was anything improper about the museum's possession of the bonnets. Unfortunately, however, they seem to have disappeared while in agency custody. Kortlander is currently suing the government over his missing property.[30]

The new federal criminal laws are important not only for their number but also for their jurisprudential character. A number of these laws differ in a very important respect from traditional American criminal statutes. In particular, many lack or have only weak *mens rea* requirements, freeing prosecutors from the obligation to prove criminal intent when they charge an individual with violating the law. *Mens rea* is, of course, one of the fundamental principles of English and American criminal law. In its most general sense, the standard of *mens rea* requires prosecutors to show that an individual charged with violating the law intentionally committed an act that a reasonable person would have known to constitute a violation of the law. The principle of *mens rea* seeks to distinguish between those who willfully commit a criminal act and those who, for example, harm another individual without malice or intent, perhaps by accident. While the latter might be sued in civil court, they would not be subject to criminal prosecution and possible imprisonment.

Unfortunately, many of the federal criminal laws enacted or amended in recent years require no showing of intent and allow individuals to be subjected to criminal prosecution and imprisonment for what most Americans would see as innocent conduct. The rationale for such laws, some of whose forebears can be found in the Progressive and New Deal eras, is said to be to establish a regulatory scheme rather than to affix blame. Indeed, the crimes defined by these statutes are sometimes called regulatory or public welfare offenses to distinguish them from more traditional criminal legislation. It is, however, probably no consolation to the individuals convicted of these offenses that the question of whether or not they are personally blameworthy is of little consequence to the government.

Take the recent and well-publicized case of Eddie Anderson, a 68-year-old former science teacher from Idaho. Anderson, who enjoyed collecting Indian arrowheads, was arrested by federal agents and charged with violating the 1979 Archaeological Resources Protection Act. Anderson and his son had been digging for arrowheads near a favorite campsite in Idaho's Salmon River Canyon on land managed by the U.S. Bureau of Land Management. The two men were unaware of the fact that removing arrowheads found on federal land was a felony punishable by up to two years in prison. Nevertheless, under the Act no knowledge or intent is required for a conviction, and the Andersons were each sentenced to one year's probation and $1,500 penalties.[31] In a similar vein, retired race car champion Bobby Unser inadvertently drove his snowmobile onto federal land when he became lost in a snowstorm in 1996. When he asked authorities for help, Unser was charged with violating the Wilderness Act, which prohibits driving snowmobiles onto protected federal land. Unser was convicted of a misdemeanor and fined $75. To cite still another case, in 2007, a District of Columbia retirement home janitor, Lawrence Lewis, was sentenced to one year's probation for temporarily diverting a backed-up sewer line into an outside storm drain so it would not flood an area where sick and elderly patients were housed. Unfortunately, the drain emptied into a creek that ultimately emptied into the Potomac River. Lewis was charged with violating the Clean Water Act.[32]

These cases may seem relatively minor, but they illustrate an important point. As law professor John Baker points out, the absence of a *mens rea* requirement in such laws as the Wilderness Act and the Archaeological Resources Protection Act is especially troublesome because the conduct outlawed by these acts could be classified as *malum prohibitum*, or wrong only because it is prohibited, rather than *malum in se*, acts that are wrong in themselves, such as murder or theft. For *malum prohibitum* crimes, as Baker argues, *mens rea* requirements as well as notice are especially important sources of protection for individuals against being prosecuted for accidental acts they could not necessarily or even reasonably be expected to know were crimes. We might add that over time, the dilution of *mens rea* does a disservice to the government's own interests by undermining the rule of law itself. As we saw above, absent a clear distinction between what is and what is not a wrongful act, the deterrence of wrongful acts is reduced.

Already, the erosion of *mens rea* requirements has opened the way for individuals to be prosecuted for acts they did not actually commit. Take the case of *U.S. v. Hanousek*, decided by the Federal Court of Appeals for the 9th Circuit in 1999.[33] Edward Hanousek was employed by the Pacific & Arctic Railway and Navigation Company, a sister company of Pacific & Arctic Pipeline, Inc., as "roadmaster" of the White Pass and Yukon Railroad running from Alaska to Yukon Territory, Canada. Among Hanousek's responsibilities was supervision of a rock-quarrying project at a site known as "6-mile," where a high-pressure oil pipeline ran parallel and adjacent to the railroad's tracks. A contractor employed by Pacific & Arctic was blasting rock at 6-mile and loading it onto rail cars for transport. On the night of October 1, 1994, at home after work, an employee of the rock-blasting contractor noticed that some rocks had fallen off a transport train and onto the railroad tracks.[34] The employee found a backhoe, drove it some 50 to 100 yards, and began to push the rocks off the track. While so doing, he accidentally punctured the pipeline, allowing some 1,000 to 5,000 gallons of oil to spill into the nearby Skagway River.

After investigating the spill, the U.S. Coast Guard, responsible for enforcing the Clean Water Act (CWA), charged Hanousek, the project supervisor, with "negligently discharging a harmful quantity of oil into a navigable water of the United States" in violation of the Act.[35] Under the CWA, which does not include a *mens rea* provision, the government need not show criminal intent. As project supervisor, Hanousek was deemed by the government to be responsible for the accidental spill. After a short trial, he was convicted and sentenced to six months of imprisonment, six months in a halfway house, and six months of supervised release, as well as a fine of $5,000. No doubt, during his period of incarceration, Hanousek was cheered by the knowledge that his personal guilt or innocence was less important than the contribution his conviction made to maintaining the integrity of an important federal regulatory scheme.

The importance of *mens rea* became all the more evident in the wake of the Supreme Court's 2010 decision in the case of *Holder v. Humanitarian Law Project*.[36] The case involved a portion of the USA Patriot Act, which prohibits U.S. citizens from providing "material support" for designated foreign terrorist organizations (FTOs). Under the Act, material support is defined broadly to include "services," "personnel," "training," and "expert advice or assistance" to FTOs. The organization in question, the Humanitarian Law Project (HLP), was a human rights organization with consultative status to the United Nations. HLP claimed that its goal was to help the Kurdistan Workers' Party (PKK) in Turkey and, before the group's collapse, the Liberation Tigers of Tamil Eelam (both designated as terrorist groups by the U.S.) to develop means of peacefully resolving conflicts. The HLP sought, for example, to advise the PKK on the proper procedures for filing human rights complaints with the UN and the most effective ways of conducting peace negotiations with the Turkish government. On its face, it seemed that the HLP's intent was to induce terrorist groups to make peace rather than war. The U.S. government, however, took a different view of the HLP's intentions and made it clear that it would prosecute the organization's members if they proceeded with their efforts.

The "material support" law was very broadly drawn and, as critics charged, the idea of "expert advice or assistance" could be used by a zealous prosecutor to pursue journalists or academics who wrote about the activities or motivations of terrorists; human rights groups that sought to bring a peaceful end to conflicts; or even former president Jimmy Carter, who monitored the 2009 Lebanese election in which Hezbollah, a designated terrorist group, was a party.[37] Indeed, the author of a newspaper or magazine article or book that presented a sympathetic view of an FTO might be said to offer material support in violation of the law. In this way, the material support statute impinges on the First Amendment.

In gauging the potential impact of the statute, though, much depends upon its *mens rea* requirement. A strong *mens rea* requirement would demand that the government show that individuals charged under the Act not only knew that the organization with which they were dealing was a designated FTO, but also that they knew that their relationship with or assistance to the organization furthered its illicit goals. Such a *mens rea* requirement would protect humanitarian groups and the First Amendment. At the other extreme, there might be no *mens rea* requirement at all, or there might be one stipulating only that the government show that those charged knew or should have known that the organization with which they dealt was a designated FTO. Even a weak requirement opens the way for prosecutions of journalists, scholars, and humanitarian groups like the HLP.

Unfortunately, it is this latter conception of *mens rea* that is embodied in the Act and that was affirmed by the Supreme Court in its 2010 decision. The Act stipulates that to violate its provisions a person must merely have knowledge that the organization to which they are said to be providing material support, which includes humanitarian advice, is a terrorist organization and has engaged or engages in terrorist activities. Reading the statute, the Court declared correctly that Congress "plainly spoke" on this matter. As Justice Breyer pointed out in his dissenting opinion, this reading of the statute also provides "no natural stopping place." Any speech or writing that seems to defend any action by an FTO might be said to provide material support and lead to criminal prosecution.[38] In this way, arrowheads, snowmobiles, accidental petroleum spills, and the First Amendment are closely related.

ABUSIVE OFFICIALS

A second source of ordinary injustice is problematic, sometimes abusive official action. This can take the form of inappropriate and violent police action. But other officials, particularly prosecutors, are often blameworthy. Especially at the federal level, prosecutorial tactics in the U.S. have become extremely aggressive and designed to make full use of the many new federal crimes for which unfortunate individuals might be prosecuted. First, of course, Congress has enacted many new federal criminal statutes dealing with such offenses as tax and securities fraud, environmental crime, antitrust, and a host of misdeeds. Some scholars have asserted that the federal government has created so many new categories of white-collar offenses that almost any American holding a managerial or professional position could find himself or herself in legal jeopardy.[39] At the same time, prosecutors have developed a number of tactics designed to overwhelm unlucky defendants. To begin with, when they find it difficult or impossible to prove the crime that initially triggered their interest, prosecutors often base their cases upon ancillary offenses. That is, they charge the defendant with such offenses as making false statements, perjury, or obstruction—crimes that are typically much easier to prove than the more complex offenses that they hoped to charge. Richman and Stuntz call these "pretextual" prosecutions.[40]

Especially important is Title 18, Section 1001 of the *U.S. Code* (known to the legal profession simply as "1001"), which makes it a crime to make false statements in matters of federal jurisdiction. Hundreds of Americans are charged with 1001 violations every year, typically when prosecutors have insufficient evidence to bring substantive charges against someone they wish to prosecute. In a well-known case, for example, Martha Stewart was successfully prosecuted for ancillary offenses, including lying to investigators, even though the central case against her turned out to be too tenuous for prosecutors to pursue successfully.[41] In a more recent case, Nancy Black, a well-known marine biologist and operator of whale-watching boats, was charged with a 1001 violation when prosecutors lacked evidence to charge her with the nominally underlying offense, namely, that one of her boat captains had whistled at a humpback whale that approached his boat. Such whistling, if proven, could constitute illegal harassment of a whale, a serious offense under the federal Marine Mammal Protection Act of 1972. The government lacked evidence to prove illegal whistling but claimed that Black had altered a video of the event—a 1001 violation. Lest anyone think that these matters are not serious, Black potentially faces a long prison term.[42]

A second prosecutorial strategy that has evolved in recent years is the tactic of discouraging defendants from fully availing themselves of legal advice. At least since 1999, the Justice Department has told corporate defendants, in particular, that they would be more likely to face criminal charges if they "lawyered up." This policy was formalized in the often-cited and well-known "Thompson Memorandum," drafted in 2003 by then deputy attorney general Larry Thompson. The Thompson Memorandum states that in deciding whether to charge a corporation with a crime, federal prosecutors should consider "the corporation's timely and voluntary disclosure of wrongdoing and its willingness to cooperate in the investigation of its agents, including, if necessary, the waiver of corporate attorney-client and work product protection." The memorandum goes on to say that the prosecutor should consider "whether the corporation appears to be protecting its culpable employees and agents" and may consider "the advancing of attorneys' fees" and sharing of information pursuant to a joint defense agreement. In other words, corporate officers are to be discouraged from retaining counsel, from refusing to disclose privileged information, or from developing complex defense strategies by the threat that the government will treat these as indications of likely guilt.[43] The policies outlined by the Thompson Memorandum were modified but not materially changed by the 2007 McNulty Memorandum.[44]

Finally, federal prosecutors have been extremely aggressive about freezing defendants' assets prior to trial or even before an actual indictment has been handed down. The ostensible reason for asset seizures is to prevent the defendant from profiting from funds that might have been the product of criminal activity. The actual reason is to deprive defendants of the financial means with which to defend themselves, often forcing them to rely upon public defenders even though the government has not yet proven their guilt or found that the assets in question were actually the fruits of criminal activity.

Though harsh, these prosecutorial strategies are within the law. But in a number of other cases that have come to light in recent years, zealous prosecutors have not been so fastidious in their regard for legal niceties. Whenever an instance of prosecutorial misconduct comes to light, the relevant government agencies are quick to declare that this is an exceptional instance and not typical of the work of prosecutorial officials. Attorneys and even judges, however, know this is not true. Questionable prosecutorial tactics are the norm, not the exception. Marvin Schechter, a defense attorney who chairs the criminal justice section of the New York State Bar Association, wrote in 2012 that prosecutorial misconduct stood revealed "not as a trickle but as a polluted river." He went on to write that misconduct by prosecutors was "learned and taught" in prosecutorial offices.[45] Be they federal, state, or local officials, prosecutors are interested in winning, not pursuing, justice.

Most readers are, of course, familiar with the so-called Duke Lacrosse case. In that 2006 case an African American woman, hired by several Duke University students to dance at an off-campus party, charged that she had been raped by several white members of the school's lacrosse team. Though the accuser's story seemed riddled with inconsistencies, the Durham County district attorney, Michael Nifong, brought rape charges against three team members. The story of privileged white students allegedly raping a poor black woman quickly became a media sensation and caused outrage in Durham's black community. Nifong, who was up for reelection that very year, was anxious to maintain good relations with Durham's black leaders and voters as well as with white progressives who quickly championed the woman's cause.

Apparently motivated by these political considerations, Nifong ignored evidence that cast any doubt upon the accuser's story and ultimately sought to hide DNA evidence in his possession that all but proved the innocence of the three lacrosse players. Nifong had sent the accuser's clothing to a private laboratory for testing. The tests revealed genetic material from several men on her clothing, as well as her body, but none from any of the lacrosse players. Nifong, in consultation with the director of the laboratory, withheld this information from defense attorneys while affirming to the court that he had disclosed all relevant evidence and telling the news media that defense efforts to obtain additional DNA evidence was a "witch hunt" aimed at the accuser. However, after a thorough document review and analysis of the DNA evidence that Nifong had given them, defense attorneys were able to surmise that critical information had been withheld and filed a motion describing the tests they knew must have been conducted and demanding to see the results.

After the judge ordered Nifong to produce the missing information and the DNA test results became public, the North Carolina bar charged Nifong with breaking the state's rules of professional conduct by making false statements to the court and the media. He was ultimately disbarred as well as cited by the court for criminal contempt and sentenced to one day in jail. The rape case was taken over by the state's attorney general and the charges were dropped. A happy ending—at a cost to the falsely accused mens' families of several million dollars in legal fees (which they sought to recover in a series of civil suits) and enormous anguish.

Nifong's efforts to hide clearly exculpatory evidence and various other forms of prosecutorial misconduct were characterized by state officials as an unfortunate and unusual example of a rogue prosecutor. Unfortunately, however, what is unusual about the Duke case is not the prosecutor's misconduct but, rather, that the prosecutor's misconduct actually came to light and led to sanctions. However reprehensible, Nifong's tactics were not particularly unusual. In 2011, for example, the U.S. Supreme Court heard a case involving a failure by New Orleans prosecutors to turn over potentially exculpatory evidence to the defense in a capital case. This marked what according to some observers was the twenty-eighth time in recent years that New Orleans prosecutors had been caught failing to turn over such evidence. Their policy was said to be "keeping away as much information as possible from the defense attorney." One inmate spent 18 years on death row while prosecutors withheld evidence pointing to his innocence.[46] In the most recent case, the Supreme Court overturned the conviction. Similarly, in a Texas case, a man convicted in 1987 of murdering his wife was released in 2011 when a court finally ordered DNA testing of evidence withheld by the original prosecutor in the case. The evidence proved conclusively that another man had committed the murder, but it and other evidence was hidden by the prosecutor—who is now a state judge.[47]

In a 2010 report, *USA TODAY* identified more than 200 recent cases in which federal prosecutors engaged in various forms of misconduct to obtain convictions—a number that may represent only the proverbial tip of the iceberg. These instances of misconduct include withholding evidence, misrepresentations to the court, improper efforts to influence witnesses, improper vouching of witnesses, and so forth.[48] Take, for example, the case of Orlando, Florida, businessman, Antonino Lyons, as reported by *USA TODAY*. In 2001 Lyons, a college graduate and respected formed basketball star with no criminal record, was arrested and convicted of selling large quantities of cocaine. The allegations and evidence against him consisted entirely of the testimony of several convicted felons who hoped to win sentence reductions and other favors from the government in exchange for their assistance. Under the U.S. sentencing guidelines in effect in 2001, Lyons faced a mandatory sentence of life in federal prison for his alleged offenses.

Fortunately, prior to his sentencing, Lyons retained the services of a new and extremely able attorney, who, after examining the government's case, concluded that the government had withheld evidence that might have exonerated Lyons and that the prosecutor had failed to correct what was probably false testimony from the witnesses against Lyons. Withholding exculpatory evidence is called a Brady violation after the 1963 case of *Brady v. Maryland*.[49] Failing to correct testimony against the accused when the prosecutor knows the testimony to be false is called a Giglio violation after the 1972 case of *Giglio v. U.S.*[50] In May 2002, a federal district judge found that, indeed, in at least one instance federal prosecutors had failed to provide the defense with exculpatory material in their possession and had, moreover, presented testimony against Lyons they knew to be false. The judge ordered a new trial. The government appealed the district judge's order, and a federal appeals court declared that Lyons was not entitled to a new trial because of the weight of other testimony against him. Prior to his sentencing, however, Lyons filed a motion to force the government to disclose additional documents that threatened to impeach all the testimony against him. For more than a year—while Lyons sat in jail without bond—the government failed to accede to the judge's order to produce the documents demanded by Lyons, engaging in what the district court judge characterized as a "concerted campaign of delay and denial . . . [as the] . . . government brazenly refused to comply with the order."[51]

When prosecutors finally produced the relevant documents, it became clear that the prosecution had committed not one but numerous Brady and Giglio violations, hiding many pieces of exculpatory evidence and remaining silent as witness after witness presented testimony prosecutors knew to be false. Forced to reveal these facts, prosecutors dropped all their charges against Lyons. Furious, the judge declared the case to have been the result of "a prosecution run amuck."[52] A new federal prosecutor assigned to the case apologized to Lyons and conceded that "The United States's prosecution of Lyons did not reflect the government at its best."[53] Subsequently, the trial judge certified that Lyons was completely innocent of all the charges brought against him, potentially opening the way for Lyons to bring a civil suit against the government.

Though Lyons was exonerated, his life was ruined. He had spent 1,003 days in jail awaiting trial and sentencing, his businesses failed, he lost his house, his wife lost her job as a school principal, and he exhausted all his savings defending himself against false charges. Lyons is a free man, but how can his life ever be repaired?

Another individual whose life was turned upside down by federal prosecutors is former U.S. Army lieutenant colonel Robert Morris. Morris was a decorated combat veteran and logistics expert who became involved in a dispute with the Defense Logistics Agency. An anonymous tipster to a Defense Department hotline had claimed that Morris had diverted for his own use $7 million of surplus medical equipment from a Marine Corps base near Morris's own base at Fort Benning, Georgia. After an investigation by the Fort Benning commander, Morris was cleared. He had sent the equipment to a charity in Rwanda approved by the Army.[54] Nevertheless, for reasons that never became clear, the Defense Logistics Agency looked for a federal prosecutor willing to take the case. After being turned down by prosecutors in Georgia and elsewhere, the agency found a federal prosecutor in Dallas, Texas, willing to file charges against Morris. The federal judge in Texas to whom prosecutors brought the case warned them that it seemed to be a very dubious effort before granting a defense motion to transfer the case back to Georgia for trial. The prosecutor was not deterred and moved the case to Georgia, where a jury deliberated for only a few minutes before acquitting Morris. Another happy ending? Not exactly. His legal defense cost Morris hundreds of thousands of dollars. The prosecution, moreover, essentially ended Morris's military career and generally upended his life—for reasons that remain difficult to understand.

Let us also consider the tragic case of the Aisenberg family. Early in the morning of November 24, 1997, the Aisenbergs, a young Florida couple, called the police to report that their 5-month-old daughter Sabrina was missing from their home. The Hillsborough County sheriff's office conducted a search and investigation. Lacking other suspects, the sheriff's office focused on the parents and obtained a court order to tap the couple's phone and install listening devices in their home. Local and state authorities concluded that there was no evidence against the couple. A federal prosecutor, however, had a federal grand jury indict the Aisenbergs on charges that they lied to investigators and conspired to deceive the authorities.[55] Federal authorities sought unsuccessfully to induce each Aisenberg to testify against the other, promising favorable treatment to the first one to cooperate.

Much of the government's case against the Aisenbergs was based upon statements allegedly captured by the various wiretaps. An assistant U.S. attorney averred in court that the government had recordings in which the Aisenbergs made incriminating statements that would be presented at trial. According to the government these statements indicated that the husband had killed the child and that the wife was conspiring to help him cover up his crime. When the Aisenbergs' defense attorney asked the U.S. District Court judge to review the tapes, the government opposed the idea, and it soon became clear why. Judge Steven Mayberry listened to the tapes in his chambers and declared that they were "inaudible" and "insubstantial as evidence."[56] He found that the disparity between the tapes' contents and the government's contentions was "shocking."[57] The judge found that even the initial warrants that had been granted for the phone taps and listening devices were based on false information "that left a trail of reckless disregard for the truth."[58] In 2001, with the tapes discredited, the government moved to dismiss the indictment against the Aisenbergs.

In 2003, the Aisenbergs joined the thirteen individuals who have succeeded in winning Hyde Amendment sanctions against the government. The 1997 Hyde Amendment was intended to provide some possibility of redress for victims of federal prosecutorial abuse. Exonerated defendants may bring a civil action against the government in which they endeavor to show that their prosecution was "vexatious, frivolous or in bad faith." With such a showing they may be awarded attorney's fees and other legal expenses they incurred. Generally speaking, the federal courts have indicated that to succeed, a Hyde Amendment case must prove that prosecutors acted maliciously and pursued a case even when they knew or should have known it was utterly without merit. This is a very high threshold, almost never met, but in 2003 a federal judge awarded the Aisenbergs more than $2 million in legal fees (later reduced to $1.5 million). Essentially, the judge found that the prosecution of the Aisenbergs had been malicious and oppressive. The government conceded the point and agreed that it was liable under the Hyde Amendment, contesting only the amount of the award. While the government focused its efforts on incarcerating the parents, the daughter was never found.

In 2011, the 11th Federal Circuit Court of Appeals significantly lessened the already remote chance that a defendant might recoup damages under the Hyde Amendment. A federal court in Florida had awarded a doctor $600,000 in damages after he was acquitted of criminal charges relating to the death of a patient. During the trial, it was revealed that federal prosecutors had engaged in a variety of forms of misconduct, including secretly taping a defense lawyer. The appeals court said that despite these matters, the prosecution had been "reasonable." A coalition of 70 former judges and civil liberties groups has asked the Supreme Court to review the 11th Circuit's decision, which, they say, amounts to excusing serious prosecutorial misconduct.[59]

As another example of ordinary injustice, let us not fail to mention the politically ambitious Massachusetts prosecutors who destroyed the Amirault family. The case began in 1984 when Gerald, his sister Cheryl, and his mother Violet Amirault, operators of a Malden, Massachusetts, daycare center, the Fells Acres School, were accused of sexually abusing several children under their supervision.[60] The charges were both sensational and fantastic. Gerald Amirault, for example, was accused of plunging a wide-blade butcher knife into the rectum of a 4-year-old boy. Surprisingly, the knife left no mark or injury. Violet was accused of tying a boy to a tree in broad daylight in full view of everyone at the school and assaulting him anally with a "magic wand," which also produced no injury.[61]

The evidence against the Amiraults consisted entirely of heavily coached testimony by the children, often memories "recovered" by counselors who claimed to specialize in helping individuals retrieve memories of which they had not been aware prior to coaching. The absence of conventional evidence did not seem to trouble the prosecutors, led by Middlesex County district attorney Scott Harshbarger, who urged jurors to strike a blow against child abuse by validating the testimony of the children who had bravely come forward. Against the backdrop of a nationwide panic over what the media called an epidemic of child abuse, all three Amiraults were convicted. Gerald was sent to prison for a term of 30–40 years, and his mother and sister to terms of 8–20 years.

Eight years later, in 1995, a judge ordered Cheryl and Violet released immediately, declaring that all the testimony against them had been the result of prosecutorial coaching. The new district attorney, Martha Coakley, appealed the judge's order and succeeded in having it reversed by the state's appeals court. Violet Amirault died before she could be returned to prison, and Coakley consented to a revision of Cheryl's sentence to time served after asking the Amiraults' attorney to agree as a condition of Cheryl's release that he would halt his efforts to win Gerald's release.[62] The attorney refused.

In 2001, the Massachusetts Board of Pardons and Paroles recommended by a 5-0 vote that the governor commute Gerald's sentence. The Board pointed to the lack of evidence against Gerald and the bizarre character of the charges. Coakley responded with a media campaign bringing the now-adult alleged victims of abuse at the Fells Acres School to interviews where they could once again tell their stories to reporters. The governor turned down the Board's recommendation, and Gerald served two more years in prison before being paroled in 2004, having spent nearly 20 years behind bars. As a convicted sex offender who had refused to "take responsibility" for his crimes, Gerald is subject to numerous restrictions and conditions, including the requirement to wear an electronic tracking device at all times.

As to the prosecutors who gained political visibility in the Amirault case, Scott Harshbarger was elected Massachusetts Attorney General and was later named president of Common Cause. Martha Coakley was later elected Massachusetts Attorney General and in 2010 was the Democratic candidate for the U.S. Senate seat vacated by the death of Edward Kennedy. Coakley lost the election but is not required to wear a tracking device.

BUREAUCRATIC INJUSTICE

As we saw in the previous chapter, bureaucratic agencies often carry out what they deem to be their missions without regard to matters of justice and humanity or even rationality. They adiaphorize the conduct in question and sometimes just do what they do because they do it, to put the matter in colloquial terms. The ultimate example might be the behavior of Nazi death camp personnel during the closing days of World War II. In some instances, with the Russian army approaching from the east and only hours away, death camp officials ordered their prisoners transported a bit farther west so that the slaughter could continue a bit longer. In this way, the bureaucracy continued to fulfill its mission even though the state that had created it had collapsed, the politicians who launched the Final Solution were mainly dead or in custody, and the camp personnel themselves might have had a better chance of escape if they simply abandoned their now irrelevant mission.

Few bureaucracies take matters to such bizarre lengths. But every established bureaucracy develops a culture and commitment to its mission that may serve internal purposes but often seems to lack external validity.[63] This idea is captured in the quip learned by every naval officer: "There is the right way, there the wrong way, and there is the Navy way."

The adherence of bureaucratic entities to their missions and routines can, and often does, lead to indifference and routine injustice. A number of pertinent, if depressing, examples are reported in Ronald Libby's recent book on the mistreatment of a number of American physicians by the nation's burgeoning health care bureaucracy.[64] Since the 1970s and 1980s, government efforts to reduce health care costs have led to an ongoing bureaucratic campaign to investigate and counter billing fraud and to recover fraudulent payments to physicians and other health care providers who receive compensation from the Medicare and Medicaid systems.

Of course, no one can object to curbing fraud. However, when a bureaucracy is assigned the task of recovering money, there is a danger that it will be indifferent to matters of innocence or guilt and will, instead, adiaphorically focus upon recovering money in the most efficient manner possible, targeting those least able to defend themselves rather than those most guilty. The Department of Health and Human Services (HHS) makes identifying fraud one of its top priorities. And under both the False Claims Act and the anti-fraud provisions of the Kennedy-Kassebaum Act (formally known as the Health Insurance Portability and Accountability Act, or HIPAA), HHS encourages private citizens to act as "whistleblowers" and to file secret complaints against doctors and other providers.[65] Thousands of these are filed every year—by patients, office employees, and so forth. Whistleblowers have every incentive to toot their whistles because they stand to obtain a percentage of any monies eventually recovered and are generally shielded from any counteraction by the targets of their complaints. Whistleblowers have been paid tens of millions of dollars in recent years.

At the same time, under amendments to HIPAA, the Centers for Medicare & Medicaid Services (CMS), the office within HHS responsible for these two programs, has issued a series of rules and regulations providing for contracts with a number of private agencies to conduct audits and investigations into the billing practices of physicians and other Medicare and Medicaid providers. Like whistleblowers, these contractors are paid a percentage of any monies they recover and have little or no liability for mistaken claims they may make. Hence, they have every incentive to identify over-billing and possible fraud whether or not it exists. Often, the contractors work with whistleblowers, and the two share whatever can be recovered from unfortunate health care providers. A third element in HHS's effort to recover funds is, of course, law enforcement, which includes the HHS Office of Inspector General (OIG), as well as the FBI's health care fraud unit. Both entities are charged with prosecuting cases of health care fraud and are financed by a fund—the Health Care Fraud and Abuse Control Program—which is funded from the fines imposed upon physicians and other health care providers.[66] Hence, like the whistleblowers and audit contractors, law enforcement agencies have an incentive to identify over-billing and fraud whether or not it exists. An OIG official quoted by Libby declares, "A doctor might say, 'Really, those were mistakes. I'm sorry.' But we'll respond, 'It did benefit you, so as far as we're concerned you're guilty of filing false claims. Now, let's sit down and talk about money.' Then the doctor might say, 'Well, I don't have that kind of money,' to which we'll reply, 'We're willing to accept your mortgage, and if you die, we'll also take your estate.'"[67]

The actions of these bureaucracies effectively criminalize billing errors in a realm where the rules are complex and subject to many interpretations. Take the case of a Massachusetts doctor accused of "massive fraud" by the OIG and told to plead guilty and accept $150,000 in fines and 3–5 years in prison. The doctor refused to accept the plea offered, and, ultimately, it turned out after many audits that he might have over-billed Medicaid by $430, but even this was not clear under the arcane billing rules. The costs of defending himself, though, left the doctor bankrupt.[68]

This doctor was relatively fortunate. He had an excellent attorney and the government's case was particularly weak. One of the government's witnesses against the doctor was described as "delusional." Other doctors have been ruined financially and sent to prison for what amounted to billing disagreements.

From a bureaucratic perspective, though, there is nothing wrong with this result. As one experienced observer noted, treating patients costs Medicare and Medicaid money and is therefore not a good thing. Finding doctors guilty of fraud brings in money and is, therefore, a good thing.[69] This seems obvious if one understands bureaucracies. And these patterns of conduct are certainly not limited to CMS, though it seems to be a particularly malevolent agency. Recently, an agent of the Environmental Protection Agency (EPA) pleaded guilty to charges that he lied under oath and obstructed justice in the case of an oil refinery manager falsely charged with illegal storage of hazardous materials. This after the agent led two dozen armed federal officers in a raid on the plant, which led to its permanent closure and unemployment for 260 workers.[70]

JUSTICE UNDER AND OVER THE LAW

What should we make of this dreary tale of ordinary injustice—unjust laws, abusive officials, and bureaucratic misconduct? Does this pattern of misdeeds on the part of the state justify violence on the part of the citizen? Perhaps not. Certainly, prudential considerations, if no other, dictate caution in this realm.

Hypothetically, the criminal and civil law offer some possibility of redress to the victims of the sorts of ordinary injustice described above. However, victims of official injustice generally find it nearly impossible to prevail in efforts to obtain requital. For example, victims of prosecutorial misconduct have virtually no avenue for relief. In the 1976 case of *Imbler v. Pachtman*, the U.S. Supreme Court upheld the long-standing principle that prosecutors were generally immune from civil suits. The Court said, "Although such immunity leaves the genuinely wronged criminal defendant without civil redress against a prosecutor whose malicious or dishonest action deprives him of liberty, the alternative . . . would prevent the vigorous and fearless performance of the prosecutor's duty." In essence, the interests of the state were more important than those of the individual. At the federal level, as we saw earlier, a victim of wrongful prosecution might obtain compensation under the Hyde Amendment, but a successful Hyde Amendment suit is extremely rare—only 13 awards were made since the adoption of the legislation in 1997. Situations like the Duke Lacrosse case, in which the state bar association took action against the prosecutor, are extremely rare.

As to misconduct by law enforcement agents, actual criminal action—beatings and so forth—will usually be punished if they become public matters and receive media attention, as in the famous Rodney King case. Law enforcement officials, of course, work assiduously to prevent such conduct from coming to light, even, as we saw, to the extent of confiscating cameras and bringing criminal action against those endeavoring to photograph police misconduct. Generally speaking, law enforcement officials are also protected by qualified immunity from civil suits arising from their official actions. Such suits may be brought against federal officials under the so-called Bivens doctrine and against state officials under 42 *U.S.C.* Section 1983, which allows individuals to seek damages from officials who have violated their constitutional rights. Bivens and Section 1983 suits were always considered the legal equivalent of a "hail Mary" pass and have seldom succeeded.

The likelihood of a successful Bivens suit was made very small, indeed, by the Supreme Court's 2007 decision in the case of *Wilkie v. Robbins*.[71] The case involved an effort, over a period of several years, by officials of the Bureau of Land Management (BLM) to force Wyoming land owner Frank Robbins to give the BLM an easement through his property. In retaliation for what BLM saw as Robbins's intransigence, BLM agents repeatedly harassed and sought to intimidate Robbins, videotaped guests at his ranch, broke into his guest house, pressured other government agencies to impound Robbins's cattle, and filed trumped-up charges against him without probable cause.[72] While recognizing that these actions constituted what the Court called "death by a thousand cuts" and conceding that some may have violated Robbins's constitutional rights, the Court refused to provide a remedy for Robbins, saying that to provide relief would open a potential flood of litigation from others asserting that a government agency had acted to retaliate against them—a rather telling admission. The case, as constitutional scholar Laurence Tribe says, "portends a bleak future . . . for the meaningful enforcement of the Bill of Rights against renegade government officials.[73]

Should citizens work to change laws and hold officials to legal account for their misdeeds? Yes, they certainly should use the political and legal processes for both these purposes, but the prospects for appropriate forms of change seem poor at best. There is, indeed, change under way, but it is change in the wrong direction. Laws, particularly at the federal level, are becoming more unjust as politicians of all stripes tell credulous voters whose understanding of justice is shaped by motion pictures and television programs in which the authorities are always heroic that their problems can be solved through a regime of harsh laws and draconian penalties. Many legal theorists point to contemporary democratic processes as a source more than a limit on injustice.[74] Abusive officials, for their part, constantly receive more, rather than less, protection from courts concerned that protecting the public from official misconduct might open a "floodgate" of litigation.

And as to bureaucratic misconduct, every year brings more regulations, more bounty-hunting contractors, and less bureaucratic accountability. Most Americans believe that government agencies are answerable to the courts as well as accountable to the citizenry through Congress and the electoral process. These are, however, rather quaint notions. In principle, as Lowi, Schoenbrod, and others have suggested, Congress could write narrowly drawn statutes that limited bureaucratic discretion. In principle, the courts could reinstitute the nondelegation doctrine and stop deferring to administrative interpretations of statutory mandates.[75] In principle, Congress might invest more time and energy in oversight of the administrative agencies. But the reality is that the more ambitious the programs and policies that Congress develops, the more power it must delegate to the bureaucracy. And the more power it delegates to the bureaucracy, the less able legislators will be to oversee their creations.

Once power is delegated to them, executive agencies inevitably have substantial control over its use and, in most instances, neither Congress nor the judiciary is able or willing to second-guess their actions. The result is that federal agencies typically write the law according to their own lights rather than those of the Congress. Indeed, whatever policy goals Congress may have had, after many years and many congresses have passed, often all that remains of a statute is its delegation of power to the executive branch. As policy analyst Jerry L. Mashaw has observed, "Most public law is legislative in origin but administrative in content."[76]

Citizens who find themselves in direct confrontations with governmental—especially federal—agencies often discover, as did Frank Robbins, that these bureaucratic entities can be relentless, without pity and without mercy. As we observed above, they adiaphorize conduct and do what they do because they do it. Those who disagree with this characterization have been fortunate enough not to have become embroiled in such a confrontation.

At any rate, our story of ordinary injustice makes it difficult to agree with Socrates's admonition to Crito. Do citizens have an obligation to a state even though the state often seems indifferent to its obligations to them? What should we say to the families of the astronauts who died after NASA assured them that there was only one chance in 100,000 of a catastrophic equipment failure when the actual chance was known to be one in one hundred?[77] What should we say to the individual harassed, as we have seen, by the CMS or BLM or some other acronymic tormentor? Putting aside prudential concerns, is there a moral basis for disobedience and resistance? These are questions always worth asking and questions that should not be ruled out of order, even in a democracy.

PRACTICING DEFENSIVE POLITICS

Disobedience and resistance, even forceful expressions of opposition and outrage, it should be said, do not necessarily require citizens to shed anyone's blood. The squeamish, scrupulous, and prudent have sometimes found that governments can also be vigorously and effectively opposed through civil disobedience and other disruptive tactics that skirt the edge but do not entail outright violence. I have characterized these elsewhere as "defensive politics."[78] Citizens practicing defensive politics, however, need to take account of the fact that governments, even democratic governments, generally have few moral qualms about shedding the blood of disobedient citizens.

The most elementary form of defensive politics is withdrawal—moving off the grid, in the contemporary vernacular. Many if not most individuals would be better off if they could avoid government and politics. They could more profitably spend the time with their families, or even singing; dancing; writing poetry; taking part in sports; attending the theater, opera, or cinema. President Lyndon Johnson, who eventually became disillusioned with politics, told the young Doris Kearns: "I'd have been better off looking for immortality through my wife and children and their children in turn."[79] "Get married," said Johnson to Kearns, "Have children, spend time with them."[80] Many Americans show by their actions, if not their words, that they agree with LBJ. Quite a few demonstrate a healthy detestation of the world of government and politics. They disdain political discussion, seldom attend political meetings, almost never seek political office, and refuse to waste time listening to the tedious Sunday-morning pundits vie with one another to rehash and puff their vapid political lines. Of course, since they are taught that politics and citizen involvement are supposed to be important, most citizens are unwilling to admit that they really have no interest in watching the politicos preen for the camera. Yet the reality is that few can bring themselves to pay serious attention to the often repulsive political spectacle.

Americans are also taught to equate political participation with personal empowerment and individual freedom. Yet the relationship between politics and freedom is more complex than the civics teachers acknowledge or know. Whatever its other virtues, popular political participation functions as a source of state power. James Wilson famously urged his fellow Constitutional Convention delegates to accept widespread popular participation as the price of raising the "federal pyramid" to a "considerable altitude."[81] But real freedom does not simply mean a formal opportunity to take part in organized political activity. Real political freedom must include a considerable measure of freedom from politics as well as the freedom to take part in politics. Freedom implies a measure of personal autonomy, a sphere within which individuals are not followers of movements, causes, candidates, or parties and are not subject to policies, initiatives, or programs. Nietzsche might have been gazing at Wilson's pyramid when he cried, "Break the windows and leap to freedom."[82]

Unfortunately, though, the government and the members of the meddlesome political class, more generally, are seldom content to leave their fellow citizens to their own devices. Officials and politicians not only want to explain things to their benighted fellows but for better or worse—too often for worse—they seem to suffer from some compulsion to interfere in everyone's lives. When not merely engaged in their normal rent-seeking endeavors, a gaggle of officials want to seize homes and turn them over to private developers. Other politicians and officials want to redistribute incomes for the benefit of their friends and supporters. Still others endeavor to impose their own moral values on everyone else. Some wish to protect marine mammals from whistlers. And, of course, there are those who insist upon sending other people's children to die on distant shores for reasons that are usually difficult to explain.

It is, alas, because the political class is relentlessly intrusive that ordinary citizens must leave their hearths and homes and gird themselves for political struggle despite their proper disdain for the activity. To be sure, neither the political class nor the state can ever truly be defeated. Occasionally one crowd of barnacles is replaced by another and one pyramid razed to make room for a new one. The new political class assures all who will listen that its slogans and mythologies are infinitely superior to the lies spun by its predecessors. Sometimes they might be, but often enough the differences are outweighed by the fundamental similarities of power and deceit. Nietzsche, after all, was not referring to any particular state when he had Zarathustra observe that "whatever the state speaks is falsehood."[83]

But even if it cannot be defeated, the political class can and should continually be subjected to embarrassment, ridicule, and harassment. Not only does constant pressure keep the politicians and officials uncertain and off balance, but the exercise reminds the citizenry of the clay feet of their erstwhile idols. This, in turn, helps individuals maintain some critical distance from the state and its rulers and preserves at least a measure of inner freedom—a sphere within which each person may remain herself or himself.[84] This effort should be understood as *defensive politics*, an attempt to maintain individual autonomy and freedom from conventional politics.

The first rule of defensive politics is always to be cynically realistic. When any politician intones, "Ask not," assume he or she has something to hide. When a politician presents himself as an advocate for children, be careful about leaving him alone with your children. The political class hides information; it lies, schemes, and manipulates. Much of what officialdom keeps secret under such rubrics as national security and executive privilege is designed to protect politicians or the bureaucracy, not the nation or the public at large. Are we to suppose that former Vice President Cheney was thinking of the public welfare when he claimed executive privilege and refused to reveal the details of his meetings with energy company executives? Was FEMA concerned with the public interest when it sought to restrict press coverage of its operations in the wake of Hurricane Katrina?[85] This seems rather unlikely. Every year, more than 20 million pieces of information are declared secret by the government. Many of these would not help America's enemies, but they might hurt America's politicians and bureaucrats. And much of what is revealed turns out to be false. What did happen to those Iraqi WMDs?

Despite frequent reminders that neither those in power nor those who aspire to power can be trusted, millions of Americans remain surprisingly credulous and hopeful. In the 1990s, Americans voted against congressional Democrats because the House banking and post office scandals proved to them that the Democratic leadership could not be trusted with power. Ten years later, many Americans voted against congressional Republicans because lobbying and moral scandals proved to them that the GOP's leadership could not be trusted with power. One lesson that might possibly be drawn from these events is that neither group of politicians can be trusted with power. Perhaps no group of politicians can be trusted with power. Politics generally does not attract good people and often brings out the worst in those it attracts. If Americans were less trusting and hopeful, they might be more difficult to deceive.

The second rule of defensive politics is to choose action over participation. Participation implies taking part in politics through the formal processes established for that purpose. In some instances this may be a worthwhile undertaking. One or another candidate for public office may, indeed, be a trustworthy champion of ideas and positions that are worth supporting at the polls. Alternatively, a candidate may be sufficiently villainous to warrant engaging in a vigorous campaign against his or her election to public office. Of course, voters may have considerable difficulty disentangling the myths created by candidates' slogans and claims from the realities of their abilities, actions, and intentions. Millions of Americans voted for Woodrow Wilson in 1916 because, according to his campaign slogans, Wilson "kept us out of war." Perhaps this slogan continued to inspire Americans as they marched to war. In 1976, Americans responded to Jimmy Carter's question "Why not the best?" Today, some might say he was the better, but surely no one examining Carter's record would confuse him with the best. Politicians lie about their plans for the future and lie about their past behavior. They lie about their intellectual abilities, experience, character, and backgrounds. Sometimes the lies are revealed, but very frequently they are not.

Short of engaging in painstaking research, which the media claim to provide but seldom deliver, what is a voter to do? One simple rule of thumb might be captured in a slogan. If politicians can have their catchwords and shibboleths, voters are certainly entitled to their own political slogans. I would propose as the voters' motto *If in doubt, vote them out*. In the absence of solid information to the contrary, voters might safely assume that their elected officials are duplicitous, venal, and self-serving. Perhaps this characterization would not be true of some, but it is true of so many that voters would seldom be wrong if they simply resolved to vote against all incumbents unless they knew some compelling reason to do otherwise. In most elections, more than 90 percent of congressional incumbents are returned to office. Given the Congress's usually abysmal record, it seems unlikely that so many actually deserved to be reelected.

Throwing the rascals out is a step in the right direction. But, as we shall see in chapter 6, electoral processes are not designed to maximize popular political influence. They are constructed, instead, to delimit popular involvement in political life and to protect the political class from popular interference. Moreover, voters often find themselves merely replacing one set of rascals with another. In 1994, Democratic congressional corruption led voters to give Republicans control of the Congress. In 2006, Republican congressional corruption persuaded voters to hand control of Congress back to the Democrats. Some of these Democrats, like Congressman John Murtha of Pennsylvania, were previously implicated in corrupt practices. It is safe to predict that in a few years, voters will be disgusted by Democratic corruption and turn again to the Republicans. Might the moral of the story be that, given a bit of power, both sides are easily corrupted? Just a thought.

The practice of defensive politics requires voters to learn to think outside the (ballot) box.[86] There are many simple forms of disruptive political action through which ordinary individuals can oblige the government to listen and, sometimes, to respond to them. These include protests, demonstrations, boycotts, embarrassing revelations, and so forth. College students are often assigned lengthy readings from the *Federalist Papers*, which, among other things, defend limited popular involvement in the political process. I have often thought that students should, instead, read Saul Alinsky's *Rules for Radicals*.[87] In chapter 7 of that book, Alinsky discusses thirteen useful political tactics designed to achieve results outside the normal participatory framework. Generally speaking, Alinsky's tactics are designed to disrupt and irritate and to subject our more pompous officials and bureaucrats to public ridicule or even shame. Thinking outside the ballot box can be remarkably effective. In one instance recounted by Alinsky, he and his followers forced Chicago authorities to yield to the demands of a black neighborhood group by threatening to send hundreds of members to form long lines that would tie up all the lavatories at Chicago's O'Hare

International Airport for an entire day. The mere threat of humiliating media coverage for what Alinsky dubbed the nation's first "shit in" forced a hurried surrender by the usually arrogant Mayor Daley.

Many of the tactics developed by Alinsky and other shrewd dissidents are aimed at exploiting the gaps between the official rhetoric and actual character of those in power. Sometimes this is called a strategy of provocation and reprisal or, in more poetic terms, a tactic designed to force the government to reveal the "mailed fist" beneath the "velvet glove" through which it pretends to rule.[88] As Alinsky puts it, the authorities, "publicly pose as the custodians of responsibility, morality, law and justice,"[89] but beneath the surface they are usually neither moral nor just. The most effective political tactics are those that use disruption and agitation to compel power holders to choose between living up to their own rhetoric or revealing that their claims are false. This was essentially the strategy employed by Dr. Martin Luther King and other leaders of America's civil rights movement. While millions of Americans watched on their television screens, King and his followers mounted peaceful boycotts, sit-ins, demonstrations, and marches that forced Southern segregationist leaders to choose between surrendering to the movement's demands or revealing the brutal reality that lurked beneath the rhetoric of "separate but equal" and similarly vacuous political claims. Analogous tactics were employed against the British by America's founders. When Samuel Adams and his "sons of liberty" dumped British tea into Boston Harbor, they provoked the authorities into undertaking harsh reprisals against innocent residents of Boston. This revealed to thousands of colonists the gaps between British claims of justice and the Crown's actual conduct. Had they not first been successful practitioners of Alinsky-style tactics, the nation's founders would never have won the opportunity to later caution against the dangers of too democratic a politics in the *Federalist*.

Today, technology is opening new avenues for popular political action. The Internet has become a powerful tool for political organization. Weblogs, popularly known as "blogs," and other Internet forums allow the rapid dissemination of information, ideas, and opinions outside the control of the government or other institutions. To be sure, many of the ideas and opinions found in the various weblogs are utterly foolish. America's always-active flying saucer community, for example, is well represented in the blogosphere. Moreover, corporations and politicians have learned to create and use blogs for their own purposes. Blogs, nevertheless, sharply lower the technological and financial barriers that previously prevented all but a few individuals and interests from reaching mass audiences and potentially increase the ability of ordinary people to engage in effective political action. In 2003, for example, bloggers took the lead in publicizing a story that cost Senate Majority Leader Trent Lott his job. Lott had praised the late Senator Strom Thurmond, a fervent segregationist, as a man who would have made a good president. Only after the blogs broke the story did the mainstream media seem to become aware of the significance of Lott's comments. In 2004, bloggers demonstrated that then CBS anchor Dan Rather had presented unsubstantiated and possibly bogus information in a major story. Rather was forced into retirement. In 2006, bloggers publicized evidence of racist comments by Florida House candidate Tramm Hudson, derailing Hudson's candidacy. And, that same year, bloggers helped to bring about Senator Joseph Lieberman's defeat in the Connecticut Democratic primary election. In 2012, bloggers publicized Mitt Romney's comments disparaging what he said were the 47 percent of Americans who depended upon government handouts.

Magnifying the power of the Internet is the universal availability of digital cameras. Particularly since cell phones are now equipped with cameras, millions of Americans have the capacity to photograph or film events that they may witness. At the same time, Internet sites like YouTube permit users to upload photos and video clips that are then viewed by hundreds of thousands of subscribers and are sometimes picked up by the mainstream media for even wider dissemination. In 2006, a YouTube video showing Virginia senator George Allen making a racist comment to one of his opponent's campaign workers caused an uproar. Allen, who had been positioning himself for a possible 2008 presidential race, was defeated for reelection to the Senate from Virginia, when his victory had previously been seen as a sure thing. His presidential aspirations were dashed. With a bit of technology, citizens had derailed the career of a once-powerful politician. This example illustrates the way in which technology can be a tool of popular political action. Because they are pervasive and intrusive, the new media technologies sometimes allow ordinary citizens to break into the private world of the political class and to observe the differences between the carefully cultivated appearance and the less attractive reality of that world. Members of eighteenth-century mobs sometimes told astonishing tales of what they saw when they stormed the gates of the lord's castle. In a similar vein, modern-day electronic rioters sometimes astonish the nation with what their cameras are able to show millions of users of the Internet.

The final rule of defensive politics is never to trust the state. Whatever ideologies they may happen to profess, those who have power will always abuse it.

On this point, Alinsky and the authors of the *Federalist* agree. Officials abuse power in petty ways—pardoning well-connected felons, for example, and they abuse power in big ways—creating phony pretexts for unnecessary wars. It is important to support restrictions on governmental power and to be wary of claims that we need more government. Occasionally we do need the protection and services of the state, but often it is only the government that needs more government. In 2006, the U.S. government cut Homeland Security funds for the protection of the citizens of New York and Washington, the most likely targets of future terrorist attacks. At the same time, though, the government funded elaborate plans for the continuation and, if necessary, relocation, of every last government agency—even the U.S. Patent and Trademark Office, in the event of some catastrophe.[90] Clearly, the government views its primary mission as protection of the government. The citizenry, it seems, is expendable.

CHAPTER 6
VIOLENCE AND CHANGE

In a recent book, noted psychologist Steven Pinker avers that the incidence of violence has been on the decline for the past several hundred years.[1] As Elizabeth Kolbert has shown in a perceptive review, Pinker's arguments and evidence are often problematic. In some instances, Pinker seems untroubled by the fact that his data seem to fly rather spectacularly in the face of his thesis. These instances include both World War I and World War II, which Pinker dismisses as historical "accidents."[2]

Leaving aside these problems and giving Pinker some benefit of the doubt, we might still ask whether, as Pinker appears to assume, an end to violence would be an unmitigated blessing. Violence is terrible, but the normal choice in political affairs is not between violence and the heavenly kingdom. Rather, the choice is between what Walter Benjamin called law-preserving and law-making violence.[3] Law-making violence is employed by those who seek to replace an established regime or system of rules with another. Law-making violence is generally public and obvious. It might entail demonstrations, riots, or more overtly violent and even bloody forms of action. It is this sort of activity that is generally thought of when we use the term political violence.

What we call peace, however, is usually the product of Benjamin's second category, law-preserving violence. Law-preserving violence is the instrument of the pillars and defenders of the established order: the violence of the *gendarme* and the prison. Law-preserving violence usually presents itself as an antidote to violence—the state's effort to prevent violence and promote law and order. But law-preserving violence is, nonetheless, violence. At this very moment, millions of Americans are serving terms in prison or are otherwise being subjected to punishment by the state. Each of these individuals was, at the very least, threatened with violence. If they escaped overtly violent treatment it was only because they refrained from resisting when arrested, tried, and jailed. Those who did resist, and some who did not, were almost certainly violently subdued. Perhaps their treatment was just, perhaps not, but it could hardly be called nonviolent.

A similar rejoinder might be made to the French historian Robert Muchembled, whose interesting book *A History of Violence* was published in France in 2008 and in the United States in 2012.[4] Like Pinker, Muchembled shows a decline in domestic violence within Europe over the past several centuries. Unlike Pinker, though, Muchembled is careful to distinguish this decline from changes in international violence or violence perpetrated by states, so we cannot hold the world wars or Mao, Hitler, and Stalin against him. Not unlike Pinker, Muchembled attributes much of the decline in violent conduct to the imposition of state authority, which was designed to supervise and pacify young males with, among other things, systems of fines and sanctions for violent conduct.[5] Again, though, what Muchembled calls peace, Benjamin would properly see as an ongoing product of law-preserving violence. Through the continuing use of superior force, states have gradually delimited the violence practiced by their citizens.

Perhaps peace can be maintained without violence or the threat of violence, but such peace is tenuous. Like the poor Moriori, those with a strong moral commitment to refrain from violence always risk being eaten by their less pacific neighbors. For the most part, apparently peaceful places tend to be those that most effectively employ law-preserving violence. Indeed, as Pinker notes, "A state that uses a monopoly on force to protect its citizens from one another may be the most consistent violence-reducer that we have encountered in this book."[6] We might restate Pinker's findings as confirming the notion that peace is less often the absence of violence than the product of effective law-preserving violence. China, these days, is an internally peaceful place, according to dissident physicist Fang Lizhi, because the government spends huge sums on "stability maintenance" to prevent protests, demonstrations, and other "mass incidents."[7] This principle also applies to the international realm, where peace is most likely to be a result of hegemonic power—the *Pax Romana*, *Pax Britannica*, and *Pax Americana* are examples.

Should we valorize the peace brought by law-preserving violence to its alternatives? Neo-Hobbesians may prefer the result of law-preserving violence to its alternatives, and they may sometimes be right—on net. They should not, however, hide from themselves the costs of this peace. "Stability maintenance" in China, as Fang Lizhi observed, included Tiananmen Square. Or, to take another example, the absence of law-preserving violence in El Salvador has produced something approaching Hobbes's war of all against all.[8] Yet, the peace brought by North Korea's very effective law-preserving violence is the peace of the labor camp, the prison, and the gallows.

For its part, law-making violence, as we saw in chapter 1, is among the world's great engines of political and social change. Through violent means, new groups, new forces, and new classes build new regimes, and states arise while consigning the old ones to historical memory. Change does not always mean progress, but it is a necessary condition for progress. Hence violence, though terrible, may be a necessary ingredient of human improvement.

To be sure, we often take comfort in the pleasant myth of peaceful change, in reform rather than revolution, as some would say. But is not reform almost by definition a mechanism for preventing or diminishing social or political change? Is not reform the technique employed by those in power to hang on to power by heading off trouble? This seems most evident if we consider the matter of democratic elections.

In the democracies, most citizens believe that elections serve as an effective alternative route to political change that makes popular violence unnecessary. Of course, governments often share this belief and view elections as useful instruments for limiting political change. In a number of contexts elections are introduced or the right to vote expanded precisely in order to redirect—sublimate—violent political impulses. As the late Walter Lippmann observed, "New numbers were enfranchised because they had power, and giving them the vote was the 'least disturbing way' of letting them exercise their power."[9]

Two examples from recent American history appear to illustrate Lippmann's proposition. One is the case of the Twenty-Sixth Amendment, added to the Constitution in 1971, which lowered the U.S. voting age from 21 to 18. This Amendment was adopted during a period of civil strife and disorder during which young people—college students in particular—engaged in sometimes violent protests over the Vietnam War, military conscription, race relations, social policy, and other aspects of American politics and society. While student protestors made many demands, their agenda did not include voting rights for young people. But even though students may not have been especially interested in voting, many political leaders seemed eager to give them the right to do so.

Senate Judiciary Committee hearings on the subject indicate a belief among Democrats and Republicans alike that the right to vote would channel students' political activities from the street into the polling places. For example, the late Senator Jacob Javits (R-NY) said, "I am convinced that self-styled student leaders who urged such acts of civil disobedience would find themselves with little or no support if students were given a more meaningful role in the political process. In short, political activism . . . is all happening outside the existing political framework. Passage of [the voting rights resolution] would give us the means, sort of the famous carrot and the stick, to channel this energy into our major political parties." In a similar vein, the late Senator Birch Bayh (D-IN) said, "This force, this energy, is going to continue to build and grow. The only question is whether we should continue to ignore it, perhaps leaving this energy to dam up and burst and follow less-than-wholesome channels, or whether we should let this force be utilized by society through the pressure valve of the franchise."[10] Three years later, the resolution under discussion became a constitutional amendment.

In a similar vein, the Kennedy administration's focus on voting rights for African Americans was, in part, an attempt to divert civil rights activists away from their militant campaign for desegregation of schools and public facilities—a campaign that was engendering violent resistance throughout the South.[11] Suspicious of the administration's purpose, some black activists initially resisted participating in the voting rights effort. One faction of the Student Nonviolent Coordinating Committee (SNCC), an important activist group of the period, vehemently refused to take part in voter registration drives on the ground that they were simply an attempt by the national government "to cool the militancy of the student movement."[12] Eventually, however, the Kennedy administration told civil rights activists that it would help them secure voting rights but would not lend them its assistance if they focused on eliminating other forms of segregation.

Perhaps citizens are better off when they can make themselves heard effectively at the polls rather than having to undertake more arduous and, perhaps, risky forms of political agitation. But citizens also lose something when their political activity is confined to the voting booth. In the same sense that legalizing the sale of alcohol allows the government to regulate its distribution and consumption—a lesson learned from the violence associated with Prohibition—the construction of a formal electoral machinery permits governments to more effectively regulate and manage popular political activity. In the absence of elections, the timing and goals of popular political activity, as well as the identity of those who will take part, are determined by the participants themselves. But elections transfer control over these and other aspects of political action from the citizen to the state, thereby reducing the uncertainty and risk that citizen involvement in politics poses to the government.

For example, anyone who decides to do so can participate in protests or demonstrations. It is the government, however, that determines who is eligible to take part in elections. Of course, when democratic electoral institutions were initially introduced in Europe and the U.S., governments sought to bar the participation of individuals whom they deemed to be undesirable. Race, religion, socioeconomic status, and a host of other factors became bases for exclusion from the electorate. While these sorts of restrictions may have served the interests of particular political forces at particular times, they also reduced the value of elections as regulatory instruments. Other things being equal, governments have a stake in seeing to it that everyone engaged in political activity is channeled into the electoral arena, and most regimes eventually acceded to this fact. Accordingly, contemporary democratic governments impose few restrictions on voting rights. In fact, most seek to make voting quite easy, establishing numerous polling places and staffing and organizing an elaborate administrative machinery for enrolling voters, selecting candidates, and counting ballots. Among the Western democracies, the United States, with its antiquated registration rules, is probably the least facilitative of voting.[13] But even in the U.S., voting is a relatively simple and painless task, as was noted above, precisely because state, local, and national governments spend hundreds of millions of dollars each year to make it so.

Ironically, electoral procedures that bring tens of millions of citizens to the polls can be seen as potent regulatory instruments. When participation involves difficulties, costs, and risks, only those with strong views and preferences are likely to be sufficiently motivated to take part. Because voting entails no risks and few costs, even those who lack firm opinions and have little interest in the outcome may be moved to respond to official and partisan exhortations and spend a few minutes at the polls. For example, every year on the anniversary of the Supreme Court's 1973 *Roe v. Wade* decision legalizing abortion, thousands of demonstrators have gathered in Washington, D.C. Some of these individuals come to affirm their support for the decision, while others come to voice their opposition. Not once in the four decades since the Court handed down its verdict have any demonstrators gathered to declare that they did not know or care much about abortion.

The don't knows and don't cares do, however, vote. In the electorate, as among those whose opinions are merely represented in the polls, individuals who do not have strong opinions usually outnumber those who do. As Philip Converse once observed, most voters' attitudes are, in fact, *nonattitudes*.[14] That is, they neither know much nor care much about most issues. By making electoral participation easy, governments can submerge those with strong views, almost always a minority, in a more apathetic majority. The virtue of this result, from the government's perspective, is that the don't knows and the don't cares, like the "silent majority" President Nixon once claimed to find in the opinion polls, also don't impose much constraint on official actions. In a sense, through electoral institutions, governments transform political activity from a collective process for the assertion of demands into what often amounts to a collective statement of permission.

Voting helps regulate political participation in other ways as well. Protestors organize themselves. Indeed, today protestors organize themselves through the Internet. The French student demonstrators whose opposition to a proposed new labor law rocked the government and forced it to rescind its proposal in March 2006 communicated nationally via a website. The proposed new labor law was known by the acronym CPE, and, hence, the website was called STOPCPE.net. Protest leaders used the site to organize rallies and disseminate information.[15] In 2011, protestors in Egypt, Tunisia, Syria, and other Middle Eastern nations made use of the Internet, particularly Facebook, to organize, schedule demonstrations, and exchange ideas and plans. Voters, though, are typically organized into districts or other electoral units by the government. Thus, while rioters are rather difficult to gerrymander, voters are subject to "electoral engineering" designed to affect the relative weights of various social groups and the outcomes of electoral contests. Protestors, moreover, may target any facet of the political process they choose. Voters, though, are usually limited to the selection of representatives. While a number of states do permit popular referenda on policy issues, at the national level America's voters are not asked to make decisions about programs, policies, budgets, and institutional arrangements. In fact, even most public officials are not subject to popular election. Voters are limited to selecting those officials who hold what are legally deemed to be elective offices. In the United States, most judges and a score of high-ranking administrative officials are immune to direct electoral scrutiny.

Similarly, protestors and rioters can assemble whenever and, as the recent "Occupy" movement suggested, wherever they want. Voting, however, takes place at regular intervals at times and in places set by law. Between these intervals, elected officials serve fixed terms in office and voters exercise no formal power. In *Federalist 71*, Alexander Hamilton explained that the purpose of limiting the frequency of popular participation and providing elected officials with fixed terms in office was to prevent the government from being forced to respond to "every sudden breeze of passion, or to every transient impulse which the people may receive."[16] Fixed terms are designed to allow elected officials to withstand the vicissitudes of public opinion and to make unpopular decisions without immediate fear of popular reprisal at the polls. Throughout the year 2005, for example, commentators noted that President Bush's popularity had dropped sharply, as had popular support for his administration's policies in Iraq. Some commentators asked whether the president, lacking popular support, would be able to continue governing effectively. President Bush, however, declared vehemently that he planned no change in policy. The president knew full well that he had no immediate reason to fear the national electorate, a body that comes into being only the Tuesday after the first Monday in November in even-numbered years and whose powers, like a mist, dissipate the next day.

Electoral institutions not only offer governments a measure of protection from the potentially negative consequences of popular political activity; they promise positive benefits as well. Just as governments derive income in the form of tax revenues from the lawful sale of alcohol, to continue the analogy, they stand to derive gain in the form of increased popular support from lawful citizen participation. Denying citizens an opportunity to participate in political life tends to alienate those who have political interests and ambitions. Indeed, the more the government attempts to harass or intimidate such individuals, the greater the chance that citizens who might have begun as mild malcontents will become full-fledged enemies of the state, working, as Senator Javits noted, to spread their seditious ideas to others as well. The history of Tsarist Russia is replete with examples of this phenomenon.[17]

However, providing those who wish to participate with a lawful outlet for their political energies, as was discussed above, is likely to have the opposite effect, generating support for rather than opposition to the regime. The benefits they hope to derive from popular voting, coupled with their desire to avoid more disturbing forms of popular political action, has impelled many governments and national political elites to encourage citizens to vote, while discouraging them from engaging in other forms of political activity. Their goal is not to stimulate participation per se. It is, rather, to make certain that those who are moved to participate are channeled into the electoral arena. In the United States, as we saw above, the virtues of voting are taught in the schools, promoted by the mass media, and touted by a host of civic institutions and foundations. And every year, state and local governments spend hundreds of millions of dollars to operate the nation's electoral machinery. Voting is the only form of popular political activity that receives this type of governmental subsidy. Those who wish to lobby or litigate must foot the bill themselves. And those who endeavor to express their views via protests, sit-ins, or demonstrations are likely to incur the displeasure of the authorities. This is what Senator Javits had in mind when he referred to the combination of carrot and stick. It is this combination that impels most Americans and Western Europeans to confine their political involvement to voting and a small number of other electoral activities.

All this does not mean that voting has no significance. Generally speaking, electoral politics helps to decide which elements within the established political elite and among the various established stakeholders surrounding that elite will wield more or less influence in government and politics. When it comes to major changes in the composition of the elite, however, violence plays a larger role than voting. Indeed, violence and political change go hand in hand. Virtually every nation on the face of the earth came into being as a result of war, civil war, or violent revolution. And, in all likelihood, most of their successors will replace them through similar means. In 2011, the world's newest nation, South Sudan, broke away from the Republic of the Sudan at the conclusion of a civil war that began in 1955 and continued, virtually without respite, for fifty-six years. The war produced millions of casualties, and fighting continues, albeit at a low level, between Sudan and South Sudan as each of these successor states endeavors to undermine the other.[18]

When the mainly black and Christian Southerners sought to part company with the largely Arab and Muslim North, Sudan's military rulers responded with vicious force—mass murder, kidnapping, rape, torture, and so forth. Though shocking, the brutality of the Sudanese regime seemed not to surprise most observers. Authoritarian governments almost invariably respond with force if dissidents attempt to bring about change. This is so whether the demand is for change in the makeup of the ruling circle, change in the character of the regime, change in the structure of society, or reconfiguration of the nation's boundaries and composition of the political community.

Hence, when it occurs in the authoritarian context, each of these forms of political change tends to be associated with violence or the threat of violence. Simple leadership transitions are typically the products of coups, while transformations of the regime or elite structure usually require political revolutions, and changes in the nation's borders or political community are generally consequences of war or secession. These forms of political change are sometimes seen as fungible. Some authoritarian rulers will agree to changes in the shape of the regime to save themselves, while their colleagues may prefer to throw the supreme leader to the wolves in order to preserve the overall power structure. Both phenomena have been evident in the recent "Arab Spring," where the leaders of Bahrain, Morocco, and Saudi Arabia, watching the collapse of the Tunisian regime, agreed to some political reforms they hoped would deflect popular antagonism. In Egypt, on the other hand, the military facilitated the ouster of President Hosni Mubarak. The generals hoped that Mubarak's departure would satisfy dissidents and bring an end to the turmoil that threatened the larger political and social order as well as the military's primacy in the corridors of power.[19] Some rulers will even agree to substantial changes in the political community and nation's borders to save their own skins. Thus, it was in the face of civil war and international pressure that threatened his rule that Sudanese leader Omar al-Bashir decided to accept the South's secession in order to firm up his own grip on the remainder of the nation.

Electoral institutions, on the other hand, promote political stability.[20] In some respects elections should be understood as instruments designed to inhibit political change by directing discontent at a small number of officials who can be ousted without disrupting the political and social structure —rather like deposing Mubarak to protect the regime. In the United States, elections some-times disturb but almost never fundamentally transform the nation's governing institutions or even cause more than a momentary disruption in the dense swarm of lobbyists, donors, interest groups, foundations, and other recognized "stakeholders" who form the government's permanent Oort Cloud.

Efforts to bring about more fundamental changes in government and society generally do not receive a friendly reception in the U.S. or the other democracies. Thus, the U.S. government is fond of recommending regime change to others. But those who advocate regime change, rather than mere electoral change, in the United States should probably prepare themselves for serious discussions with the FBI. And, of course, while the United States government urged Sudan to agree to the secession of its South, it did not display the same forbearance when its own South sought to secede a century and a half earlier.

Not surprisingly, the most important changes in American political history are associated with violence, not the ballot box. These include the Revolution, the Civil War, the labor strife of the late nineteenth and early twentieth centuries, and the Civil Rights era. Take the Revolution. The literature of the Revolution seems to emphasize philosophical questions as though it was an academic debate. In fact, the American Revolution began when a segment of the colonial elite, namely a coalition composed of a portion of New England's mercantile stratum along with a substantial fragment of the Southern gentry, embarked upon a campaign to free itself from British mercantilist and other restrictions on its entrepreneurial activities. These restrictions were embodied by the various Navigation Acts, the 1751 Currency Act, the Proclamation of 1763, and the Tea Act of 1773—as well as taxes on their commercial enterprises such as the Sugar Act, Stamp Act, and Townshend Duties. This coalition was joined and radicalized by politicians like Samuel Adams, Patrick Henry, Paul Revere, Robert Yates, Arthur Fenner, Melancton Smith, and Thomas Paine, who spoke for the aspirations of a stratum of educated professionals, tradesmen, printers, craftsmen, agriculturalists, and so forth. Members of this group came to believe that separation from the mother country would provide them with an opportunity to enhance their own political rights and standing vis-à-vis the elites, generally supported by the Crown, who dominated local government in most of the colonies.

The violence of the Revolution claimed as many as 100,000 lives among colonists who fought in the revolutionary army and in the various militias that supported both the revolutionary and British causes. Many others died in fighting in New York and the Carolinas as a virtual civil war broke out between rebels and loyalists after British forces withdrew.[21] Since the colonial population was under 3 million individuals, the Revolution may have claimed the lives of nearly 3 percent of the populace. After the Revolution, nearly 100,000 loyalists fled to Canada and other parts of the British realm to escape threats and reprisals from the victorious patriots.

The result of this revolutionary violence was not only independence for the colonies but a significant change in the balance of power within the former colonies. The pre-revolutionary colonial elite had divided on the question of breaking from the mother country and was now weakened by the departure of those of its members who had supported the British cause. Subsequent elections were held within the context of the regime established by the Revolution until a new episode of political violence—the Civil War—significantly altered the character of the regime once again. Violence, not voting, was the driving force of political change. Absent violence, the likelihood of what politicians like to call "change we can believe in" is reduced.

Violence is terrible, but its alternative is not the Kingdom of Heaven. Not only is violence a great engine of political change but, much as we dislike admitting it, violence is also the great driver of science and even culture. After all, along with love, violence inspires poetry, art, music, and literature. In Anthony Burgess's dystopian novel *A Clockwork Orange*, the protagonist Alex DeLarge loses his love of Beethoven when a government clinic subjects him to a therapy that cures his violent impulses. And in Carol Reed's superb 1949 film *The Third Man*, Harry Lime (Orson Welles) famously declares, "In Italy, for thirty years under the Borgias they had warfare, terror, murder, bloodshed—but they produced Michelangelo, Leonardo da Vinci, and the Renaissance. In Switzerland they had brotherly love, 500 years of democracy and peace, and what did that produce? The cuckoo clock." Would a peaceful world, particularly a Hobbesian world, be a world of Beethoven or a realm of cuckoo clocks?

Of course, it may be presumptuous to think that the choice is entirely ours. Walter Benjamin introduced not only the categories of law-making and law-preserving violence to which I alluded above, but also a third category. This he called "divine violence," a form of violence that was, he said, neither an end nor a means but was, instead, pure violence without reason or explanation, as if the work of God. For Benjamin, law-making and law-preserving violence reflect the ordinary ebb and flow of human affairs. Regimes arise, developing laws and institutions through which to affirm their power and are, in turn, assailed by opponents who seek to impose their own laws and practices.

Outside this cycle, though, is pure and spontaneous violence. Benjamin appears to have in mind the sort of unplanned and uncoordinated paroxysm of rage, looting, rape, and murder sometimes associated with the final collapse of an empire or civilization. Divine violence sweeps away the existing order of things and without any particular design or pattern opens the way for a new world. For better or worse, divine violence is also part of human history. Indeed, if we consider violence emanating from the natural world to be a species of divine violence, we can learn from the jurist Richard Posner and the historian William McNeill that such violence is a recurrent and inevitable phenomenon that dramatically changes the course of history.[22] Sooner or later, God scourges the world and gives it an opportunity to begin again.

NOTES

INTRODUCTION. VIOLENCE OFTEN *IS* THE ANSWER

1. Mason L. Weems, *The Life of George Washington*, ed. Marcus Cunliffe (Cambridge, MA: Belknap Press of Harvard University, 1962).

2. Mary Ann Akers, "Heard on the Hill," *Roll Call*, January 4, 2007, p. 1.

3. Pew Center for the People and the Press, "The State of the News Media 2004."

4. Joseph Nye, Philip Zelikow, and David King, *Why People Don't Trust Government* (Cambridge, MA: Harvard University Press, 1997), p. 5.

5. Kevin Mattson and Richard C. Leone, *Engaging Youth: Combating the Apathy of Young Americans toward Politics* (New York: Century Foundation Press, 2003).

6. Ilene Grossman, "To Combat Cynicism and Voter Apathy, States Turn to Civic Education," in the Midwestern Council of State Governments, *Firstline* 7, no. 5 (May 2000): 1.

7. Dale Turner, "Cynical Voices Can't Sing a Song of Peace," *Seattle Times*, March 29, 2003.

8. For recent examples, see Frank Rich, *The Greatest Story Ever Sold* (New York: Penguin, 2006).

9. Quoted in Alexander Cockburn and Jeffrey St. Clair, eds., "Weapons of Mass Destruction: Who Said What When," in *Counterpunch*, May 29, 2003, p. 1.

10. Ambrose Bierce, *The Unabridged Devil's Dictionary* (Athens: University of Georgia Press, 2001).

11. The National Election Studies, Center for Political Studies, University of Michigan, 1952–2002.

12. According to a 2002 Roper Poll, 70 percent of all Americans believe the government is hiding information about UFOs.

13. The phrase is associated with Fang Lejun, Liu Wei, and other artists working in the aftermath of the 1989 Tiananmen Square massacre.

14. Niccolò Machiavelli, *The Prince* (New York: Mentor, 1952), p. 50.

15. Ibid., ch. 17, p. 90.

16. Steven Pinker, *How the Mind Works* (New York: W. W. Norton, 1997), p. 495.

17. Vamik Volkan, "Narcissistic Personality Disorder and Reparative Leadership," *International Journal of Group Psychotherapy* 30 (1980): 131–52.

18. Donald Kagan, *The Peloponnesian War* (New York: Penguin, 2003), p. 212.

19. Henry A. Turner, *General Motors and the Nazis* (New Haven, CT: Yale University Press, 2005).

CHAPTER 1. VIOLENCE: THE DRIVING FORCE OF POLITICAL LIFE

1. Steven Pinker, *The Blank Slate: The Modern Denial of Human Nature* (New York: Penguin, 2003), ch. 17.

2. Winston Churchill, "Shall We Commit Suicide?" *Nash's Pall Mall Magazine*, September 24, 1924.

3. Thomas Hobbes, *Leviathan* (New York: Oxford University Press, 1957), p. 185.

4. Carl von Clausewitz, *On War* (New York: Brownstone, 2009).

5. James Randall, "The Blundering Generation," *Mississippi Valley Historical Review* 27 (June 1940): 2–28.

6. Steven Pinker, *The Better Angels of Our Nature: Why Violence Has Declined* (New York: Viking, 2011).

7. E. Marshall, "The Shots Heard Round the World," *Science* 289 (2000): 570–74.

8. Hannah Arendt, *On Violence* (New York: Harcourt, 1969), p. 9.

9. Roderick MacFarquhar and Michael Schoenhals, *Mao's Last Revolution* (Cambridge, MA: Belknap Press, 2008).

10. Charles Tilly, *Coercion, Capital and European States* (Oxford, UK: Blackwell, 1990).

11. Victor Davis Hanson, *Carnage and Culture* (New York: Doubleday, 2001).

12. Jacqueline Rose, *The Question of Zion* (Princeton: Princeton University Press, 2005).

13. Walter Benjamin, "Critique of Violence," in Marcus Bullock and Michael W. Jennings, *Walter Benjamin: Selected Writings, Vol. 1* (Cambridge, MA: Belknap Press of Harvard University, 1996), p. 240.

14. Barrington Moore Jr., *Social Origins of Dictatorship and Democracy* (Boston: Beacon Press, 1966).

15. Nicholas Kulish, "As Scorn for Vote Grows, Protests Surge around Globe," *New York Times*, September 28, 2011.

16. Robert Putnam, *The Comparative Study of Political Elites* (Englewood Cliffs, NJ: Prentice Hall), 1976.

17. Richard Zuczek, *State of Rebellion: Reconstruction in South Carolina* (Columbia: University of South Carolina Press, 1996).

18. Vasil N. Zlatarski, *Istoria na Bulgarskata* (Sofia, Bulgaria: Akademichno uzd-vo Marin Drinov, 1994) vol. 2, pp. 1–41.

19. Jake Sherman, "Steny Hoyer: Members Are at Risk," *Politico.com*, March 24, 2010, http://www.politico.com/news/stories/0310/34953.html.

20. Niccolò Machiavelli, *The Prince* (New York: Mentor, 1952), ch. 7.

21. Erica Chenoweth and Maria J. Stephan, *Why Civil Resistance Works: The Strategic Logic of Nonviolent Conflict* (New York: Columbia University Press, 2011).

22. Saul D. Alinsky, *Rules for Radicals* (New York: Vintage Books, 1971).

23. David Garrow, *Bearing the Cross: Martin Luther King, Jr., and the Southern Christian Leadership Conference* (New York: Random House, 1986).

24. Hugh Davis Graham, *The Civil Rights Era* (New York: Oxford University Press, 1990).

25. David Garrow, *Protest at Selma* (New Haven, CT: Yale University Press, 1968).

26. Stephen Lawson, *Black Ballots* (New York: Columbia University Press, 1976).

27. Howell Raines, *My Heart Is Rested* (New York: Putnam's, 1977).

28. Mary Boykin Chesnut, *A Diary from Dixie*, ed. Ben Ames Williams (Cambridge, MA: Harvard University Press, 1980), p. 38.

29. Mao Zedong, "On Contradiction," *Selected Works of Mao Tse-Tung* (Peking, China: Foreign Languages Press, 1937), vol. 1, p. 344.

30. Steven Cohen and William Eimicke, *The New Effective Public Manager* (San Francisco: Jossey-Bass, 1995), ch. 10.

31. Kai T. Erikson, *Wayward Puritans* (New York: Wiley, 1966).

32. Charles Tilly, "War Making and State Making as Organized Crime," in Peter Evans, Dietrich Rueschemeyer, and Theda Skocpol, eds., *Bringing the State Back In* (New York: Cambridge University Press, 1985), pp. 169–85.

33. Charles Tilly, *Coercion, Capital and European States, AD 990–1992* (Malden, MA: Blackwell, 1992), p. 67.

34. Barrington Moore Jr., *Terror and Progress USSR* (Cambridge, MA: Harvard University Press, 1954).

35. Harold Lasswell and Daniel Lerner, eds., *World Revolutionary Elites* (Cambridge, MA: MIT Press, 1966).

36. Peter Merkl, *Political Violence under the Swastika* (Princeton: Princeton University Press, 1975).

37. In Fascist Italy. Social mobility was most pronounced in what Lasswell and Sereno call "rising agencies"—governmental agencies either established by, or whose powers were enlarged by, the Fascist regime. Harold D. Lasswell and Renzo Sereno, "The Fascists: The Changing Italian Elite," in Lasswell and Lerner, *World Revolutionary Elites*. Social transformation in Nazi Germany is discussed in David Schoenbaum, *Hitler's Social Revolution* (New York: Norton, 1980).

38. H. H. Gerth and C. Wright Mills, *From Max Weber: Essays in Sociology* (New York: Oxford University Press, 1946), p. 228.

39. Cornelius M. Kerwin, *Rulemaking*, 3rd ed. (Washington, DC: CQ Press, 2003), ch. 6.

40. Philip Selznick, *TVA and the Grass Roots* (Berkeley: University of California Press, 1949).

41. Harold Seidman, *Politics, Position and Power: The Dynamics of Federal Organization*, 5th ed. (New York: Oxford University Press, 1998), ch. 8.

42. James Q. Wilson, *Bureaucracy: What Government Agencies Do and Why They Do It* (New York: Basic Books, 1989), p. 91.

43. Robert M. Fogelson, *Violence as Protest* (New York: Doubleday, 1971), p. 62.

44. Ibid.

45. Ibid., p. 55.

46. Leonard N. Moore, *Black Rage in New Orleans: Police Brutality and African American Activism* (Baton Rouge: Louisiana State University Press, 2010).

47. Fogelson, *Violence as Protest*, p. 52.

48. Ibid., pp. 50–51.

49. Ibid., p. 54.

50. Robert C. Wadman and William T. Allison, *To Protect and to Serve: A History of Police in America* (Upper Saddle River, NJ: Pearson, Prentice Hall, 2004), ch. 9.

51. MacFarquhar and Schoenhas, *Mao's Last Revolution*.

52. Goran Therborn, "The Rule of Capital and the Rise of Democracy," *New Left Review*, no. 103 (May 1977): 3–41.

53. Catherine Lyle Cleverdon, *The Woman Suffrage Movement in Canada* (Toronto: University of Toronto Press, 1950).

54. Pinker, *Blank Slate*, ch. 17.

55. Peter Pulzer, *The Rise of Political Anti-Semitism in Germany and Austria* (Cambridge, MA: Harvard University Press, 1988), pp. 315–16.

56. Martha Crenshaw, "The Causes of Terrorism," in Catherine Besteman, ed., *Violence: A Reader* (New York: New York University Press, 2002), p. 108.

57. Gilles Kepel, *Jihad: The Trail of Political Islam* (Cambridge, MA: Belknap Press of Harvard University, 2002), p. 159.

58. Oskar Verkaaik, *Migrants and Militants* (Princeton: Princeton University Press, 2004).

59. Pinker, *Blank Slate*, p. 308.

60. Slavoj Žižek, *Violence* (New York: Picador, 2008), p. 9.

61. James Q. Wilson and George Kelling, "Broken Windows," http://www.manhattan-institute.org/pdf/_atlantic_monthly-broken_windows.pdf.

62. Thomas Hobbes, *Leviathan*, ed. Ian Shapiro (New Haven, CT: Yale University Press, 2010).

63. Immanuel Kant, "Perpetual Peace: A Philosophical Sketch," http://www.mtholyoke.edu/acad/intrel/kant/kant1.htm.

64. Pinker, *Better Angels*, p. 680.

65. Thomas Hobbes, *Leviathan*, ed. Michael Oakeshott (New York: Collier, 1962), p. 132.

66. Charles D. Tarleton, "The Despotical Doctrine of Hobbes, Part II: Aspects of the Textual Substructure of Tyranny in Leviathan," *History of Political Thought* 23, no. 1 (Spring 2002): 82.

67. Hobbes, *Leviathan*, p. 141.

68. Ibid., p. 133.

69. James Lee Ray, "Wars between Democracies: Rare, or Nonexistent?" *International Interactions* 18, no. 3 (February 1993). Also, Joanne Gowa, *Ballots and Bullets: The Elusive Democratic Peace* (Princeton: Princeton University Press, 1999) and Sebastian Rosato, "The Flawed Logic of Democratic Theory," *American Political Science Review* 97 (2003): 585–602.

70. Reinhold Niebuhr, *Christianity and Power Politics* (New York: Scribner's, 1940), p. 16.

CHAPTER 2. BUREAUCRACY AND VIOLENCE

1. Martin Van Creveld, *Supplying War: Logistics from Wallenstein to Patton* (New York: Cambridge University Press, 1977).

2. Hannah Arendt, *Eichmann in Jerusalem: A Report on the Banality of Evil* (New York: Viking Press, 1964), p. 106.

3. Iver Bernstein, *The New York City Draft Riots* (Lincoln: University of Nebraska Press, 1990).

4. Ibid., pp. 62–63.

5. Linda Melvern, *Conspiracy to Murder: The Rwandan Genocide* (London: Verso, 2001).

6. "Organizations and Functions of the Department of Defense," http://odam.defense.gov/omp/Functions/Organizational_Portfolios/Organization_and_Functions_Guidebook.html.

7. John J. McGrath, *The Other End of the Spear: The Tooth-to-Tail Ratio (T3R) in Modern Military Operations* (Fort Leavenworth, KS: Combat Studies Institute Press, 2007), http://www.cgsc.edu/carl/download/csipubs/mcgrath_op23.pdf.

8. D. Robert Worley, *Shaping U.S. Military Forces* (Westport, CT: Praeger, 2006), ch. 3.

9. Harold Seidman, *Politics, Position and Power*, 5th ed. (New York: Oxford University Press, 1998), p. 209.

10. Jacob N. Shapiro, "Bureaucracy and Control in Terrorist Organizations," http://www.princeton.edu/~jns/papers/Shapiro_Bureaucracy_Control_Terrorism_2.pdf (2008).

11. James Q. Wilson, *Bureaucracy* (New York: Basic Books, 1989), ch. 1.

12. Martin Van Creveld, *Supplying War*, 2nd ed. (Cambridge: Cambridge University Press, 2004), p. 205.

13. Donald W. Engels, *Alexander the Great and the Logistics of the Macedonian Army* (Berkeley: University of California Press, 1990).

14. Timothy May, *The Mongol Art of War* (Yardley, PA: Westholme Publishing, 2007).

15. Victor Davis Hanson, *Carnage and Culture* (New York: Doubleday, 2001), p. 77.

16. Van Creveld, *Supplying War*, 2nd ed., p. 82.

17. Ibid., p. 97.

18. Geoffrey Perrett, *A Country Made by War* (New York: Random House, 1989), p. 230.

19. Russell F. Weigley, *The American Way of War* (Bloomington: Indiana University Press, 1973), p. 131.

20. Ibid.

21. Perrett, *Country Made by War*, p. 322.

22. Joanne E. Johnson, "The Army Industrial College and Mobilization Planning between the Wars," Industrial College of the Armed Forces, National Defense University, Fort McNair, District of Columbia, 1993.

23. Randall Collins, *Violence: A Micro-Sociological Theory* (Princeton: Princeton University Press, 2008).

24. Karl Marlantes, *What It Is Like to Go to War* (New York: Atlantic Monthly Press, 2011).

25. The exception involves what Collins calls "forward panic," most often associated with military confrontations when armies in retreat are slaughtered by their advancing foes. Collins, *Violence*, ch. 3.

26. S. L. A. Marshall, *Men against Fire: The Problem of Battle Command* (Norman: University of Oklahoma Press, 1947).

27. Collins, *Violence*, p. 61.

28. John Keegan, *The Face of Battle* (New York: Random House, 1976), pp. 311–13.

29. Collins, *Violence*, p. 63.

30. Ibid., p. 376.

31. David A. Grossman, *On Killing* (Boston: Little, Brown, 1995), p. 180.

32. Warren Christopher, ed., *Report of the Independent Commission on the Los Angeles Police Department* (Los Angeles: Dane Publishing, 1991).

33. Marvin Wolfgang, Robert Figlio, and Thorsten Sellin, *Delinquency in a Birth Cohort* (Chicago: University of Chicago Press, 1972).

34. Collins, *Violence*, p. 370.

35. Grossman, *On Killing*, p. 30.

36. Ibid., p. 107.

37. Thomas Ricks, *Making the Corps* (New York: Touchstone, 1997).

38. Grossman, *On Killing*, p. 177.

39. Ibid., p. 260.

40. Ibid., p. 258.

41. Stanley Milgram, *Obedience to Authority* (New York: Harper, 1974).

42. Christopher Browning, *Ordinary Men: Reserve Police Battalion 101 and the Final Solution in Poland* (New York: Harper, 1998).

43. Ibid., p. 176.

44. Grossman, *On Killing*, p. 160.

45. Ibid., p. 145.

46. Wilson, *Bureaucracy*, ch. 1.

47. Daniel Goldhagen estimates that at least 100,000 Germans but possibly more were directly involved in physical assaults against Jews and in actual murders. See Daniel Goldhagen, *Hitler's Willing Executioners: Ordinary Germans and the Holocaust* (New York: Vintage, 1997), p. 166.

48. Goldhagen, *Hitler's Willing Executioners*, p. 167.

49. Ibid.

50. Raul Hilberg, *Perpetrators, Victims and Bystanders* (New York: HarperCollins, 1992).

51. Milgram, *Obedience to Authority*, p. 48.

52. Zygmunt Bauman, *Modernity and the Holocaust* (Ithaca, NY: Cornell University Press, 2000), p. 215.

53. An adiapharon was something declared indifferent, neither good nor evil—by the Church. Ibid., p. 215.

54. In recent years, the public's fear of crime, fueled by claims of ambitious politicians that their opponents were "soft on crime," did indeed play a role in the enactment of harsh sentencing policies and a decay of prison conditions. See David Garland, *The Culture of Control: Crime and Social Order in Contemporary Society* (Chicago: University of Chicago Press, 2001). Also, Jonathon Simon, *Governing through Crime: How the War on Crime Transformed American Democracy and Created a Culture of Fear* (New York: Oxford University Press, 2007).

55. James E. Robertson, "A Clean Heart and an Empty Head: The Supreme Court and Sexual Terrorism in Prison," *N.C.L. Rev.* 81, no. 433 (January 2003): 477.

56. Human Rights Watch, World Report 2000, part 1, p. 5.

57. Stephen Donaldson, "The Rape Crisis Behind Bars," *New York Times*, December 29, 1993.

58. Robertson, "Clean Heart," p. 441.

59. Ibid., p. 435.

60. David Kaiser and Lovisa Stannow, "Prison Rape: Obama's Program to Stop It," *New York Review*, October 11, 2012, p. 51.

61. Lynette Clemetson, "Links between Prison and AIDS Affecting Blacks Inside and Out," *New York Times*, August 6, 2004.

62. Will A. Smith, "Civil Liability for Sexual Assault in Prison," *Cumb. L. Rev.* 34, no. 289 (2003/2004).

63. Robertson, "Clean Heart," p. 446.

64. Ibid., p. 447.

65. Ibid.

66. Ibid., p. 448.

67. Quoted in ibid.

68. Olga Giller, "Deliberate Indifference and Male Prison Rape," *Cardozo Women's L.J.* 10, no. 659 (Summer 2004).

69. Shara Abraham, "Male Rape in U.S. Prisons," *Hum. Rts. Br.* 9, no. 5 (Fall 2001).

70. Ibid., p. 7.

71. See *Hudson v. McMillan*, 503 U.S. 1 (1992).

72. 509 U.S. 25 (1993).

73. 429 U.S. 97 (1976).

74. 501 U.S. 294 (1991).

75. 511 U.S. 825 (1994).

76. *Bounds v. Smith*, 430 U.S. 817 (1977).

77. 403 U.S. 388 (1971).

78. Abraham, "Male Rape," p. 7.

79. *Farmer v. Brennan*, at 858.

80. Abraham, "Male Rape," p. 7.

81. *Estelle v. Gamble*, 429 U.S. 97 (1976).

82. *Bencon v. Cady*, 761 F.2d. 235 (7th Cir. 1985).

83. *McGill v. Duckworth*, 944 F.2d 344, 350 (1991).

84. *Farmer*, at 835.

85. Id. at 834.

86. Ibid.

87. *Pope v. Shafer*, 86 F.3rd 90 (7th Cir. 1996).

88. *Berry v. Muskogee*, 900 F.2d 1489 (10th Cir. 1990).

89. *Benny v. Pipes*, 799 F.2d 489 (9th Cir. 1996).

90. 917 F.2d. 1449 (6th Cir. 1990).

91. Id. at 1453.

92. No. 94-6916, 1995 U.S. App. Lexis 13283 (4th Cir. 1995).

93. *Arnold v. Jones*, 891 F.2d 1370 (8th Cir. 1989).

94. 467 F.Supp. 1339 (D. Md. 1979).

95. Leo Carroll, *Hacks, Blacks and Cons* (Long Grove, IL: Waveland Press, 1982).

96. 390 U.S. 333 (1968).

97. 995 F.2d 1526 (11th Cir. 1993).

98. 845 F.2d 763 (8th Cir. 1988).

99. Robertson, "Clean Heart," pp. 453–54.

100. *Turner v. Sufley*, 482 U.S. 78 (1987).

101. *Redman v. County of San Diego*, 942 F.2d. 1435 (9th Cir. 1991).

102. 254 F.3d 617 (6th Cir. 2001).

103. 100 F.3rd 1235 (7th Cir. 1996).

104. Id. at 1239.

105. Id. at 1241.

106. 183 F. Supp. 2d 814 (E.D. Va. 2001).

107. See *Kish v. County of Milwaukee*, 441 F.2d. 901 (7th Cir. 1971).

108. Id. at 822.

109. *Hedrick and Jones v. Roberts*, at 822.

110. 107 F.3rd 549 (7th Cir. 1997).

111. Id. at 554.

112. 385 F.3d 503 (2004).

113. *Johnson v. Johnson*, at 513.

114. Id. at 513.

115. Ibid.

116. Id. at 526.

117. 161 F3d. 1127 (8th Cir. 1998)

118. Id. at 1129.

119. 149 F.3rd 783 (8th Cir. 1998).

120. Id. at 786, quoting *Farmer*.

121. See Justice Blackmun's *Farmer* concurrence at 854.

CHAPTER 3. FORCE AND GOVERNANCE

1. Barrington Moore Jr., *Terror and Progress USSR* (New York: Harper, 1954), p. 175.

2. James Madison, *Federalist No. 62*, in Clinton Rossiter, ed., *The Federalist Papers* (New York: Mentor, 1961), p. 381.

3. Alexei Anishchuk, "Medvedev Says Poor Rule of Law Holds Russia Back," Reuters, May 20, 2011, www.reuters.com.

4. Randall Peerenboom, *China's Long March toward Rule of Law* (Cambridge: Cambridge University Press, 2002).

5. See Jonathan Simon, *Governing through Crime: How the War on Crime Transformed American Democracy and Created a Culture of Fear* (New York: Oxford University Press, 2007) Also, David Garland, *The Culture of Control* (Chicago: University of Chicago Press, 2001).

6. James Madison, "Concerning Public Opinion," *National Gazette*, December 19, 1791.

7. Hannah Arendt, *On Violence* (New York: Harcourt, 1969), ch. 2.

8. Leon Trotsky, *The Russian Revolution* (New York: Simon & Schuster, 1932), ch. 7.

9. Gary Bruce, *The Firm: The Inside Story of the Stasi* (New York: Oxford University Press, 2011).

10. Tom R. Tyler, *Why People Obey the Law* (Princeton: Princeton University Press, 2006).

11. Samuel E. Finer, "State and Nation-Building in Europe: The Role of the Military," in Charles Tilly, ed., *The Formation of National States in Western Europe* (Princeton: Princeton University Press, 1975), pp. 84–163.

12. Kai Erikson, *Wayward Puritans* (New York: Wiley, 1966).

13. Charles Tilly, "War Making and State Making as Organized Crime," in Peter Evans, Dietrich Rueschemeyer, and Theda Skocpol, eds., *Bringing the State Back In* (Cambridge: Cambridge University Press, 1985).

14. Geoffrey W. Conrad and Arthur A. Demarest, *Religion and Empire* (Cambridge: Cambridge University Press, 1984), p. 186.

15. A. Barahona de Brito, P. Aguilar, C. Gonzalez Enriquez, Introduction, in *The Politics*

of Memory: Transitional Justice in Democratizing Societies (Oxford: Oxford University Press, 2001), pp. 1–39; Priscilla B. Hayner, *In Pursuit of Justice and Reconciliation: Contributions of Truth Telling. Comparative Peace Processes in Latin America*, ed. C. J. Arnson (Washington, DC: Woodrow Wilson Center Press, 1999), pp. 363–83; David Pion-Berlin, "To Prosecute or to Pardon? Human Rights Decisions in the Latin American Southern Cone," *Human Rights Quarterly* 16, no. 1 (1994): 105–30.

16. Eugen Weber, *Peasants into Frenchmen* (Stanford: Stanford University Press, 1976), p. 70.

17. Benjamin Ginsberg and Robert Weissberg, "Elections as Legitimizing Institutions," *American Journal of Political Science* (February 1978).

18. Sar Levitan and Diane Werneke, *Productivity: Problems, Prospects and Policies* (Baltimore: Johns Hopkins University Press, 1984), ch. 3.

19. Max Farrand, ed., *The Records of the Federal Convention of 1787* (New Haven, CT: Yale University Press, 1966), vol. 1, p. 49.

20. Ibid., p. 132.

21. Matthew A. Crenson and Benjamin Ginsberg, *Downsizing Democracy* (Baltimore: Johns Hopkins University Press, 2002).

22. Goran Therborn, "The Rule of Capitalism and the Rise of Democracy," *New Left Review*, no. 103 (May 1977): 3–41.

23. Julie Mason, "Obama Invokes Faith as Campaign Nears," *Washington Examiner*, February 6, 2011.

24. "Clergy's Wages Not to Decrease Next Year," *Prague Daily Monitor*, December 9, 2010, http://praguemonitor.com/2010/12/09/clergys-wages-not-decrease-next-year.

25. Luis E. Lugo, "International Obligations and the Morality of War," *Society* 44 (2007): 109–12.

26. James K. Wellman, *Evangelical vs. Liberal* (New York: Oxford University Press, 2008).

27. Andrew Higgins, "Putin and Orthodox Church Cement Power in Russia," *Wall Street Journal*, December 18, 2007.

28. Alex Inkeles and Raymond Bauer, *The Soviet Citizen* (Cambridge, MA: Harvard University Press, 1959), ch. 10.

29. Meyer Kestnbaum, "Citizen Soldiers, National Service and the Mass Army: The Birth of Conscription in Revolutionary Europe and North America," in Lars Mjøset and Stephen Van Holde, eds., *The Comparative Study of Conscription in the Armed Forces* (New York: Elsevier, 2002), p. 118.

30. Ibid.

31. Ira Katznelson, "Flexible Capacity: The Military and Early American Statebuilding," in Ira Katznelson and Martin Shefter, eds., *Shaped by War and Trade: International Influences on American Political Development* (Princeton, NJ: Princeton University Press, 2002), pp. 82–110.

32. Margaret Levi, *Consent, Dissent and Patriotism* (Cambridge: Cambridge University Press, 1997), p. 64.

33. Khaled Fahmy, "The Nation and Its Deserters: Conscription in Mehmed Ali's Egypt," in Erik J. Zurcher, ed., *Arming the State: Military Conscription in the Middle East and Central Asia 1775–1925* (London: I. B. Tauris, 1999), pp. 59–78.

34. Levi, *Consent, Dissent and Patriotism*, p. 65.

35. Iver Bernstein, *The New York City Draft Riots* (Lincoln: University of Nebraska Press, 1990).

36. George Q. Flynn, *The Draft, 1940–1973* (Lawrence: University Press of Kansas, 1993).

37. Damien Cave, "Desperate Guatemalans Embrace an 'Iron Fist,'" *New York Times*, September 10, 2011, http://www.nytimes.com/2011/09/10/world/americas/10guatemala.html?_r=1&ref=world.

38. Joseph S. Nye Jr., *Soft Power: The Means to Success in World Politics* (New York: Public Affairs Press, 2004), p. 7.

39. Ibid.

CHAPTER 4. AMERICA: A TOUGH NATION

1. *Never Give In!: The Best of Winston Churchill's Speeches* (New York: Hyperion, 2003), p. 352.

2. William Smith, *Dictionary of Greek and Roman Antiquities* (Boston: Little, Brown, 1870), vol. 3, p. 750.

3. Stephen M. Kohn, *Jailed for Peace* (New York: Praeger, 1987), ch. 3.

4. Benjamin Ginsberg and Martin Shefter, *Politics by Other Means*, 3rd ed. (New York: W. W. Norton, 2002), p. 92.

5. Daniel Wirls, *Irrational Security: The Politics of Defense from Reagan to Obama* (Baltimore: Johns Hopkins University Press, 2010).

6. Marie Gottschalk, *The Prison and the Gallows: The Politics of Mass Incarceration in America* (New York: Cambridge University Press, 2006). Also, James Q. Whitman, *Harsh Justice: Criminal Punishment and the Widening Gap between America and Europe* (New York: Oxford University Press, 2003).

7. Alfred Blumstein and Allen J. Beck, "Reentry as a Transient State between Liberty and Recommitment," in Jeremy Travis and Christy Visher, eds., *Prisoner Reentry and Crime in America* (New York: Cambridge University Press, 2005).

8. Robert Goldstein, *Political Repression in Modern America* (New York: Schenkman, 1978), ch. 1.

9. Ibid., p. 72.

10. Elaine Cassell, *The War on Civil Liberties* (New York: Lawrence Hill Books, 2004).

11. Geoffrey Perret, *A Country Made by War* (New York: Random House, 1989), p. 558.

12. Frances Fox Piven and Richard A. Cloward, *Regulating the Poor: The Functions of Public Welfare* (New York: Vintage, 1971).

13. For example, see Steven D. Levitt, "Why Do Increased Arrest Rates Appear to Reduce Crime: Deterrence, Incapacitation, or Measurement Error? *Economic Inquiry* 36, no. 3 (July 1968): 353–72; David Downes and Kristine Hansen, "Welfare and Punishment: The Relationship between Welfare Spending and Imprisonment," *Crime and Society* (November 2006); Junsen Zhang, "The Effect of Welfare Programs on Criminal Behavior: A Theoretical and Empirical Analysis," *Economic Inquiry* 35, no. 1 (January 1997): 120–37.

14. Whitman, *Harsh Justice*.

15. Ibid., p. 27.

16. "The Welfare State and Military Power," *Wall Street Journal*, December 4, 2009, http://online.wsj.com/article/SB10001424052748704107104574573711965511326.html.

17. Works include Louis Hartz, *The Liberal Tradition in America* (New York: Harcourt, 1955); Daniel Boorstin, *The Genius of American Politics* (Chicago: University of Chicago Press, 1953); and Seymour Martin Lipset, *American Exceptionalism: A Double-Edged Sword* (New York: Norton, 1997).

18. Alberto Alesina and Edward Glaeser, *Fighting Poverty in the U.S. and Europe: A World of Difference* (New York: Oxford University Press, 2006).

19. Piven and Cloward, *Regulating the Poor*, p. 46.

20. Theda Skocpol, *Protecting Soldiers and Mothers: The Political Origins of Social Policy in the United States* (Cambridge, MA: Harvard University Press, 1996), p. 103.

21. Ibid., p. 102.

22. Richard Bensel and Elizabeth Sanders, "The Impact of the Voting Rights Act on Southern Welfare Systems," in Benjamin Ginsberg and Alan Stone, eds., *Do Elections Matter?* (Armonk, NY: M. E. Sharpe, 1986), pp. 52–70.

23. Martin Gilens, *Why Americans Hate Welfare* (Chicago: University of Chicago Press, 1999).

24. See, for example, the testimony of Cato Institute analyst Michael Tanner before the Senate Judiciary Committee, June 7, 1995, http://www.cato.org/publications/congressional-testimony/relationship-between-welfare-state-crime-0.

25. Andrew J. Bacevich, *Washington Rules: America's Path to Permanent War* (New York: Metropolitan Books, 2010), p. 33.

26. Lewis Anthony Dexter, "Congressmen and the Making of Military Policy," in *New Perspectives on the House of Representatives*, ed. Robert Peabody and Nelson Polsby (Chicago: Rand McNally, 1963), pp. 305–24.

27. Allan R. Millett, Peter Maslowski, and William Feis, *For the Common Defense: A Military History of the United States from 1607 to 2012*, 3rd ed. (New York: Free Press, 2012), ch. 10.

28. Allan R. Millett, *Semper Fidelis: The History of the United States Marine Corps* (New York: Free Press, 1991), pp. 292–96.

29. Millett, Maslowski, and Feis, *For the Common Defense*, p. 366.

30. Ibid., p. 515.

31. Michael Hogan, *A Cross of Iron* (New York: Cambridge University Press, 1998), p. 151.

32. George Q. Flynn, *The Draft* (Lawrence: University Press of Kansas, 1993), p. 141.

33. Millett, Maslowski, and Feis, *For the Common Defense*, p. 517.

34. Aaron L. Friedberg, "American Antistatism and the Founding of the Cold War State," in Ira Katznelson and Martin Shefter, eds., *Shaped by War and Trade: International Influences on American Political Development* (Princeton, NJ: Princeton University Press, 2002), p. 254.

35. Paul Koistinen, *The Hammer and the Sword: Labor, the Military and Industrial Production, 1920–1945* (New York: Arno Press, 1979), p. 580.

36. Ken Silverstein, *Private Warriors* (London: Verso, 2000), ch. 5.

37. Harold Seidman, *Politics, Position and Power*, 5th ed. (New York: Oxford University Press, 1998), pp. 208–11.

38. Ann Markusen, Peter Hall, Scott Campbell, and Sabina Deitrick, *The Rise of the Gunbelt: The Military Remapping of Industrial America* (New York: Oxford University Press, 1991), ch. 10.

39. John P. Burke, *The Institutional Presidency*, 2nd ed. (Baltimore: Johns Hopkins University Press, 2000), pp. 37–40.

40. Joel R. Paul, "The Geopolitical Constitution: Executive Expediency and Executive Agreements," *University of California Law Review* 86 (July 1998): 713–14.

41. Ibid., pp. 720–21.

42. Ibid., sect. 3. Also, Louis Fisher, *The Politics of Shared Power*, 4th ed. (College Station: Texas A&M University Press, 1998), pp. 190–91.

43. Harold W. Stanley and Richard Niemi, *Vital Statistics on American Politics, 2001–2002* (Washington, DC: Congressional Quarterly Press, 2001), p. 334.

44. John C. Yoo, "Laws as Treaties?: The Constitutionality of Congressional-Executive Agreements," *University of Michigan Law Review* 99, no. 757 (February 2001).

45. Phillip J. Cooper, *By Order of the President* (Lawrence: University Press of Kansas, 2002), p. 144.

46. Ibid., p. 158.

47. Rhodri Jeffreys-Jones, *The CIA & American Democracy* ((New Haven, CT: Yale University Press, 1989), pp. 55–56.

48. Arthur Schlesinger, *The Imperial Presidency* (Boston: Houghton-Mifflin, 1973), p. 167.

49. Robert J. Donovan, *Conflict and Crisis: The Presidency of Harry S. Truman, 1945–1948* (New York: W. W. Norton, 1977), pp. 296–97.

50. Athan Theoharis, ed., *The Truman Presidency: The Origins of the Imperial Presidency and the National Security State* (Stanfordville, NY: E. M. Coleman, 1979), pp. 257–61.

51. Schlesinger, *Imperial Presidency*, ch. 10.

52. Margaret Myers, *A Financial History of the United States* (New York: Columbia University Press, 1970), ch. 15.

53. Friedberg, "American Antistatism," p. 250.

54. Sidney Ratner, *American Taxation: Its History as a Social Force in Democracy* (New York: W. W. Norton, 1942), p. 72.

55. Joseph A. Pechman, *Federal Tax Policy*, 5th ed. (Washington, DC: Brookings, 1987), pp. 355–63. Also, B. Guy Peters, *The Politics of Taxation* (Cambridge, MA: Blackwell, 1991), pp. 1–15.

56. Todd Sandler and Keith Hartley, *The Economics of Defense* (Cambridge: Cambridge University Press, 1995), ch. 10. Also, Michael T. Klare, *American Arms Supermarket* (Austin: University of Texas Press, 1984), p. 34.

57. David Gold, "The Changing Economics of the Arms Trade," in Ann Markusen and Sean Costigan, eds., *Arming the Future* (New York: Council on Foreign Relations Press, 1999), pp. 249–68.

58. Larry Neal, *War Finance* (Brookfield, VT: Edward Elgar Publishing, 1994), vol. 1, p. 3.

59. Dean Acheson, *Present at the Creation* (New York: W. W. Norton, 1987), ch. 26.

60. Malcolm Chalmers, *Sharing Security: The Political Economy of Burdensharing* (London: Macmillan, 2000), p. 33.

61. Millett, Maslowski, and Feis, *For the Common Defense*, p. 519.

62. Schlesinger, *Imperial Presidency*, p. 165.

63. Ibid., pp. 200–207.

64. Ibid., pp. 132–33.

65. Edward C. Luck, *Mixed Messages: American Politics and International Organization, 1919–1999* (Washington, DC: Brookings, 1999), pp. 61–62.

66. Ibid., ch. 7.

67. Schlesinger, *Imperial Presidency*, pp. 132–35.

68. Ibid., pp. 156–58.

69. Louis Fisher, *Congressional Abdication on War and Spending* (College Station: Texas A&M Press, 2000), pp. 49–52.

70. Flynn, *The Draft*, p. 265.

71. Douglas Bandow, "Fixing What Ain't Broke: The Renewed Call for Conscription," *Policy Analysis*, no. 351 (August 31, 1999): 2.

72. Bacevich, *Washington Rules*, p. 244.

73. Charles B. Rangel, "Bring Back the Draft," *New York Times*, December 31, 2002.

74. Thomas E. Ricks, *Making the Corps* (New York: Simon & Schuster, 1997), ch. 5.

75. Ole R. Holsti, "Of Chasms and Convergences: Attitudes and Beliefs of Civilians and Military Elites at the Start of a New Millennium," in Peter D. Feaver and Richard H. Kohn, *Soldiers and Civilians* (Cambridge, MA: MIT Press, 2001), pp. 15–100.

76. Jonathan Turley, "The Military Pocket Republic," *Northwestern University Law Review* 97, no. 1 (Fall 2002).

77. David M. Halbfinger and Steven A. Holmes, "Military Mirrors a Working-Class America," *New York Times*, March 30, 2003. Also, David Shiflett, "An Army That Drawls: Johnny Reb Goes to Iraq and Everywhere Else," *National Review*, May 5, 2003, pp. 29–30.

78. In the aftermath of the Vietnam War, some generals supported placing critical specialties in the reserves to prevent presidents from asking the army to fight without popular support. See Greg Jaffe, "Today, Military Kids Often Say Goodbye to Dad—and Mom," *Wall Street Journal*, March 11, 2003.

79. Thom Shanker, "U.S. Considers Limits on Role of the Reserves," *New York Times*, January 26, 2003.

80. Vernon Loeb, "Rumsfeld Turns Eye to Future of Army," *Washington Post*, June 8, 2003.

81. James R. Locher III, *Victory on the Potomac: The Goldwater-Nichols Act Unifies the Pentagon* (College Station: Texas A&M Press, 2002).

82. Franklin C. Spinney, "Notes on Close Air Support," in Donald Vandergriff, ed., *Spirit, Blood and Treasure: The American Cost of Battle in the 21st Century* (Novato, CA: Presidio Press, 2001), pp. 199–213.

83. Perret, *Country Made by War*, pp. 305–308.

84. George Friedman and Meredith Friedman, *The Future of War* (New York: St. Martin's, 1996), ch. 10.

85. Matthew Brzezinski, "The Unmanned Army," *New York Times Magazine*, April 20, 2003, pp. 38–80.

86. P. W. Singer, *Wired for War: The Robotics Revolution and Conflict in the Twenty-First Century* (New York: Penguin, 2009).

87. MacGregor Knox and Williamson Murray, *The Dynamics of Military Revolution, 1300–2050* (New York: Cambridge University Press, 2001), pp. 188–92.

88. Christopher Palmeri, "A Predator That Preys on Hawks?" *Businessweek*, February 17, 2003, p. 78.

89. David Halberstam, "Televising the Vietnam War," in Doris A. Graber, ed., *Media Power in Politics* (Washington, DC: Congressional Quarterly Press, 1984), pp. 290–95.

90. Jennifer Harper, "Journalists Prepare to See War from the Battlefield," *Washington Times*, March 4, 2003.

91. Tim Reid, "Texan Sent to Be Voice of War," *Times* (London), November 14, 2002.

92. Michael Massing, "The Unseen War," *New York Review*, May 29, 2003, pp. 16–19.

93. John Lehman, *Making War: The 200-Year-Old Battle between the President and the Congress Over How America Goes to War* (New York: Scribner's Sons, 1992), p. 263.

94. Ibid., p. 265.

95. Louis Fisher, "The Spending Power," in David Gray Adler and Larry N. George, *The Constitution and the Conduct of American Foreign Policy* (Lawrence: University Press of Kansas, 1996), p. 234.

96. Neal, *War Finance*, p. 18.

97. Fisher, *Congressional Abdication*, p. 76.

98. Joseph Stiglitz and Linda J. Bilmes, *The Three Trillion Dollar War* (New York: W. W. Norton, 2008).

99. Gordon Silverstein, *Imbalance of Powers: Constitutional Interpretation and the Making of American Foreign Policy* (New York: Oxford University Press, 1997), p. 145.

100. Lori F. Damrosch, "Covert Operations," in Louis Henkin, Michael J. Glennon, and William D. Rogers, eds., *Foreign Affairs and the U.S. Constitution* (Ardsley-on-Hudson, NY: Transnational Publishers, 1990), pp. 87–97.

101. 171. 453 U.S. 654 (1981).

102. 462 U.S. 919 (1983).

103. Harold H. Koh, *The National Security Constitution* (New Haven, CT: Yale University Press, 1990), pp. 46–47.

104. Christopher N. May, *In the Name of War: Judicial Review and the War Powers since 1918* (Cambridge, MA: Harvard University Press, 1989), p. 256.

105. Thomas M. Franck, "Rethinking War Powers: By Law or by 'Thaumaturgic Invocation'?" in Henkin, Glennon, and Rogers, *Foreign Affairs*, p. 59.

106. Caspar W. Weinberger, "Dangerous Constraints on the President's War Powers," in L. Gordon Crovitz and Jeremy Rabkin, eds., *The Fettered Presidency: Legal Constraints on the Executive Branch* (Washington, DC: American Enterprise Institute, 1989), pp. 95–116.

107. Fisher, *Congressional Abdication*, p. 68.

108. Ibid., pp. 75–76.

109. Ibid., p. 77.

110. George Bush and Brent Scowcroft, *A World Transformed* (New York: Knopf, 1998), p. 441.

111. Robert J. Delahunty and John C. Yoo, "The President's Constitutional Authority to Conduct Military Operations against Terrorist Organizations and the Nations That Harbor Them," *Harvard Journal of Law and Public Policy* 25, no. 487 (Spring 2002).

112. For an analysis of the Act, see Michael T. McCarthy, "USA Patriot Act," *Harvard Journal on Legislation* 39, no. 435 (Summer 2002).

113. Mark Danner, "After September 11: Our State of Exception," *New York Review*, October 13, 2011, p. 44.

114. James Forman Jr., "Exporting Harshness: How the War on Crime Helped Make the War on Terror Possible," *NYU Review of Law and Social Change* 33 (2010): 331.

115. Radley Balko, "A Decade after 9/11, Police Departments Are Increasingly Militarized," *HuffPost*, September 12, 2011, http://www.huffingtonpost.com/2011/09/12/police-militarization-9-11-september-11_n_955508.html.

116. Christian Caryl, "Predators and Robots at War," *New York Review*, September 29, 2011, pp. 55–58. Also, Ana Campoy, "The Law's New Eye in the Sky: Police Departments' Use of Drones Is Raising Concerns over Privacy and Safety," *Wall Street Journal*, December 13, 2011. Also, Andy Pasztor and John Emshwiller, "Drone Use Takes Off on Home Front," *Wall Street Journal*, April 20, 2012.

CHAPTER 5. MORALITY AND VIOLENCE

1. Georges Sorel, *Reflections on Violence* (Glencoe, IL: Free Press, 2004), ch. 6.

2. Susan A. Brewer, *Why America Fights: Patriotism and War Propaganda from the Philippines to Iraq* (New York: Oxford University Press, 2009).

3. See Michael Walzer, *Just and Unjust War*, 3rd ed. (New York: Basic Books, 2000).

4. Jeremy Waldron, "Special Ties and Natural Duties," in W. A. Edmundson, ed., *The Duty to Obey the Law* (Lanham, MD: Rowman & Littlefield, 1999).

5. *Crito*, 54c, in G. M. A. Grube, *The Trial and Death of Socrates*, 3rd ed. (Indianapolis: Hackett Publishing, 2000), p. 54.

6. Edmundson, *Duty to Obey the Law*. Also, Joseph Raz, *The Authority of Law*, 2nd ed. (Oxford: Oxford University Press, 2009).

7. 686 F.2d. 616 (7th Cir. 1982).

8. See, for example, Katherine Florey, "Sovereign Immunity's Penumbras: Common Law, Accident and Policy in the Development of Sovereign Immunity Doctrine," *Wake Forest L. Rev.* 43, no. 765 (Winter 2008).

9. See Natalie Banta, "Death by a Thousand Cuts or Hard Bargaining?: How the Court's Indecision in Wilkie v. Robbins Improperly Eviscerates the Bivens Action," *BYU J. Pub. L.* 23, no. 119 (2008).

10. Jeremy R. Lacks, "The Lone American Dictatorship: How Court Doctrine and Police Culture Limit Judicial Oversight of the Police Use of Deadly Force," *N.Y.U. Ann. Surv. Am. L.* 64, no. 391 (2008).

11. "New Orleans Cops Convicted in Post-Katrina Shootings Case," CNN.com, August 5, 2011, http://www.cnn.com/2011/CRIME/08/05/louisiana.danziger.bridge.shooting/index.html?eref=mrss_igoogle_cnn.

12. Jennet Kirkpatrick, *Uncivil Disobedience* (Princeton: Princeton University Press, 2008). See also, Henry David Thoreau, "On the Duty of Civil Disobedience," 1849, http://www.gutenberg.org/files/71/71.txt.

13. Luke Ryan and Molly Strehorn, "Adjutant and Internal Affairs: Making the Case for Access to Evidence of a Police Officer's Propensity for Violence," *W. New Eng. L. Rev.* 32, no. 73 (2010).

14. Jennifer Peltz, "Patrick Pogan, Biker Shove Cop, Gets No Jail," *HuffPost*, July 14, 2010, http://www.huffingtonpost.com/2010/07/15/patrick-pogan-biker-shove_n_646517.html.

15. Todd Wright, "Charges Dropped against Woman Framed by Cops: Police Seen Plotting to Pin Car Accident on Woman They Hit," NBC Miami, July 29, 2009, http://www.nbcmiami.com/news/local/Cops-Set-Up-Woman-After-Crash.html.

16. Jeffrey Wolf, Deborah Sherman, and Nicole Vap, "Videotape Shows Man Beaten by Denver Police," 9News.com, August 12, 2008, http://www.9news.com/news/story.aspx?storyid=97466&catid=222.

17. "Did Cops Intend to Cover Up Videotaped Beating?" CBS News, April 14, 2010, http://www.cbsnews.com/stories/2010/04/14/earlyshow/main6394678.shtml.

18. William K. Rashbaum, Joseph Goldstein, and Al Baker, "Trouble Found in Police Department by the Outside," *New York Times*, November 3, 2011.

19. Cato Institute, National Police Misconduct Reporting Project, 2010, http://www.policemisconduct.net/2010-npmsrp-police-misconduct-statistical-report/.

20. Ryan Gallagher, "Study: Police Abuse Goes Unpunished," *Medill Reports*, April 4, 2007, http://news.medill.northwestern.edu/chicago/news.aspx?id=6125

21. Matthew Walberg and William Lee, "Burge Found Guilty," *Chicago Tribune*, June 28, 2010, http://articles.chicagotribune.com/2010-06-28/news/ct-met-burge-trial-0629-20100628_1_burge-chicago-police-cmdr-special-cook-county-prosecutors.

22. Gallagher, "Study."

23. Radley Balko, "The War on Cameras," *Reason*, January 2011, http://reason.com/archives/2010/12/07/the-war-on-cameras.

24. "Oakland Remains Calm as Johannes Mehserle Is Freed," *San Francisco Examiner*, June 13, 2011, http://www.sfexaminer.com/local/bay-area/2011/06/oakland-remains-calm-johannes-mehserle-freed.

25. Radley Balko, "Chicago State's Attorney Lets Bad Cops Slide, Prosecutes Citizens Who Record Them," *HuffPost Politics*, June 8, 2011, http://www.huffingtonpost.com/2011/06/08/chicago-district-attorney-recording-bad-cops_n_872921.html.

26. John S. Baker, "Measuring the Explosive Growth of Federal Crime Legislation," Federalist Society for Law and Public Policy Studies, 2004, http://fedsoc.server326.com/Publications/practicegroupnewsletters/criminallaw/crimreportfinal.pdf. Also, John S. Baker, "Revisiting the Explosive Growth of Federal Crimes," Heritage Foundation, 2008, http://www.heritage.org/research/reports/2008/06/revisiting-the-explosive-growth-of-federal-crimes. See also, Harvey A. Silverglate, *Three Felonies a Day: How the Feds Target the Innocent* (New York: Encounter Books, 2009).

27. Gary Fields and John R. Emshwiller, "As Criminal Laws Proliferate, More Ensnared," *Wall Street Journal*, July 23, 2011.

28. Louise Radnofsky, Gary Fields, and John R. Emshwiller, "Federal Police Ranks Swell to Enforce a Widening Array of Criminal Laws," *Wall Street Journal*, December 17, 2011.

29. Susan Jones, "After Two Raids, DOJ Decides No Criminal Charges against Gibson Guitar Company," http://cnsnews.com/news/article/after-two-raids-doj-decides-no-criminal-charges-against-gibson-guitar-company.

30. Radnofsky, Fields, and Emshwiller, "Federal Police Ranks Swell."

31. Fields and Emshwiller, "As Criminal Laws Proliferate."

32. Gary Fields and John R. Emshwiller, "A Sewage Blunder Earns Engineer a Criminal Record," *Wall Street Journal*, December 12, 2011.

33. 176 F.3rd 1116 (9th Cir. 1999).

34. Whit Davis, "Water Criminals: Misusing Mens Rea and Public Welfare Offense Analysis in Prosecuting Clean Water Act Violations," *Tul. Envtl. L.J.* 23, no. 473 (Summer 2010).

35. 176 F.3rd at 1119.

36. 561 U.S. (2010).

37. Michael Price, "Mens Rea and Material Support of Terrorism: How Congress Should Respond to Holder v. Humanitarian Law Project," *Champion* 34, no. 53 (August 2010).

38. Price, "Mens Rea," p. 54.

39. Harvey Silverglate, *Three Felonies a Day* (New York: Encounter Books, 2009).

40. Daniel Richman and William Stuntz, "Al Capone's Revenge: The Political Economy of Pretextual Prosecution," *Colum. L. Rev.* 105, no. 583 (2005).

41. Michael Siegel and Christopher Slobogin, "Prosecuting Martha: Federal Prosecutorial Power and the Need for a Law of Courts," *Penn St. L. Rev.* 109, no. 1107 (2005).

42. John R. Emshwiller and Gary Fields, "For Feds Lying Is a Handy Charge," *Wall Street Journal*, April 10, 2012.

43. Peter J. Henning, "The Politics of Crime: Targeting Legal Advice," *Am. U.L. Rev.* 54, no. 671 (2005).

44. Sarah Helene Duggin, "The McNulty Memorandum, the KPMG Decision and Corporate Cooperation: Individual Rights and Legal Ethics," *Geo. J. Legal Ethics* 21, 341 (Spring 2008).

45. Michael Powell, "Misconduct by Prosecutors, Once Again," *New York Times*, August 14, 2012.

46. Campbell Robertson and Adam Liptak, "Louisiana Prosecutors' Methods Raise Scrutiny Again," *New York Times*, November 3, 2011.

47. John Schwartz and Brandi Grissom, "Exonerated of Murder, Texan Seeks Inquiry on Prosecutor," *New York Times*, December 19, 2011.

48. "Justice in the Balance," *USA Today*, September 23, 2010, http://projects.usatoday.com/news/2010/justice/cases/.

49. 373 U.S. 83 (1963).

50. 405 U.S. 150 (1972).

51. *U.S. v. Antonio Lyons*, U.S. District Court, Middle District of Florida, Orlando Division. Case No. 6:01-cr-134-Orl-31DAB. Filed 7/20/10, http://s3.documentcloud.org/documents/6687/united-states-v-lyons-district-court-granting-motion-for-a-certificate-of-innocence.pdf.

52. "Justice in the Balance."

53. Ibid.

54. Kevin McCoy and Brad Heath, "Not Guilty but Stuck with Big Bills, Damaged Career," *USA Today*, September 28, 2010, http://www.usatoday.com/news/washington/judicial/2010-09-27-hyde-federal-prosecutors_N.htm.

55. "Justice in the Balance."

56. Ibid.

57. Ibid.

58. Ibid.

59. Molly McDonough, "Coalition of Nearly 70 Former Judges, Prosecutors Urge High Court to Hear Gov't Misconduct Dispute," *ABA Journal Weekly Newsletter*, August 17, 2012, http://www.abajournal.com/news/article/coalition_of_nearly_70_former_judges_prosecutors _urge_high_court/.

60. The best account of the Amirault case is Dorothy Rabinowitz, *No Crueler Tyrannies* (New York: Free Press, 2004).

61. Dorothy Rabinowitz, "Martha Coakley's Convictions," *Wall Street Journal*, January 14, 2010, http://online.wsj.com/article/SB10001424052748704281204575003341640657862.html.

62. Rabinowitz, "Martha Coakley's Convictions."

63. Benjamin Ginsberg, *The American Lie* (Boulder, CO: Paradigm Publishers, 2007), ch. 4.

64. Ronald T. Libby, *The Criminalization of Medicine: America's War on Doctors* (Westport, CT: Praeger, 2008).

65. Thomas Stanton, "Fraud and Abuse Enforcement in Medicare: Finding Middle Ground," *Health Affairs* 20, no. 4 (2001): 28–42.

66. Libby, *Criminalization of Medicine*, p. 39.

67. Ibid., p. 25.

68. Ibid., p. 38.

69. Ibid., p. 32.

70. Radnofsky, Fields, and Emshwiller, "Federal Police Ranks Swell."

71. 127 S.Ct. 2588 (2007).

72. Laurence H. Tribe, "Death by a Thousand Cuts: Constitutional Wrongs without Remedies after Wilkie v. Robbins," *Cato Sup. Ct. Rev.* 23 (2006/2007).

73. Ibid., p. 76.

74. David Garland, *The Culture of Control* (Chicago: University of Chicago Press, 2001), ch. 4., and Jonathan Simon, *Governing through Crime* (New York: Oxford University Press, 2007), ch. 3.

75. Theodore J. Lowi, *The End of Liberalism* (New York: W. W. Norton, 1969).

76. Jerry L. Mashaw, *Greed, Chaos and Governance: Using Public Choice to Improve Public Law* (New Haven, CT: Yale University Press, 1997), p. 106.

77. Freeman Dyson, "The 'Dramatic Picture' of Richard Feynman," *New York Review of Books*, July 14, 2011, pp. 39–40.

78. Ginsberg, *American Lie*.

79. Doris Kearns Goodwin, *Lyndon Johnson and the American Dream* (New York: St. Martin's, 1991), p. i.

80. Ibid., p. ii.

81. Max Farrand, ed., *The Records of the Federal Convention of 1787* (New Haven, CT: Yale University Press, 1966), vol. 1, p. 49.

82. Friedrich Nietzsche, *Thus Spake Zarathustra* (Mineola, NY: Dover, 1999), p. 31.

83. Ibid., p. 30.

84. Herbert Marcuse, *One-Dimensional Man* (Boston: Beacon Press, 1964), p. 10.

85. MediaMatters.org, September 8, 2005.

86. Matthew A. Crenson, "Guest Editorial," *Baltimore Urbanite*, October 2006.

87. Saul D. Alinsky, *Rules for Radicals: A Pragmatic Primer for Realistic Radicals* (New York: Vintage, 1971).

88. See, for example, Antonio Gramsci, *Prison Notebooks*, Vol. I (New York: Columbia University Press, 1991).

89. William Arkin, "Back to the Bunker: Don't Worry: Washington Has a Plan to Save Itself," *Washington Post*, June 14, 2006.

90. Ibid.

CHAPTER 6. VIOLENCE AND CHANGE

1. Steven Pinker, *The Better Angels of Our Nature: Why Violence Has Declined* (New York: Viking, 2011).

2. Elizabeth Kolbert, "Peace in Our Time: Steven Pinker's Theory of Violence," *New Yorker*, October 3, 2011, pp. 75–78.

3. Walter Benjamin, "Critique of Violence," in Marcus Bullock and Michael W. Jennings, eds., *Walter Benjamin: Selected Writings* (Cambridge, MA: Belknap Press, 1996), pp. 236–52.

4. Robert Muchembled, *A History of Violence* (Malden, MA: Polity Press, 2012).

5. Ibid., p. 3.

6. Pinker, *Better Angels*, p. 680.

7. Fang Lizhi, "The Real Deng," *New York Review of Books*," no. 10, 2100, p. 8.

8. Alma Guillermoprieto, "In the New Gangland of El Salvador," *New York Review of Books*, November 10, 2011, pp. 45–48.

9. Walter Lippmann, *The Essential Lippmann*, ed. Clinton Rossiter and James Lare (New York: Random House, Vintage Books, 1965), p. 12.

10. United States Senate, Committee on the Judiciary, Hearings before the Subcommittee on Constitutional Amendments on S.J. Res. 8, S.J. Res. 14 and S.J. Res. 78, relating to lowering the voting age to 18. May 14, 15, and 16, 1968 (Washington, DC: U.S. Government Printing Office, 1968), p. 12.

11. Frances Fox Piven and Richard A. Cloward, *Poor People's Movements* (New York: Random House, 1979), pp. 231–35.

12. Ibid., p. 233.

13. Steven Schier, *You Call This an Election?: America's Peculiar Democracy* (Washington, DC: Georgetown University Press, 2003).

14. Philip E. Converse, "Attitudes and Non-Attitudes: Continuation of a Dialogue," in Edward R. Tufte, ed., *The Quantitative Analysis of Social Problems* (Boston: Addison-Wesley, 1970), pp. 168–89.

15. Andrew Higgins, "Careful Planning Pays Off for French Protestors," *Wall Street Journal*, March 17, 2006.

16. *Federalist 71*, p. 432.

17. For example, see Martin Malia, *Alexander Herzen and the Birth of Russian Socialism* (Cambridge, MA: Harvard University Press, 1961).

18. Michael Gerson, "As South Sudan Becomes New Nation, Old Conflicts Remain," *Washington Post*, July 7, 2011, http://www.washingtonpost.com/opinions/as-south-sudan -becomes-new-nation-old-conflicts-remain/2011/07/07/gIQATARk2H_story.html.

19. Joshua Hammer, "Egypt: Who Calls the Shots?" *New York Review of Books*, August 18, 2011. Also, David Kirkpatrick, "Egypt Military Moves to Cement a Muscular Place in Government," *New York Times*, July 17, 2011.

20. Andrew Milnor, *Elections and Political Stability* (Boston: Little, Brown, 1969).

21. Rosemary H. T. O'Kane, *The Revolutionary Reign of Terror* (London: Edward Elgar, 1991), p. 125.

22. Richard Posner, *Catastrophe: Risk and Response* (New York: Oxford University Press, 2005), and William McNeill, *Plagues and Peoples* (New York: Anchor, 1977).

INDEX